Monetary Policy, Central Banking and Economic Performance in the Caribbean

Monetary Policy, Central Banking and Economic Performance in the Caribbean

Derick Boyd and Ron Smith

University of the West Indies Press
Jamaica • Barbados • Trinidad and Tobago

University of the West Indies Press
7A Gibraltar Hall Road   Mona
Kingston 7   Jamaica
www.uwipress.com

© 2011 by Derick Boyd and Ron Smith

All rights reserved. Published 2011

A catalogue record of this book is available from the National Library of Jamaica.

ISBN: 978-976-640-252-5

Cover design by Robert Harris.
Printed in the United States of America.

Contents

Illustrations	vii
Preface	ix
Acknowledgements	x
Abbreviations	xi

1	**Introduction to Monetary Policy in the Caribbean**	1
2	**Country Characteristics, Monetary Institutional Background, Central Banks and Economic Performance**	8
	2.1 Country Characteristics	9
	2.2 Monetary Historical Institutional Background	13
	2.2.1 The Early Monetary Foundations	14
	2.3 Central Bank Characteristics	27
	2.3.1 The Eastern Caribbean Central Bank	27
	2.3.2 Central Bank of Barbados	28
	2.3.3 Central Bank of the Bahamas	29
	2.3.4 Central Bank of Jamaica	30
	2.3.5 Central Bank of Trinidad and Tobago	30
	2.3.6 Central Bank of Guyana	31
	2.3.7 Central Bank of Belize	31
	2.4 Comparative Country Performance	32
	2.5 Conclusions	38
3	**Monetary Policy Transmission Mechanisms in Developing Countries**	42
	3.1 Monetary Policy in Industrialized Countries	44
	3.2 Objectives of Monetary Policy	46
	3.3 Policy Instruments	47
	3.4 Short-Run Transmission Mechanisms in Developing Countries	49
	3.4.1 Interest Rate Channel	50
	3.4.2 Exchange Rate Channel	50
	3.4.3 Domestic Asset Price Channel	51
	3.4.4 Credit Channel	52
	3.5 Recent Empirical Developing Country Studies	53
	3.6 Conclusions	57
4	**The Data**	59
	4.1 Data Sources and Variables	60
	4.2 The Country Data	61

	4.3 Interpolation	62
	4.4 Annual Data for External Balance Estimates	65
5	**Econometric Methods and Issues**	**67**
	5.1 Unit Roots and Cointegration	68
	5.2 Vector Autoregressions (VARs)	69
	5.3 Identification	70
	5.4 An Example	71
	5.5 Impulse Response Functions	74
	5.6 Cointegration	74
6	**Estimating the Monetary Policy Effects on Inflation and Output: Closed Economy Unrestricted Vector Autoregression Modelling**	**77**
	6.1 Inflation Dynamics	78
	6.2 Vector Autoregression	84
	6.3 Money, Income and Prices	85
	6.4 Conclusions	93
7	**The Monetary Transmission Mechanism: Vector Error Correction Modelling and Cointegration**	**96**
	7.1 Cointegration Modelling	96
	7.2 Conclusions	105
8	**Caribbean External Balance Adjustment: The Marshall-Lerner Condition and J-Curve Effects**	**107**
	8.1 The Model	108
	8.2 Investigating Balance of Trade Effects	110
	8.3 Unrestricted VAR Estimations, Results and Interpretation	110
	8.3.1 ADF Test for a Unit Root	110
	8.3.2 Granger Block Non-causality Tests	111
	8.3.3 Engle-Granger Test for Cointegration	112
	8.4 Cointegrated VAR and VECM Estimations, Results and Interpretation	112
	8.4.1 Johansen ML Tests for Number of Cointegrating Vectors	112
	8.4.2 Johansen ML Estimates of the Cointegrating Vector and the Marshall-Lerner Condition	113
	8.4.3 Generalized Impulse Responses and the J-Curve Effects	114
	8.4.4 VECM Feedback Coefficients	115
	8.5 Conclusions	117
9	**Conclusions**	**119**
	9.1 The Substantive Objective	120
	9.2 The Methodological Objective	122
	9.3 Lessons and Policy Implications	125
References		**131**
Index		**139**

Illustrations

Figures

2.1	Money supply and inflation, 1980–2003	34
2.2	Real GDP: all countries, 1980–2003	36
2.3	Rate of growth of GDP and inflation, 1980–2003	38
4.1	Jamaica: GDP volume index, annual (1995 = 100)	63
4.2	Jamaica: GDP volume index, quarterly (1995 = 100)	64
4.3	Jamaica: GDP volume index, quarterly (1995 = 100) annualized	64
6.1	Mean inflation and inflation persistence	83
6.2	Mean inflation and inflation variation	83
6.3	Impact effect of a one standard error money and price shock: unrestricted VAR	91
7.1	Orthogonalized impulse response to one standard error money supply shock	99
7.2	Generalized impulse response to one standard error price shock	100
7.3	Impact effect of a one standard error monetary and price shock: VAR and VECM	103
8.1	Generalized impulse response of balance of payments and income to a real exchange rate shock	116

Tables

2.1	Country Characteristic Variables	12
2.2	Jamaica: Annual Rate of Growth in Money Supply (%)	31
2.3	Rate of Growth in Money Supply (M2), Prices and Output: Annual Average	33
2.4	Average and Variation in Real Interest Rates and GDP Growth Rates	35
4.1	Annual Data Series Used in Open Economy Estimations	65
6.1	Unrestricted ADF Estimates from Equation 6.7	81
6.2	Restricted ADF Estimates from Equation 6.8	81
6.3	Unrestricted Second Order VAR (y_t, p_t, m_t): Granger Non-Causality p Values	87
6.4	Unrestricted VAR: Orthogonalized Impulse Response Functions	89
6.5	Unrestricted VAR: Generalized Impulse Response Functions	89
6.6	Cumulative Orthogonalized Impulse Response	92
6.7	Cumulative Generalized Impulse Response	92
7.1	Cointegration and Adjustment Coefficients	99
7.2	Cointegrating VAR: Orthogonalized Impulse Response Functions	101
7.3	Cointegrating VAR: Generalized Impulse Response Functions	101
7.4	Cointegrating VAR: Cumulative Orthogonalized Impulse Response	104

7.5	Cointegrating VAR: Cumulative Generalized Impulse Response	105
8.1	ADF Test for Order of Integration of Variables	111
8.2	Unrestricted VAR Estimates: Granger Block Non-Causality Tests and Engle-Granger Test for a Unit Root	113
8.3	Cointegrated VAR (1) Vector Estimates and VECM Error Correction Coefficients Estimates: SE and Probability Values	114

Preface

Our interest in the role of monetary policy in economic development led us to investigate how monetary policy influences growth and inflation. We also wanted to examine the effectiveness of economic theory and econometric tools in providing a description and explanation of the diverse economic experience. The group of Caribbean countries on which we focus is interesting because all countries, for a time, had a common monetary background. In recent years, however, they have evolved to a variety of monetary systems and experienced widely varying economic outcomes.

The literature on the Caribbean tends to concentrate on Barbados, Guyana, Jamaica, and Trinidad and Tobago. We wanted to extend the list of Caribbean countries examined, so we included Antigua and Barbuda, the Bahamas, Belize, Dominica, Grenada, St Kitts and Nevis, St Lucia, and St Vincent and the Grenadines. We did so particularly because in some of these countries, monetary policy is shaped by their membership in a currency union administered by the Eastern Caribbean Central Bank.

We developed an analysis of monetary policy in the Caribbean, starting with an examination of the transmission mechanisms through which monetary policy influences the economy. We soon realized, however, that an analysis of Caribbean monetary policy and institutional framework has its origins in a common colonial administrative infrastructure, and as such, the structure of the analysis must be built on foundations of political economy. Contemporary Caribbean monetary institutions evolved from these roots in various ways in different countries. Consequently, despite the common origins of their monetary systems, the Caribbean countries now provide an interesting variety of institutional arrangements and economic experiences.

Some of the material in this text is technical. However, we have tried to make the first two chapters and concluding chapter accessible to the general reader. In chapter 2, we present the main thesis of the research and provide a readable explanation of the fundamental monetary features of these Caribbean economies. We have also tried to provide university students of all levels with a source from which they could draw on for quantitative courseworks, dissertations and theses. There is considerable scope, for example, to develop single-country or comparative studies for the countries in this study, or for other countries, following elements of our economic and statistical approach.

The application of statistical techniques to developing economies should not only help us understand the economies concerned, but also allow us to judge the efficacy of the econometric tools in aiding understanding.

Derick Boyd, Trinidad and Tobago
Ron Smith, London, England
June 2010

Acknowledgements

We would like to express our sincere thanks to all who helped us along the way: Maureen Allgrove of the University of the West Indies (UWI), Mona, Jamaica; Sir Courtney Blackman, founding governor of the Central Bank of Barbados; Roseann Collymore of CARICOM; Natalie Haynes of the Bank of Jamaica; Richard Hart, historian and author; Giles Robbins of AMC Group PLC, City of London; Vindelyn Smith-Hillman of the Law Commission, London, England; Patrick Watson of the University of the West Indies, St Augustine, Trinidad and Tobago; and Sheila Williams of the Eastern Caribbean Central Bank.

Special thanks to Alaa Suliman, University of East London (UEL), for his research assistance on this project. Thanks also to Vasileios Kazakos (UEL), Georgios Nastos (UEL), Ioanna Xagorari (UEL), Pamela Joseph of the Caribbean Centre for Money and Finance (CCMF), Julia Jhinkoo (CCMF) and Simeon Wu-Kwai (CCMF), who assisted us at various stages of the project. Thanks also to Edsel Thompson of the Department of Geography, UWI St Augustine, Trinidad and Tobago, who prepared the map.

We have benefited from discussions that took place when parts of the book were presented at conferences, including the Fifth Annual International Academy of African Business and Development Conference, Atlanta, Georgia, 7–10 April 2004; the Fifth Annual Sir Arthur Lewis Institute for Social and Economic Studies Conference, UWI St Augustine, 31 March–2 April 2004; the thirty-fifth annual Caribbean Centre for Monetary Studies Conference, Eastern Caribbean Central Bank, St Kitts, 24–28 November 2003; and at research seminars at the University of East London.

We are grateful for financial support from an ESRC Research Award, R000 22 3500.

Abbreviations

ADF	augmented Dickey-Fuller equation
AIC	Akaike Information Criterion
BCCB	British Caribbean Currency Board
BWI	British West Indies
CBB	Central Bank of the Bahamas
CVAR	cointegrating vector autoregression
EC	Eastern Caribbean
ECCA	East Caribbean Currency Authority
ECCB	Eastern Caribbean Central Bank
GDP	gross domestic product
GIRF	generalized impulse response function
IMF	International Monetary Fund
LDC	less developed country
MDC	more developed country
MLC	Marshall-Lerner condition
OLS	ordinary least squares
OECD	Organisation for Economic Co-operation and Development
OECS	Organisation of Eastern Caribbean States
SBC	Schwartz Bayesian Criterion
VAR	vector autoregression
VECM	vector error correction model

Country List

AB	Antigua and Barbuda
DOM	Dominica
GRE	Grenada
SKN	St Kitts and Nevis
SLU	St Lucia
SVG	St Vincent and the Grenadines
BAH	The Bahamas
BAR	Barbados
GUY	Guyana
BEL	Belize
JAM	Jamaica
TT	Trinidad and Tobago

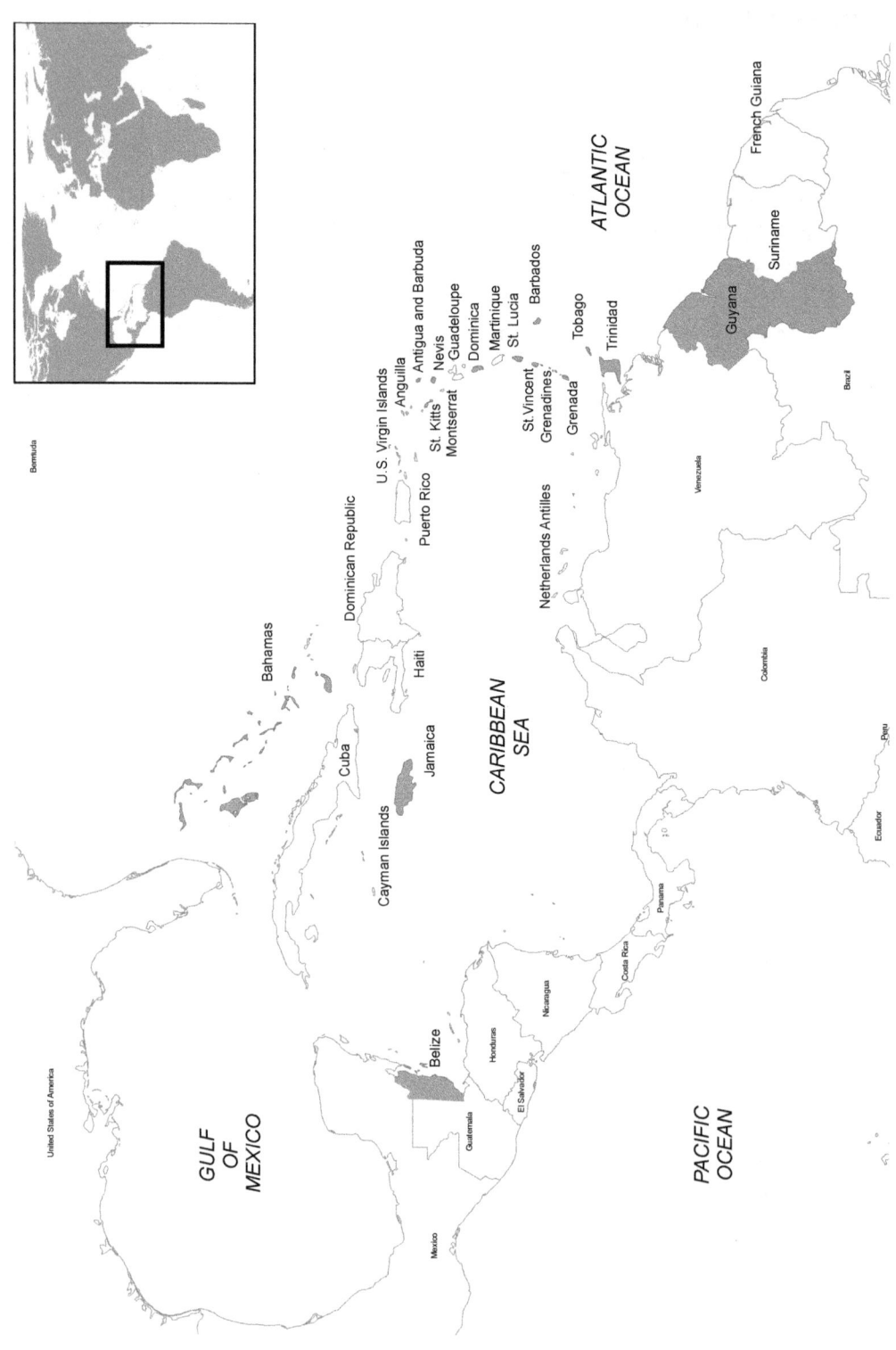

Map of the Caribbean. (Map drawn by the GIS Research Lab, Department of Geography, University of the West Indies, St Augustine, Trinidad and Tobago.)

Chapter 1

Introduction to Monetary Policy in the Caribbean

Introduction

This book presents an analysis of monetary policies and their effect in twelve Caribbean economies. We carry out a detailed examination of the evolution of the monetary framework, the resulting policy and its effects on economic performance. The book is motivated by our interest in the characteristic features of sound monetary and fiscal policies that may form the basis for sustained economic growth and development. The group of twelve Caribbean economies that we examine provides a variety of economic performance experiences, making it an interesting group on which to compare monetary policies and their effects.

Applied economics involves the synthesis of many elements. We have tried to provide a comprehensive and relatively self-contained description of the elements that go into our analysis. This will allow readers to evaluate them, replicate them and apply the procedures in different circumstances. Therefore, before we present empirical results, we provide a fairly detailed description of the historical origins of the monetary framework in these countries; the theory of the monetary transmission mechanism; the sources and characteristics of the data used; and the econometric techniques employed.

Monetary and fiscal policies lie at the core of how government influences the economy. As such, they are central to the success or failure of a country's economic development. This study examines the contribution monetary policy has made to domestic economic performance and financial stability over time. From the 1990s, there has been a growing consensus among academics and policymakers that monetary policy occupies a primary position in macroeconomic management and the progress of economic development. There have been considerable advances, both theoretically and in the application of economic policies, aimed at stabilizing economies in terms of prices and real variables. Some argue that the change in central banks' attitude toward inflation is largely based on their "recently obtained ability to conduct monetary policy with independence, transparency and credibility" (Loayza and Soto 2002). Other works on monetary policy rules (Taylor 1993) and inflation targeting (Mishkin 1997) have also identified broad monetary policy approaches that have been employed in some industrial countries and in a growing number of developing countries, in their quest for financial stability and sustained economic growth and development.

Central banks can have multiple functions. These may include maintaining convertibility against another currency; controlling the money supply; financing the government deficit; prudential regulation to maintain financial stability; and intervening in financial crises through lender of last resort facilities. At the risk of some oversimplification, we can think of central banks in these countries operating within one of three broad frameworks. The first is a classical framework, within which the central bank tightly controls the money supply to maintain convertibility at a fixed rate against gold or some reserve currency. Interest rates may or may not play a central role in the control of the money supply. The second is an accommodating framework, within which the central bank supplies the money necessary to finance the government deficit and maintain full employment and growth. This framework was often labelled Keynesian, though this may represent a misreading of Keynes. The third is an inflation targeting framework, within which the central bank adjusts interest rates in a floating exchange rate regime to ensure that inflation stays within a target range. All three frameworks occur in our sample of countries at different times, being implemented with different degrees of prudence and discretion. These differences occur despite the fact that all twelve of our countries had a history as British colonies with monetary frameworks provided by currency boards that operated in a classical manner and, on becoming independent, all established central banks that were nominally modelled on the Bank of England.

Since the 1990s, a dominant view in the literature has been that policy rules have major advantages over discretion in improving economic performance. The Friedman Rule, based on fixing the rate of growth of a monetary aggregate, and the Taylor Rule, based on changing a short-term interest rate primarily in response to inflation, are two often identified policy approaches in this regard. The policy rules that have emerged from recent research are not necessarily rigid and may allow some scope for the speed of adjustment in the responses of the instruments to movements in the target. The rules of this research refer more generally to changes in the money supply, the monetary base, or, more usually, a short-term interest rate, in response to changes in the price level or real income (Taylor 1993). Policy rules are seen as accomplishing three tasks:

1. Ensuring a technical link between the target and the policy instrument
2. Providing consistent policy response over time
3. Enhancing the credibility of monetary policy and institutions

Even if there is no explicit policy rule, some monetary frameworks may, in certain circumstances, be seen as functioning as policy rules. They provide a rigorous link between a policy target and a policy instrument, and serve to ensure a consistent policy response to events, and thus enhance the credibility of policymaking. A currency board, for example, can be seen as functioning in important respects like a policy rule. It establishes a rigorous link between the target (exchange rate stability) and the instrument (the issuance of the "backed" currency). The policy responses are consistent over time. The credibility of policy can be maintained. Therefore, the currency board operations of some central banks are an example of binding constraints imposed on monetary policy behaviour.

On the other hand, monetary authorities that follow a more discretionary approach often give rise to examples of time inconsistency and non-credible policies that damage the credibility of monetary policymaking institutions. Of course, this does not have to be the case, but it is often so, which gave rise in the literature to the notion that rule-based approaches are likely to provide more desirable economic outcomes.

One of the interesting features of our sample countries is that they provide examples of both discretionary-prudent and discretionary-imprudent monetary policy effects. The empirical analyses provide textbook examples of these different effects: growth and stability in the case of the former (the Bahamas, Barbados and Belize provide some evidence of prudent policymaking with positive effects), and stagnation and financial instability in the case of the latter (Guyana and Jamaica provide evidence of imprudent discretionary policy with adverse effects).

The 1990s saw substantial growth in the view that low inflation should be promoted as the primary objective of economic policy, and low and stable inflation is increasingly regarded, in both industrial and developing countries, as an important precondition for economic growth and development. This is especially the case for open economies. To this end, a growing number of countries have adopted "inflation targeting" as the primary monetary policy strategy. Inflation targeting, like policy rules, is not a rigid specific procedure that has to be followed, but rather a policy framework within which monetary authorities can develop and implement policy. In this regard, the monetary authority follows what Mishkin (1997) calls "constrained discretionary" policies, and does not provide a magic bullet monetary policy mechanism. Inflation targeting as a strategy significantly reduces the role of intermediate targets, such as the exchange rate or money growth, although intermediate targets may remain important. Its particular feature is that, in case of conflict, the implementation of an inflation targeting strategy generally means that the low inflation goal takes precedence (Mishkin 1997).

So far, the literature on policy rules and inflation targeting is mostly developed with respect to monetary policy in industrial economies, where the main instrument is short-term interest rate. The repo rate set by the Bank of England Monetary Policy Committee and the official cash rate set by the Reserve Bank of New Zealand are prime examples of these (Blinder 1999; McCullum 2003). Emerging and developing countries are increasingly adopting anti-inflation strategies. Both Chile and Brazil have implemented inflation targeting approaches (Loayza and Soto 2002; Mishkin 2000). Interest rates in many developing countries, however, do not play a major role in short-term policymaking. In many cases, nominal interest rates are constant, as we shall see in the sample of countries in this study. Nevertheless, rules may be developed that function equivalently in seeking to control inflation. Small open economies are particularly vulnerable to the impact of external deficits. Experience has shown that the primary macroeconomic determinant of such imbalances is inflation. There are well-established links between inflation and the external account, and prolonged relative inflation inexorably leads to devaluation and foreign exchange crises. Indeed, the general finding in this regard is that low inflation seems to be a necessary, though not sufficient, condition for economic growth and development.

The evidence from this sample of countries supports the view that a regulatory system *can* distinctly encourage monetary stability through certain mechanisms within a reserve banking framework. Within a currency board arrangement, for example, this is so because the *backing of a currency* effectively prioritizes monetary responses, which ensures monetary adjustment in response to the external accounts constraint. Or perhaps, even more effectively, it seeks to ensure that monetary policy is not likely to initiate the external disequilibrium in the first place. Timely adjustments to external imbalances are often achieved by a short-term decline in output along with increasing fiscal balance constraints – so-called tightening monetary and fiscal policies.

The balance of payment–output trade-off secured through a reserve backed currency stands in contrast to discretionary policies that often seek not to make the adjustment and so build up destabilizing pressures for the future. That is, slack or expansionary monetary and fiscal policies serve to build up inflationary and adverse balance of payment pressures that will result in higher adjustment costs in terms of deterioration in both output and balance of payments. Discretionary policies that are prudent can be consistent and credible. We shall see evidence of this in this study in the case of Barbados. Discretionary approaches are, however, not often associated with prudent policies. In the sample of countries in this study, we are able to observe clear empirical examples of discretionary approaches giving rise, in some cases, to prudent monetary policies (the Bahamas, Barbados and Belize), and the all too familiar imprudent monetary policies (Guyana, Jamaica, and Trinidad and Tobago).

The quest for financial stabilization in both developing and emerging market economies has given rise to a resurgence of interest in the institutional framework of currency boards. This has formed a part of the corner solution or bipolar view of exchange rate regimes as a conditional choice between a hard peg (through a currency board arrangement, a currency union or some form of dollarization) and a float (Fischer 2001). Hong Kong adopted a currency board in 1983 and has been followed by Argentina, Estonia, Lithuania and Bulgaria (Gulde 1999; Ghosh 1998).

Currency board systems are typically seen as contributing to financial and macroeconomic stability (Honohan 1994). Some advocates have argued that countries such as Mexico and Russia, with longstanding financial problems, should follow such systems. However, others forward important arguments why currency boards are not always the ideal monetary framework (Williamson 1995). Indeed, the recent experience of Argentina shows that hard pegging through a currency board is not a panacea for economic ills or foreign exchange crises (Edwards 2002).

A currency board arrangement within a currency union links a group of six countries in this study. This is particularly interesting because the group of six countries have had a form of currency board arrangement since the nineteenth century, as a by-product of the quest for financial stability in the establishment of the gold standard in 1844. The currency board and currency union arrangement was formalized into a sterling area agreement in 1939 (Clauson 1944), through which the colonial territories were obliged to hold sterling as their reserve assets. The economic motive for the establishment of the British monetary system shall be examined in chapter 2. We shall examine the historical foundation and the subsequent development of the associated currency board system that was the foundation of monetary policy not only throughout the Caribbean countries but throughout the British Empire. We shall see that the essential motive arose out of the quest for financial stability and the fear of excessive monetary expansion of the British pound (£), and this was translated and expanded into the administration of the currencies in colonial territories being hardwired to sterling, that was itself hardwired to a gold standard. We shall show that the foundation for this was established in the 1844 Bank Charter Act that established the gold standard. That historical hard peg of a currency continues to be the foundation of monetary policy in some Caribbean countries, and there is evidence this has served these countries well. In other cases, there is evidence that the feared currency over expansion led, predictably, to economic collapse and prolonged financial crises, even in the presence of significant mineral resource endowments.

The establishment of the European Monetary Union has focused attention on the effect of currency unions and renewed interest in the many, mostly small, currency unions that have been established for some time (Honohan and Lane 2000). Some analysts, such as Rose (2000), have argued that currency unions can have a significantly positive effect on trade. Rose (2000) sought to provide evidence of this on the basis of cross-section regressions that currency unions increase trade by a factor of three. A central issue in the European Monetary Union is the consequences of a single monetary policy. If the shocks hitting the various members are similar, then a one-size-fits-all monetary policy may be adequate. If, however, the shocks are different, with some countries inflating while others are in recession, a single monetary policy is unlikely to be adequate. It is also possible that a monetary union across a single market will synchronize the cycles of the members, making the correlation of shocks post-union much greater than pre-union, increasing the appropriateness of a single monetary policy. The synchronizing of cycles among these Caribbean micro-states may well be determined by large external forces, which may provide interesting insights. The composition of the Caribbean currency union has changed over time. As countries became politically independent, the larger and more resourced endowed countries left the union to pursue their economic ambitions. The less resource endowed and significantly more vulnerable micro-states – tiny rather than small open economies – continued in the union as their more optimistic ex-colonial counterparts set out on independent courses. Interestingly, the crucial difference is not between those countries that stayed in the currency union (the Eastern Caribbean Central Bank [ECCB]) and those that left. The crucial difference is between the countries that followed prudent constrained monetary policies and those that did not.

For the most part, the evidence shows that the financial constraints hardwired into the currency union and currency board arrangements have served the smaller micro-states well, delivering a currency that has never been devalued against its pegged currency, even through the turbulent oil crisis international conditions of the 1970s and 1980s. As this group of Caribbean countries increasingly became politically independent, the monetary arrangements of the smallest micro-states have delivered economic welfare gains well above their larger Caribbean counterparts. Our analysis indicates that this may be attributed, in important part, to the anti-inflation mechanisms endemic in the monetary framework implicit in the currency board arrangements.

In recent decades, developing countries have confronted severe economic problems in general and foreign exchange crises in particular with the need to implement financial stabilization policies. These, in turn, have focused attention on the role of monetary and fiscal policies in the generation of such crises. Against a background of inappropriate monetary and fiscal policies, the development objective is increasingly seen as constrained by such financial instability. It is clear that the nature and type of the constraints imposed by the institutional framework within which monetary and fiscal policies take place are also of fundamental importance. As such, the institutional framework within which the monetary authorities operate is of fundamental interest. In examining the institutional framework, the historical development of the framework shall form a basic part of our examination, since the historical developments often serve to provide context to the nature and function of the contemporary framework.

All the countries in our sample have a common colonial currency board monetary background. However, in the last quarter of the twentieth century, they underwent a varied economic performance experience arising partly from the pursuance of independent monetary policies formed on the basis of a variety of institutional arrangements: a currency union; stand alone central banks; currency boards to varying degrees; and a variety of experiences in discretionary central bank activities, such as the enthusiastic financing of government deficit to being more cautious of such activity, for example. The common monetary historical background, the development of independent monetary policy from around the 1960s, the variety of monetary frameworks and the varied economic performance, make this sample of countries particularly interesting for our examination of economic policy effects arising from monetary policies.

In many central banks, quantitative modelling plays a role in the formation of monetary policy. Such quantitative modelling involves a synthesis of economic theory with detailed knowledge of the data and institutions and a variety of econometric techniques. In the latter chapters we investigate the effectiveness of particular modelling strategies in estimating the ways and mechanisms through which monetary policies may have an impact on the real economy. This is the area of estimating the monetary transmission mechanisms of these countries. In this econometric analysis we use structural cointegrating vector autoregression (CVARs), which are designed to have long-run properties consistent with economic theory and flexible short-run dynamics. We also investigate whether a common analytical framework can be applied to this range of countries. This is of particular interest since the results in Boyd and Smith (2002) suggest that it is quite difficult to get standard equations to work on developing country data. In a sample of fifty-seven developing countries estimating four standard monetary policy transmission equations, we found that by averaging across countries, reasonably plausible estimates could be obtained, but the dispersion across countries was so substantial as to make the individual country equations unreliable for policy purposes.

Following this overview, chapter 2 begins by examining the economic characteristics of the twelve countries of the study and the historical development of their monetary frameworks from colonial origins to the contemporary characteristics of their central banks. It then reports a comparative analysis of the countries, focusing on the relationship between changes in their money supply, inflation and output. Chapter 3 reviews the theory on monetary policy and the monetary transmission mechanism in developing countries. Chapter 4 describes the data, its sources and its interpolations, which will be used in the subsequent econometric exercises. Chapter 5 sets out the econometric modelling framework that we use. A central econometric issue is how many variables to use in the analysis and we steadily increase the range of variables covered. Chapter 6 starts from a univariate of inflation dynamics in the countries and proceeds to an unrestricted vector autoregression (VAR) in the three main variables, output inflation and money, and uses impulse response functions to examine the impact of monetary policy on inflation and output. Chapter 7 extends the analysis to an open economy model to examine balance of payments and exchange rate effects arising from monetary policy shocks. It uses a vector error correction modelling (VECM) technique to examine long-run relationships within an open economy. It estimates impulse responses arising from a money shock and a price shock for each of the countries from a cointegrating VAR and a VECM. This is a further development of the monetary policy transmission mechanisms analysis. The balance of payments plays a crucial role within the classical framework. Chapter 8 extends the open economy modelling exercise by estimating six specifications to search for evidence of the Marshall-Lerner condition (MLC) and J-Curve balance of payments effects. Chapter 9 pulls together the main conclusions of the research.

Chapter 2

Country Characteristics, Monetary Institutional Background, Central Banks and Economic Performance

Introduction

In this chapter, we provide an introduction to the twelve countries in our sample. History matters and their current monetary frameworks reflect to differing degrees their origins in colonial structures. Therefore, we consider the development of monetary institutions in some detail. We analyse the aims and objective (currency stability), the economic linkages (control of the money supply and inflation) and the institutional framework (asset backed and convertibility) used to attain the primary objective of monetary stability. We examine these with respect to the gold standard and the underlying economic theories, and trace the linkages between these and the monetary framework administered by the British Currency Authority. This study was, in important part, motivated by the notion that the institutional framework within which monetary policy is developed is likely to have a defining impact on the nature of the monetary policy and the policy effects that result. As such, this chapter establishes the theoretical bases on which the study is developed.

The context of the Caribbean economic policies under study may be described as follows: After centuries of colonial rule that put their interest a poor second to the interests of the colonial British, there was a drive for social and economic development in the Caribbean following World War Two. Political independence from the 1960s brought about self-rule, and saw monetary and fiscal policy increasingly used to pursue the economic development ambitions of Caribbean nation states (Downes 2004a; Downes 2004b; Girvan 1980; Jefferson 1972). Arguably, influenced by the dominance of pro-fiscal Keynesianism, among other things, monetary management in some countries failed to reflect the importance of monetary stability in the quest for economic development (King 2000; Girvan, Bernal and Hughes 1980; Bourne 1977). However, where there is evidence of cautious and prudent monetary management, this seems to be reflected in success in economic performance over a long period. The high degree of openness of these economies to international trade exacerbated the adverse impact of any overvalued currency, resulting in long-term social and financial problems.

The structure of this chapter is as follows: In section 2.1 we begin by providing some background to the countries in the study. In section 2.2 we analyse the foundations of monetary management in Britain, that is, the aims, economic principles and theories underlying its management. We argue that an appreciation of this is not only fundamental to understanding the historical structure of the monetary management in the Caribbean, it is also vital to appreciate the priority and importance given to that structure and the aims it was to satisfy. In section 2.3 we trace the transition of Caribbean colonies to independent nation states and observe the variety of economic experiences as a result of the differing monetary institutional framework and policy trends that were adopted. In section 2.4 we analyse the comparative country performance and examine the statistical evidence in support of the argument that links the rate of money supply to price inflation and growth in real output. The evidence suggests that although low inflation is not a sufficient condition for economic growth, it appears to be a necessary condition. Section 2.5 contains the conclusions, where we pull together the main argument, theories and evidence. In this section we note that this group of small open economies provide notable examples of monetary management:

1. The ECCB group of countries provide a remarkably successful example of a currency board within a monetary union – a notable achievement for such micro-states.
2. The Bahamas, Barbados and Belize provide remarkable examples of discretionary policies conducted within different regimes of prudency producing notable monetary stability over a period of considerable international trade and financial instability. In the economics literature, discretionary frameworks for monetary policy are often associated with excessive monetary expansion and stagflation (Greenspan 1997; Mankiw 1994). The economic managements of the Bahamas, Barbados and Belize, however, provide differing examples of good monetary management within a discretionary framework.
3. On the other hand, a considerable part of the economic and social problems of Guyana and Jamaica are associated with excessive increases in the money supply and inflation. Fiscal deficits that were accommodated through the printing of money played a central role in undermining the currencies of Guyana and Jamaica (King 2000; Worrell and Bourne 1989; Thomas 1972). An interesting feature of these three countries is the extent to which oil- and gas-rich Trinidad and Tobago has been able to mitigate adverse outcomes over the long run, while the mineral resources of Guyana and Jamaica have not provided such mitigation.

2.1 Country Characteristics

The twelve Caribbean countries in our empirical analyses are Antigua and Barbuda; Dominica; Grenada; St Kitts and Nevis; St Lucia; St Vincent and the Grenadines; the Bahamas; Barbados; Guyana; Belize; Jamaica; and Trinidad and Tobago. Most of them are islands in the long chain stretching in an arc from Miami, Florida, in the United States to Venezuela on the eastern coast of South America (see the map of the Caribbean). Belize and Guyana are Caribbean countries on the north-eastern side of the South American continent. The Bahamas, Nassau and Cuba lie to the north. Grenada and Trinidad and Tobago lie to the south. The overall chain of islands provides the eastern boundary of the Caribbean Sea.

Some small British ex-colonies or territories in the region had to be excluded for lack of data. However, the sample of countries in this study includes all of the major historically British territories and may therefore be regarded as highly representative of such territories.

All of the sample countries were at one time a part of the British colonial empire. They all functioned as primary commodity-producing outposts, producing sugar and bananas among other things, and provided markets for various UK products. Within the colonial experience, they were not countries that were governed with economic growth and development as governmental objectives. Economic growth and development as objectives of Caribbean government policy are an important part of post–World War Two phenomena. This is generally true of all British colonial possessions. Prior to their political independence, productive investments required the permission of the colonial office of the UK government. Permission was not generally forthcoming if such investments were perceived as leading to competition with the industries or products imported from the United Kingdom. Richard Hart (1999, 107–12; Hart 1998, 1990) provides an illustrative example of this process at work in the case of the Jamaican businessman James Gore's quest to establish a cement factory in Jamaica.

Hart writes that the "sordid story" of the setting up a cement factory in Jamaica provides an example of the extent to which the colonial government could provide obstacles to frustrate industrial development initiatives. In 1941, a local businessman named James Gore requested permission to establish a cement factory. Hart (1999, 110) explains that the then governor of Jamaica "informed the Colonial Office by telegram that, in view of the war time interruptions of supplies, it was important that a cement factory should be erected in Jamaica, . . . but he added, 'I do not favour Gore's proposal.' Instead he would 'prefer a local company to be formed in which Cement Marketing Company would have interest.'" The Cement Marketing Company was the UK firm that exported cement to Jamaica.

> The cement saga ended in 1948, with the enactment of legislation granting a monopoly to manufacture cement in Jamaica to Caribbean Cement Company Ltd. This was a locally incorporated company in which British cement manufacturers had a substantial financial stake. Gore, the entrepreneur who had originally proposed the establishment of a local cement factory, had been forgotten. The group of local investors involved in the project was headed by the Ashenheims who, as solicitors, had done the legal work. (Hart 1990)

This highly restrictive investment process was the case until well after World War Two, as the Gore case illustrates. It was the movement to self-government, in the post-war years and the attainment of political independence that provided the basis for the process of economic development to be meaningfully pursued. The quest for economic development in the Caribbean through the application of policies explicitly designed to do so in a general manner is therefore a fairly young one, not much more than fifty years old. From the early 1960s, as the territories gradually became politically independent, they were able to pursue economic policies aimed, ostensibly, at increasing the general welfare of their populations.

Within the twelve countries in this study, six of the smallest island states (Antigua and Barbuda, Dominica, Grenada, St Kitts and Nevis, St Lucia, St Vincent and the Grenadines) are in a currency union with a single monetary authority (the ECCB), with a single currency (the Eastern Caribbean [EC] dollar). Prior to their political independence in the 1960s, these countries, along with Barbados, British Guyana, and Trinidad and Tobago, were in a British colonial currency union administered by the British Caribbean Currency Board (BCCB), which introduced the EC dollar. The currencies of all the Caribbean territories, as British colonies, were governed within a common British Currency Board system that was, with minor variations, applied to all British colonies worldwide. (The historical development of this currency union will be examined later in the book.)

Following their independence, the other six countries (the Bahamas, Barbados, Guyana, Belize, Jamaica, and Trinidad and Tobago) developed stand-alone central banks with individual currencies, largely following the model of the Bank of England of the time. However, they soon developed individual characteristics (table 2.1) based on different policy response to the economic environment in which they functioned.

The countries of the ECCB group are micro-states in almost any terms, especially in terms of land mass and population. St Lucia has the largest ECCB population, with 152,000 people, and the second-largest landmass at 610 kilometres square. This is approximately the equivalent of 39 per cent of the Greater London Area, or 3.5 times the size of Washington, DC. Among the ECCB group, Dominica has the largest landmass, with an area of 754 kilometres square. St Kitts and Nevis has a population of 40,820, making it the smallest ECCB population included in this study (see table 2.1). The two ECCB countries excluded from this study have between them the smallest population and the smallest land area: Montserrat has a population of 7,574 and a land area of 100 kilometres square and Anguilla has a population of 12,132 and is 91 kilometres square.

The ECCB populations are mainly rural populations, with three of the six having less than 40 per cent urbanized population (see table 2.1). They also rely heavily on revenues from international tourism. International tourism receipts ranged from 30 per cent to 76 per cent as a percentage of exports for 1998 in the ECCB islands. In comparison, tourism receipts as a percentage of total exports for the United Kingdom and United States, both with important tourism sectors, were 7 per cent and 10 per cent, respectively. Therefore, there is a heavy reliance on international tourism revenues. These ECCB islands do not earn significant revenues from mineral resource endowment, such as oil, gas or bauxite. The export revenues of these countries, as a consequence of their heavy reliance on international tourism, are highly vulnerable to demand and supply shocks. All of these countries are in a geographical region subject to annual hurricanes. Therefore, for these very small countries, a hurricane can constitute a large negative supply shock, which would be reflected in the value of their national output (Bluedorn 2002).

There are six non-ECCB countries (the Bahamas, Barbados, Belize, Guyana, Jamaica, and Trinidad and Tobago) in this study. The non-ECCB countries are also physically small, although all are larger than the individual states of the ECCB. Four of these non-ECCB countries are

Table 2.1 Country Characteristic Variables

	Total Population 2004	Urban Population (% of total) 2004	International Tourism Receipts (% of exports)	GDP (per capita) PPP (US$) 2004	Growth of Real GDP (%, per capita, per annum) 1990–2003
ECCB					
Antigua and Barbuda	80,084	38	60[a]	10,095	1.6
Dominica	71,459	72	30[a]	5,188	1.2
Grenada	105,747	41	44[a]	7,355	2.4
St Kitts and Nevis	46,984	32	53[a]	11,800	3.1
St Lucia	163,650	31	76[a]	5,548	0.3
St Vincent and the Grenadines	118,428	59	46[a]	6,110	1.8
Non-ECCB					
The Bahamas	318,762	90	69[c]	16,210[d]	0.3
Barbados	268,881	52	53[b]	14,851[e]	1.4
Belize	282,600	49	30[a]	6,201	2.2
Guyana	750,232	38	4[c]	3,973	3.6
Jamaica	2,644,592	52	44[c]	3,657	0.4
Trinidad and Tobago	1,301,307	76	7[b]	11,022	3.2
United Kingdom	59,866,864	89	7[c]	28,545	2.5
United States	293,655,392	80	10[c]	36,665	2.1

Source: World Bank 2007.
International Tourism Receipts years:
[a]1998
[b]2003
[c]2004
[d]This figure for the Bahamas is for 2002.
[e]This figure for Barbados is for 2003.

island states, and two are on the South American subcontinent (Belize and Guyana). Guyana has by far the largest land area at 196,850 kilometres square. However, its population is only 750,232, and has been falling in recent decades due to economic hardship. The island of Jamaica has the next largest land area at 10,990 kilometres square, considerably larger than any ECCB country. With 2.6 million people, it has by far the largest population of all the countries in this study. The Jamaican population is twice the size of the next largest population, that of Trinidad and Tobago, which has just over 1.3 million people.

The urban–rural distribution of the populations in the non-ECCB group of countries is not different from that of the ECCB group. The non-ECCB group ranges from 38 per cent to 90 per cent urban, as compared to the ECCB group at 31 per cent to 72 per cent. Both groups, therefore, remain importantly rural, with the exception of the Bahamas that has 88 per cent of its population urbanized.

International tourism is also an important part of the economy of this non-ECCB group, with the notable exceptions of Trinidad and Tobago, and Guyana. Trinidad has an oil- and gas-based economy with some tourism in Tobago. Tobago has an important tourism sector, whereas Trinidad does not. In the aggregation, however, the relative size of the two islands hides the importance of tourism to Tobago. Guyana is an agro-based society with a history of economic decline and generally poor infrastructure. It does not have a significant international tourist industry. Among this non-ECCB group (with the exceptions of Guyana, and Trinidad and Tobago), the range of tourism receipts relative to total export earnings (44 to 69 per cent) was similar to that for the ECCB group (see table 2.1).

The three countries with the largest land area (Guyana, Jamaica, and Trinidad and Tobago) have significant mineral resource endowments relative to the rest of the countries in the study. Guyana has agricultural, bauxite, gold and various other resources; Jamaica has bauxite; and Trinidad and Tobago has oil and gas. In spite of their resource advantages, however, Guyana and Jamaica have by far the lowest per-capita incomes among all the countries of this study. Jamaica recorded the lowest per-capita GDP among the countries in 2004 with $3,657. Guyana was the next lowest, with $3,973 (see table 2.1). These low per-capita incomes are associated with prolonged and sustained economic crises in both Jamaica and Guyana (Downes 2003, 2004b; Handa and King 2003; King 2000). The next lowest per-capita income of $5,188 for Dominica was over 40 per cent greater than that of Jamaica. The Bahamas and Barbados recorded the highest per-capita GDP with $16,210 and $14,851, respectively.

A snapshot of the Caribbean economies at the turn of the twenty-first century shows a group of small nation states with very low per-capita income, at levels associated with widespread poverty and deprivation. Only the Bahamas ($16,210) and Barbados ($14,851) had per-capita income that approached half that of the United Kingdom ($28,545) and the United States ($36,665). These low per-capita incomes, combined with the relative rural composition of their population and high dependence on tourism receipts, make the small open economies of all these countries vulnerable to internal shocks from political crises and external international shocks.

2.2 Monetary Historical Institutional Background

In this section, we carry out a detailed examination of the motives and economic principles underlying certain monetary reforms. This is done to explain the institutional mechanisms set in place for currency management and monetary policy that affected Caribbean countries. From what may be regarded as the initial beginnings of modern monetary developments in 1597, the asset backing and convertibility of a currency were regarded as essential features in *restricting the excessive printing of banknotes* by the then authorized banks. Control of the supply of currency improved as the Bank of England, established in 1694, gradually became the primary and then the sole supplier of currency. The benchmark act in this regard was the 1844 Bank Charter Act, which restricted the powers of the English banks, gradually removing their issuing powers and giving the Bank of England exclusive issuing powers. The *gold standard* ushered in by this act provided full asset backing for the currency issued by the Bank of England. This act was regarded as a victory for the British Currency School, which argued that the issue of new banknotes was a major cause of price inflation.

The backing provided by the gold standard or a currency board was regarded as important in providing stability to a currency, by providing important mechanisms that seek to guard against excessive money growth and price inflation. In this post-Friedman era, the link between excessive money growth and price inflation is well established. Moreover, in our sample of countries we have evidence that such mechanisms have proved important in minor economies in fostering confidence in a currency. Nowadays, the adverse impact of high relative inflation on a country's balance of payments is well established. Mechanisms that guard against excessive monetary expansion (such as those of a currency board or monetary policy rules) are identified as crucial in establishing the conditions for economic growth and development in all economies – industrial or developing. The evidence from our sample of countries serves to demonstrate the efficacy of such mechanisms for highly vulnerable small open economies.

As a part of the British colonial empire, the twelve countries of our study were governed within a common monetary institutional framework. This 1844 Bank Charter Act linked the currency to a fixed amount of gold, and in doing so, served to establish the principles and mechanism that would govern monetary matters throughout the British Empire. Arguably, it provided the foundation for monetary policy in the Caribbean into the twenty-first century, to a greater or lesser degree. As we will discuss later in this book, the countries that have stayed closest to the colonial monetary principles and mechanism (that is, the Organisation of Eastern Caribbean States, with their common currency known as the Eastern Caribbean dollar, administered through the ECCB) have the most stable currency in the group, and are arguably among the most stable in the world (Obstfeld and Rogoff 1995). The motive underlying the 1844 act is worthy of examination because the principles that it established still influence the practice of monetary policy in the region in the twenty-first century, and indeed are relevant to macroeconomic policy in general.

The monetary policy history of Britain is characterized by attempts at reforms made to establish a monetary system, as the political economy of the times demanded, consistent with the rise of Britain to become the first industrial nation. How a country manages its currency was seen from early on as crucial to the growth and development of the nation's trade and wealth, and at various times attracted considerable attention both from scholars and government. Around the 1840s, as Britain's industrial development began to outstrip her competitors, it was widely recognized that international trade would be central in the quest for economic growth. The British pound[1] (£) was seen as playing a central role in establishing British hegemony in world trade. Establishing a reliable measure of value and medium of exchange was long agreed upon as central to the economic development of Britain. What was not agreed upon was how this was best achieved (New School 2006).

2.2.1 The Early Monetary Foundations

From 1597, *bills of exchange* and *promissory notes* issued through early merchant banks were linked to silver "of a certain fineness" at a fixed rate. This established a *silver standard,* wherein a certain amount of silver of a standardized quality was linked to a British pound. The pound sterling

---

[1] Throughout this text we will use the term British pound and £ interchangeably. Pound sterling is also used equivalently, although less often. The £ sign is particularly useful in order to provide clear in-line text, especially in this chapter, and to obviate the confusion between currency and weight.

currency – associated with a given sterling silver – was moreover *convertible* into silver. This ability to convert paper currency into silver at a fixed rate at the issuing bank was known as *convertibility* and was long regarded as an important quality for a currency to provide security for the holders of the issued banknotes, among other things, and to prevent the excessive printing of banknotes by the legally permitted banks. From its start in 1694, the Bank of England was primary among banks that were legally enabled to issue *banknotes*.[2] Convertibility was a feature of its operations from the start. "The Bank's royal charter allowed the bank to operate as a joint-stock bank with limited liability and granted the right to issue notes payable on demand" (Trev 2006). Convertibility could be, and was, suspended by the government when economic and political circumstances demanded.

The 1797 Suspension of Cash Payments by the Bank of England Act suspended the convertibility of currency into precious metals. This was a major monetary policy move that was implemented when the country was in the midst of the 1792–1815 Napoleonic Wars that threatened the survival of the nation state. As is usually the case in times of unrest or war, there was considerable capital flight and runs on banks as people sought to convert paper into *specie*. Two factors lay behind this policy. First, convertibility made capital flight easy. Second, and more important, the government needed to finance the war effort to pay for munitions and European armies to fight the French in Europe. Such international payments had to be made in the most part in *specie*, not by banknotes. The government's reaction to this was the 1797 act that suspended convertibility for private transactions, leaving the precious metals for use by the government. The French wars ended with the decisive defeat of Napoleon's army in 1815. In the following year, the 1816 Coinage Act fixed the gold content of a British pound as the standard unit of currency[3] and the 1819 Resumption of Cash Payments Act that restored convertibility in 1821 completed the establishment of the gold standard in practice and in law in Britain for the first time (Davies 2002; Keynes 1925). The 1833 Bank of England Act awarded the bank some further temporary monopoly privileges and continued the obligation of the bank to redeem its notes in gold and silver, but it was the 1844 Bank Charter Act that established the long-term foundation for monopoly central banking of the modern Bank of England.

The 1844 Bank Charter Act set out the principles and objectives that would underpin the operations of monetary authorities, not only in Great Britain, but throughout the British Empire. The historical importance of this act was always evident. At its introduction, Prime Minister Sir Robert Peel said that the matters covered in the act were of "vast and manifest importance", and sought to set down in the act "matters of fundamental principles". He was clear that what he sought to do was to re-establish the link between the pound (£) as a "measure of value" and a "medium of exchange . . . according to the ancient monetary policy of the country, according to the law, according to the practice that prevailed at all time, excepting during the period of

---

[2] "A banknote is a form of promissory note, which developed from the bill of exchange – an open letter requesting one person to pay a stated sum of money to another on behalf of the person who wrote the letter. A development was to make the notes 'payable to bearer', rather than to a named individual" (Trev 2006). This enabled the issued paper to be freely exchanged, as long as people had confidence in the banks' willingness and ability to honour the notes.

[3] This bill established the British pound (the sovereign) as the standard unit of currency and confirmed the valuation of one standard ounce of gold (11/12 fine) at £3.17.10½ (http://www.gold.org/value/reserve_asset/history/monetary_history/vol1/1816may31.html).

inconvertible paper currency, that a certain quantity of the precious metals, definite in point of weight and fineness, has constituted, and ought to constitute the measure of value". This reform was aimed at inspiring confidence in the currency so that "legislation could ensure the just reward for industry, and the legitimate profit of commercial enterprise conducted with integrity and controlled by provident calculations" (Peel 1844).

The 1844 act not only began the process of granting longstanding monopoly note issuing powers to the Bank of England, but also established the principle that the issue of new banknotes would be 100 per cent backed by gold. It is this act, more than any other, that may be seen as establishing the classic period of the Gold Standard in Britain's modern economic history. This act, however, did not only determine the principles underlying the management of money in Britain, it importantly determined how the management of money would function throughout the British Empire, hence its relevance to this study. The principles underlying the functioning of monetary matters in the colonies were no less governed by the principles established in this 1844 Bank Charter Act for Britain. Convertibility and the full backing of currency were to be central features of that management.

The fundamental motive in Prime Minister Peel's reform was to establish a stable currency and a credible monetary system. He sought as a primary objective to ensure that the currency would function effectively as a *measure of value* and *medium of exchange*. The link to gold, through its full backing, and the security of knowing that the Bank of England banknotes could be converted to bullion, was specifically designed to bring about this objective. By giving this goal the highest priority, the government sought to establish and maintain the long-term credibility of its primary monetary institution, its currency and its financial structure. Such a monetary framework, based on a gold standard and a currency board with a fully backed currency, should provide support to the maintenance of a low-inflation regime, it was argued, and thus enhance confidence in the monetary system. Although the act laid down longstanding fundamental principles, the government nevertheless retained the power to suspend the act in case of financial crises. This, in fact, happened several times: in 1847; in 1857; and during the Overend-Gurney crisis in 1866. In the process, the Bank of England improved its management of financial crises. The Overend-Gurney crisis saw the last major run on an English bank until the bank run on Northern Rock 141 years later.

The monetary system set in place by the 1844 act formed the framework for monetary policy throughout the British Empire until the suspension of gold standard with the outbreak of World War One in 1914. In response to the monetary demands of the war, the gold standard and convertibility was suspended in Britain. Other countries' money supply was determined through fiduciary issue, and exchange rates were allowed to float against each other, instead of being linked to gold.

Inflation was relatively high during the war years. "If 1914 is taken as the base year (= 100), wholesale prices in December 1918 were: France 355; United Kingdom 246; United States 202" (http://www.econ.iastate.edu/classes/econ355/choi/golds.htm). With wages and prices significantly higher after the war than prior to the war, attempts by the United Kingdom and United States governments, among others, to re-establish their currencies at the pre-war gold standard parities, in effect, significantly overvalued their currencies.

This concept of the overvaluation of a currency and the economic instability that it can generate is crucial in explaining some of the difficulties faced by many countries, including those of the

Caribbean, during the latter part of the twentieth century. It is, therefore, worthwhile to explain the primary transmission mechanisms that could be set into play through an overvaluation.

The primary source of currency overvaluation is usually differences in inflation rates across countries that conduct international trade. The overvaluation transmission mechanism may be illustrated in terms of a closed economy as follows: Prior to the war, a pound could buy a basket of goods and services value-indexed at 100, and could also buy gold at £1 = 113 grains[4] – *1 troy ounce = 480 grains* (http://www.econ.iastate.edu/classes/econ355/choi/golds.htm). After the war, a pound could buy a basket of goods valued at 40.65 per cent of the pre-war basket: (100/246 = 0.4065). However, the move to re-establish the gold standard to its pre-war parity would still mean that a pound could buy gold at £1 = 113 grains of gold. This meant that the currency, which had lost nearly 60 per cent of its value in terms of its purchasing power of labour, goods and services, would lose *none* of its purchasing power with respect to gold. Under such circumstances, the printed paper money is said to be *overvalued*. It is overvalued with respect to the *gold standard*.

The market-determined value of the pound indicated that the value of the pound should also fall nearly 60 per cent with respect to gold, as it had with domestic purchases. Under such circumstances, it is entirely rational for holders of gold not to exchange the gold for currency, especially because gold has an intrinsic value and paper money has none. It is the intrinsic value of gold that has made it historically a store of value and medium of exchange. Moreover, it was this precise quality that made governments seek to tie the issue of bank notes to a precious metal. It would be entirely rational and a source of significant fortune for holders of paper currency to be able to convert paper money into gold at the old rate, but for reasons discussed above, holders of gold would be justly reluctant to make such a trade.

The macroeconomic impact of such a currency overvaluation would be a reduction in the supply of gold-backed money, since holders of gold would be reluctant to exchange it for paper currency. The gap between the supply of money and the demand for money would tend to grow, and this would increase interest rates. This would, in turn, tend to generate a slowdown in investment, economic activity and output, and result in deflation and growing unemployment. Such monetary conditions are not conducive to economic growth, but rather to economic stagnation and unemployment.

The overvaluation transmission mechanism also extends to stagnation effects arising from international trade, so that there is an internal and external dimension to the effects. This may be illustrated in an open economy context as follows:

Prior to the war, the Coinage Act of 1816 fixed the value of £1 = 113 grains of pure gold, and one dollar ($) was defined to be equal to 23.22 grains of pure gold. Thus, the par exchange rate between the dollar and the pound was £ = 113/23.22 = $4.866. At home, prior to the war a pound could buy a basket of goods and services value-indexed at 100. After the war, when the

---

[4] The reference in the act referred not to a single pound (£) as the point of reference but to a troy ounce, so that reference is made not to a £, but to £3.17.10½ for an ounce of gold, "as the standard unit of currency and confirms the valuation of one standard ounce of gold (11/12 fine) at £3.17.10½" (http://www.econ.iastate.edu/classes/econ355/choi/golds.htm). The 1925 Gold Standard Act that re-established that parity stated: "the Bank of England shall be bound to sell to any person who makes a demand . . . gold bullion at the price of three pounds, seventeen shillings and ten pence halfpenny per ounce troy of gold of the standard fineness prescribed for gold coin by the Coinage Act, 1870" (Keynes 1925).

gold standard was re-adopted by the United States (1919) and by the United Kingdom (1925) at its pre-war parity, the pound and the dollar were freely convertible into gold at £1 = $4.866. In the United States, the dollar was only able to buy 49.5 per cent (roughly half) of its pre-war basket of goods and services (1914 = 100, 1918 = 202). The re-establishment of the pre-war parity, however, would cause the pound to be considerably overvalued, since inflation in the United Kingdom was greater than the inflation in the United States. During the war, the dollar lost 50.5 per cent of its domestic value, but the loss of value in the pound was greater, at 59.1 per cent of its value. This meant that a pound could in effect increase its purchasing power by buying goods and services in the United States. A pound that would purchase $4.866 goods in real terms prior to the war would, in effect, be valued in real terms at £ = 4.866 (246/202) = $5.9259 after the war at the re-established pre-war gold standard rates. Conversely, the overvaluation of the pound meant an undervaluation of the dollar. The purchasing power of the dollar fell in real terms with respect to the pound. A dollar that was worth $ = 1/4.866 = £0.2055 prior to the war fell to $ = 1/5.9259 = £0.16875 after the war at the re-established pre-war gold standard rates. This represented an effective fall in the purchasing power of the dollar with respect to the pound of almost 18 per cent (1 − (0.16875/0.2055) = 0.179).

The significant relative inflation across different countries and the quest to re-establish the gold standard, and thus effectively, the exchange rates between currencies at the pre-war rates, caused a misalignment between currencies that affected the international trade competitiveness between countries. This resulted in countries with an overvalued currency, such as Britain, incurring balance of payment deficits, whereas countries such as France, which had an undervalued currency, ran a balance of payments surplus. The deficits resulted in a reduction in output and investment and an increase in unemployment. The standard expectation following consistent balance of payments deficits is stagnation and unemployment that may, in the absence of suitable macroeconomic adjustment, also develop into a currency crisis. Evidence of such effects among our sample countries will be discussed later when we examine the impact of high inflation associated with high growth in the money supply.

In his authoritative account of the British colonial currency system published in the *Economic Journal* in 1944, G.L.M. Clauson noted that the colonial territories, or dependencies, as he terms them, may be seen as comprising four groups:

1. The sterling group (comprising all the dependencies not otherwise enumerated)
2. The rupee group (Aden, Ceylon, Mauritius, the Seychelles and Somaliland)
3. The ex-silver group (Malaya, the British dependencies in Borneo and Hong Kong)
4. The US dollar colony (British Honduras)

"By far the biggest of the four groups enumerated above", stated Clauson, "is the 'sterling group'". Although conditions varied widely between the different colonial territories, Clauson (1944, 2) noted the following:

> Whatever the precise situation of the currency, all the Dependencies alike can best be described as being on a sterling (or rupee or United States dollar) exchange basis, and all share the characteristics of not having independent currencies. There is in them no

central bank or other institution which can issue or withdraw currency at will; the function of the Currency Authority (which is the most convenient collective title for the Currency Boards, Commissioners of Currency and other responsible authorities) is simply that of a money-changer, issuing physical currency on demand in exchange for bank payments in the principal or parent currency (sterling, rupees or United States dollars, as the case may be) or redeeming it as required, by payments in that currency. These functions are automatic, not discretionary, and are performed under the sanction of Orders-in council, local Ordinances or other legislative enactments.

The British Caribbean dependencies were on what was in essence a sterling area and was so formalized in 1939. Monetary policy based on the adherence to the principles that sought to ensure monetary stability was then effected through administrative mechanisms based on colonial currencies being fully backed in a currency board arrangement, managed through the British civil service. As such, this arrangement was in essence an equivalent derivative of the British pound being on a gold standard.

In a work entitled *The History of Colonial Currency* by Lord Chalmers, published fifty years earlier, Barbados was used as the representative case study to illustrate the colonial sterling group. In his 1944 study, however, the West African dependencies comprised of Gambia, the Gold Coast, Nigeria and Sierra Leone are used as representative of the sterling group of countries. The arrangements governing the monetary arrangements of the colonies were essentially the same, as he explains, so adopting Barbados or the West African dependencies would make no essential difference to the analysis. Clauson (1944, 4) writes:

> In 1912 there was presented to Parliament as Cd. 6426 the "Report of a Departmental Committee appointed to inquire into matters affecting the Currency of the British West African Colonies and Protectorates". It starts by stating the existing currency position in those Dependencies. The legal tender in all of them was gold, silver and copper coinage of the United Kingdom . . .
>
> At this time the ordinary arrangement in regard to the British Colonies was that any banker, merchant, or other person requiring silver coin in a Colony could have it delivered to him in the Colony by paying the face value in London, the Government bearing the cost of delivery. Special arrangements . . . had recently been terminated, and the position now was the same as that in the other Dependencies.
>
> Thus in 1912 . . . the coinage and monetary system of the West African Dependencies was indistinguishable from that of, say, any English county or the Isle of Man, except that, although there were British banks in the area, there were no bank notes.

In their analysis of money and banking in British Colonial Africa, Newlyn and Rowan (1954, 43) remarked on the essential effect of the linkage of the colonial currency to sterling:

> The currency system inaugurated with the establishment of the West African Currency Board provided the four West African territories with a variety of "managed money" as this concept is defined by Keynes (1930, 7–8).

> The intention of the Committee was to institute a gold exchange standard under which reserves would be held partly in gold and partly in sterling securities. Keynes, indeed, in referring to the system in his *Indian Currency and Finance*, described it in precisely these terms (Keynes 1913, 35). In fact, however, appearances were deceptive, and what was really established was a sterling exchange standard. This was plainly demonstrated when sterling depreciated in terms of gold. As a consequence, not of the exchange standard itself but of the form it has taken in West Africa, the West African pound has no independent existence but is merely the pound sterling by another name.

Clauson (1944, 7–10) noted some modification to the monetary system associated with the wartime suspension of the gold standard:

> By 1922 the permanent arrangements for expanding and contracting the currency in circulation had been fully worked out and tested in practice . . . [T]hese are, except in one respect, the standard arrangements for all Colonial currencies . . . In effect the creation of the [West African Currency] Board provided both a depository in the Dependency in which surplus currency could be placed, and a source in the Dependency from which extra currency could be obtained, at short notice, and currency in the depository was a completely sterilised as unissued Bank of England notes in the Bank . . . The arrangement made for issue and withdrawal in West Africa is exceptional, in that the Board, unlike the other Colonial Currency Authorities, deals in practice only with banks. The reasons for this special arrangement arise from the previous history of currency in West Africa, and it is possible that they will not continue indefinitely. With this exception the West African arrangements are entirely typical. The Board is under an obligation to instruct its Currency Officers in West Africa to issue coin and notes on a £ for £ basis to the local branch of any bank in West Africa, on receiving from the head office in London the equivalent amount in sterling plus a small commission . . . It is also under an obligation, if a bank branch in West Africa lodges coin or notes with one of its Currency Officers, to pay the equivalent amount, less the same small commission, to the head office of the bank in London. The functions of the Board are wholly passive in the matter, they can neither refuse nor initiate transactions; the only element of discretion which they possess is that they can, subject to the approval of the Secretary of State for the Colonies, discourage the excessive use of the facilities provided by increasing the rate of commission. But the permissible maximum rate is quite a low one, and they must, of course, charge the same rate to all customers . . .
>
> It must be emphasised that this system, though it guarantees the conversion of any Colonial currency presented for redemption into sterling, makes no provision for its conversion into any other currency . . .
>
> As has been stated already, the description just given is equally applicable to any other Colonial currency in the "sterling group", except that in other Dependencies the Currency Authority offers the same facilities to any member of the public as the West African Board offers to the bank alone . . .

> [T]here are only three Currency Boards proper, located in London: the West African currency Board (covering the Gambia, the Gold Coast, Nigeria and Sierra Leone), the East African Currency Board (covering Kenya, Tanganyika Territory, Uganda and Zanzibar), and the Palestine Currency Board (covering Palestine and Trans-Jordan).
>
> In nearly all other Dependencies, both in the "sterling group" and the other groups mentioned above, the functions of currency control are exercised by a local commissioner of Currency, or a Board of Commissioners of Currency, located at the capital of the Dependency concerned. The system operates in exactly the same way as that described above, except that the Commissioners, instead of the Board's Currency Officers, issue and redeem currency, and the Crown Agents for the Colonies, acting as the Commissioners' London agents, instead of the Board, issue and receive sterling and invest moneys not immediately required, under the general instructions of the Commissioners.

It is clear from the historical literature that the arrangements governing monetary management in the colonies arose from the quest to ensure monetary stability through the imposition of a gold standard where the pound would be fully backed by gold, although convertibility would be suspended at times of significant financial crises and war. The monetary framework governing the colonies was no less strict in the adherence to the principles established for the homeland British pound. Although the circumstances and the situation of each of the colonial territories varied, the essential framework governing money throughout the colony was based on a bullion or sterling standard, thus effectively meeting the principles forwarded in the 1844 act. In concluding his comprehensive analysis of the West African Currency Board operations, Clauson (1944, 13) states:

> The rest of the "sterling group" need less full description. In most of these dependencies the present sterling exchange systems have developed out of note issues of an older pattern under which the notes were redeemable in local standard coin (normally United Kingdom coin) and reserves against them were held partly in bullion and partly in sterling securities. The bullion portions were reduced at various stages, and during the period 1918–39 the present system of issue and redemption against sterling and the holding of all reserves in sterling securities or deposits was substituted.

Clauson (1944, 14–15) covers the particular monetary features of the Caribbean, noting that the West Indies "are eccentric in many respects". But these eccentricities are systemic in their nature and are concerned mainly with the particular coins and their denominations, and the curiosity of an imperial and metric system being simultaneously employed in some Caribbean countries.

> In some Colonies, notably Jamaica, Bermuda and the Falkland Islands, both the Government and the public keep their accounts in £ s.d. In other colonies, notably British Guiana, Trinidad and the Windward Islands, although the coinage is expressed

> in shillings and pence, accounts are kept both by the Government and by the public in dollars and cents . . . In the remainder (Barbados, the Bahamas and the Leeward Islands) the Governments keep their accounts in £ s.d. and the public usually in dollars and cents . . . In most Colonies certain United Kingdom and Canadian Banks have, and exercise, the right to issue bank-notes. There has been some tendency towards . . . the gradual substitution of Government notes for the bank notes. (Clauson 1944, 15)

A Board of Commissioners was constituted in Jamaica in 1904 to issue notes. Successive laws gave additional responsibilities to the Board of Commissioners and it functioned until it was replaced by the establishment of the Jamaican central bank, the Bank of Jamaica, in October 1960.

The British West Indies dollar (BWI$) was adopted in 1935 and administered by a regional currency authority. The West Indies was not to have a currency board until 1950. The currency was originally used regionally by the various British West Indies territories and was later to be adopted by the ill-fated Federation of the West Indies.

In 1950, the British government established the British Caribbean Currency Board (BCCB) as the central monetary authority for British colonies in the Caribbean. The BCCB did not cover Jamaica and the Bahamas, which had their own Board of Commissioners that administered monetary policy in those countries. The BCCB introduced the Eastern Caribbean dollar (EC dollar) on its establishment in 1950 to serve Barbados, Guyana, Trinidad and Tobago and the current member states of the ECCB (Antigua and Barbuda, Dominica, Grenada, Montserrat, St Kitts and Nevis, Anguilla, St Lucia, and St Vincent and the Grenadines). These comprised the British colonies of the Caribbean, excluding Jamaica and the Bahamas, which are geographically distant from these other colonies (see the map of the Caribbean). The BCCB functioned as a standard British currency board with every BWI dollar put into circulation backed 100 per cent by foreign reserves, which were invested in British government securities and treasury bills, in much the way described above. To obtain BCCB currency, banks in the region had to deposit with the Currency Board's agents in London, the equivalent amount of sterling for the currency required.

Thus, the governing colonial monetary institution in the Caribbean was a long established fully backed system (a currency board system), and although it evolved, it essentially remained in place well into the post–World War Two period (Schuler 1992). "Under the old Currency Board system, colonial governments were authorised to issue new currency only against the equivalent holding of sterling securities . . . Barbados, Guyana, Trinidad and Tobago and the present Organisation of Eastern Caribbean States (OECS) shared the same currency under the British Caribbean Currency Board (BCCB)" (Blackman 1998, 248).

In 1958, the quest for political autonomy by some of the British Caribbean colonies led to the formation of the short-lived 1958–1962 Federation of the West Indies (Lewis 1968). The BWI dollar was the federation currency, but it was not introduced in Jamaica, which was always administered through its own Currency Board of Commissioners. The intention of Jamaica to leave the federation, following a referendum in that island to decide between continued membership or the setting up of an independent Jamaican state, led to the threat that Trinidad and Tobago would also leave, if Jamaica, the largest economy, left the federation. In 1962 Jamaica, closely followed by Trinidad and Tobago, left the federation and obtained political independence from Britain. This led to the dissolution of the federation, despite a determined effort by W. Arthur Lewis to convince the other countries to continue with a smaller federation of states that excluded the two largest economies.

Following the break-up of the federation, Jamaica (1962), Trinidad and Tobago (1962), Guyana (1966) and Barbados (1966) obtained their political independence from Britain and established independent nation states.

Jamaica was the first Caribbean country to gain its independence from Britain in 1962. As a part of that self-governing process, the Bank of Jamaica was established in that year with a regulatory framework modelled on the Bank of England. The Bank of Jamaica was, like the Bank of England at that time, not an independent central bank, but subject to the discretionary demands that the government of the day placed on it. On its establishment, however, the Bank of Jamaica announced its intention to follow the full backing of its currency as under its predecessor, the Currency Board of Commissioners. C.Y. Thomas (1972) provides clear evidence of this in his invaluable account of early central banking in the Caribbean. Quoting a Bank of Jamaica document on its establishment:

> None of this, however, has affected the basic advantage of the sterling exchange system. The whole of the money supply (active currency circulation plus bank deposits) is still effectively backed pound for pound by sterling. The Central Bank has to be prepared to provide sterling to meet on demand any Jamaican currency offered for redemption and this also applies to the commercial banks' deposits with the Central Bank . . . The significance of the existence of the Central Bank and the fiduciary issue is that great care has to be exercised in the creation of money not backed by sterling assets – in other words, Central Bank lending to Government, whether by way of taking up Treasury Bills or by direct advances. (Thomas 1972, 35–36)[5]

In analysing the performance of the Bank of Jamaica from its inception to 1969, the bank came under considerable criticism for its continuation of the "open economy stable money" policy of its Currency Board predecessor. The monetary policy that gave priority to monetary stability, which came from backing the currency with foreign but mainly sterling reserves, was seen as evidence of the dereliction of duty to the domestic economy in its early quest to secure a path to economic and social development. Professor Thomas, a leading commentator at the time, writing from the University of the West Indies and the University of Guyana, provides a clear statement of this criticism:

> In a most fundamental sense, the policies pursued here were really externally oriented. Stable exchange rates, easy and free convertibility of the local currency into sterling, together with minimum state intervention, except for fostering the growth of financial markets which would make private enterprise more efficient, were the foundations of these policies. This approach was also consistent with the Government's views of the

---

[5] Thomas (1972, 36) footnotes this as a quote from *Annual Report,* Bank of Jamaica 1961, 14.

> development process, which relied heavily on the unencumbered inflow of private foreign capital and unhampered private decisions about the allocation of resources. It was this type of development policy which accounted for the original creation of Currency Boards, and which serves to explain why the Central Bank was so determined to minimize the differences between its powers and those of the Currency Board. (Thomas 1972, 39)

The brunt of Thomas's criticism rests on the quest to give primacy to effectively linking the Jamaican currency with a *sterling standard,* thus continuing the process described above that gave primacy to monetary stability – maintaining constancy in the currency as a *medium of exchange* and a *store of value*. From this distance in time, it is more easily seen that this type of criticism that was being developed especially by the emerging economists of the new independent developing nations, arose from the confluence of the policies and historical role that the colonial territories played over preceding centuries, and the newly developed Keynesian macroeconomics that gave governments a more influential role in the determination of the macroeconomic outcome.

With respect to the historical role, it was clear to this first generation[6] of economists that the ambition of colonial governments had never extended to the social and economic development of their territories (Hart 1990). The Caribbean countries, like many countries at the time were not democracies. Governments in the Caribbean did not represent the majority of inhabitants of the islands. The basic instrument of productive domestic investments required the permission of the Colonial Office in London. This was not given if such domestic investments were perceived as against the interest of homeland British firms.

Richard Hart (1998, 107) notes: "One of the most convincing arguments for self-government was that if Jamaicans were able to elect their own government such a government would give priority to local interests and encourage industrialisation." The social and economic condition in the Caribbean was a residual of the quest to enrich the British colonial interests who influenced and controlled production and trade in and out of the countries. This was no hidden agenda, but the general state of affairs for all colonized territories. The appeal to the self-interest of the people of the Caribbean in particular, and colonized people in general, rested on the assertion that they would be best off in this arrangement. This assertion meant that, in general, the colonized people were best served by the peripheral benefits of the colonial regime than any other governing arrangements.

It is noteworthy that they all, at first (including the new fully independent nations), adopted fixed exchange rate regimes pegged to the British pound, but from the 1970s they all pegged their currencies to the US dollar in a variety of exchange regimes (fixed, floating and currency board). This arose because, initially, all these countries were members of the so-called *sterling area,* comprised mainly of British Commonwealth countries. The main feature of the sterling area was that its members were prepared to accept sterling freely, and to settle any deficit with each other in sterling. These arrangements grew out of the British Empire colonial trading and banking relationships of the nineteenth century, and were formalized in exchange controls introduced in Britain in 1939.

---

[6] Nobel laureate Sir W. Arthur Lewis, from the Caribbean island of St Lucia, from work done during this early period was later acknowledged as among the primary founders of what is now known as "development economics".

Following the unexpected devaluation of sterling by the British government in November 1967, they all signed up to the Basle Facility in 1968, which required each member of the sterling area to agree to hold a certain minimum proportion of its exchange reserves in sterling for a period of three to five years. The Basle Facility sought to protect sterling and was costly to its signatories as sterling fell in value against other reserve currencies. The support of the newly independent countries marked a watershed in their transition from colonial territories to politically independent states. This is evident by the fact that at the end of the agreement period the countries quickly de-linked their currencies from sterling and pegged them to the US dollar, which had replaced sterling as their major trading currency.

As economists of the newly independent states developed their understanding of how the economic system worked, and found evidence of deliberate policies and indeed an institutional structure, designed in particular to retard its growth and development, increasing attention was given to seeing how such structural constraints could be broken. The establishment of a central bank that had as a primary aim growth and development objectives was seen as a vital plank to social and economic progress. In Jamaica, however, the maintenance of a currency board system was the primary ambition of the newly developed central bank, and this was not a unique experience. The Bank of Jamaica records the following:

The main objectives of the Central Bank were defined by the Bank of Jamaica Act to be:

- to issue and redeem notes and coins
- to keep and administer the reserves of Jamaica
- to influence the volume and conditions of supply of credit so as to promote the fullest expansion in production, trade and employment, consistent with the maintenance of monetary stability in Jamaica and the external value of the currency
- to foster the development of money and capital markets in Jamaica
- to act as banker to the government

Increasingly among economists, and especially so among many development economists, social and economic development came to be more widely seen as requiring a more general role for central banks. In the case of Jamaica, the bank records the following: "In the earlier years, the Central Bank's role tended to be of a largely reactive nature as the institution grappled with several national and international developments. However, in recent years, monetary policy implementation has been characterized by a more proactive stance, as the Central Bank has actively sought to encourage the appropriate environment for economic growth and development" (Bank of Jamaica 2007).

From the 1930s to the 1970s, the demand for economic development abetted by an atmosphere dominated by Keynesian economics. One of its central tenets was that, through demand management, government could influence the operation of the economy, led in many countries to what we would nowadays regard as *reckless deficit financing*. This phenomenon was by no means confined to developing countries. At various times, it was significant in industrial countries. Caribbean evidence of the movement to a developmental role for monetary policy soon emerged on the establishment of central banks. Thomas (1972, 20) writes the following:

> During its four years of full operations the Central Bank of Guyana has had to encounter four major crises. The first of these centred on its ability to impose effective limits on public sector credit. This crisis can be seen from developments in 1966 in which the Central Bank clearly felt, and indeed argued in its Annual Report for that year, that the indiscriminate use of its credit-creating powers had led to huge increases in government deficit financing.

Thomas notes that the law under which the Central Bank of Guyana is constituted "does not permit the Bank much room for manoeuvre in the *restraint* of credit" (Thomas 1972, 24).

Trinidad and Tobago showed evidence of imprudent government deficit financing right from the start of its central bank operations. In the case of Trinidad and Tobago Thomas (1972, 28) writes the following: "As with its Guyana counterpart, the Central Bank of Trinidad-Tobago also ran into what it interpreted to be a very serious financial crisis in 1966, its first year of full operations, and which it attributed to the injudicious use of its capacity to grant credit to the public sector." Although the Bank of Jamaica showed some effort to retain the currency board framework at the start, it also soon joined the Bank of Guyana and the Central Bank of Trinidad and Tobago in financing large government deficits that resulted in inflation generating increases in their money supplies. The cases of the remaining members of the defunct Federation of the West Indies, however, were different.

In 1964, the BCCB was dissolved and replaced by the East Caribbean Currency Authority (ECCA), established in January 1965 with headquarters in Barbados, and the Eastern Caribbean dollar (EC dollar) was introduced. During the early years of the ECCA's operation, commercial banks wanting to obtain cash had to continue to deposit the sterling equivalent with the Authority's agents in London. Thus, by regulation, the EC dollar was backed 100 per cent by sterling (ECCA 1982). In this regard, the ECCA acted much like its BCCB predecessor (ECCA 1982). Over time, however, the ECCA began lending to its member governments, and the 100 per cent foreign asset backing was formally reduced to requiring it to maintain a minimum of 60 per cent external assets backing of the currency in circulation, and other demand liabilities. In reality, however, the ECCA continued to maintain reserves at its previous levels, although it had the ability to, in practice, substantially reduce the backing of the currency. This cautionary practice, as we will discuss later on, has carried over to the successor of the ECCA, the Eastern Caribbean Central Bank (ECCB).

When the ECCA was established in 1964, its member states were not independent states, they were still British dependencies. As such, "there was not a great deal of scope for the Authority to perform even those functions which were provided for in its statute" (ECCA 1982). However, as member states became increasingly politically independent, the role of the Authority increased to support government monetary and fiscal activities, both nationally and internationally.

As its role developed, the ECCA was able to lend to member governments by investing in publicly issued Treasury Bills, but its holding of such bills was limited to 10 per cent of the estimated recurrent revenue of the particular government for the financial year. This was designed to provide short-term fiscal support while limiting the extent to which any fiscal deficit could be financed. The Authority also invested in longer-term securities, but this was also limited to

15 per cent of the Authority's demand liabilities. These statutory limitations constrained the ECCA in its support of member governments' fiscal programmes, constraints that were conspicuously absent in some of the other Caribbean central banks, as we will discuss.

For the small open economies of the ECCA member states, the above arrangements worked to stabilize its foreign assets by curbing foreign currency demand, since the ECCA was limited in the amount of credit it could create. This arrangement effectively constrained not only the size of the budget deficit in any particular year, but also constrained domestic demand. Under these arrangements, the level of foreign reserves is determined significantly by currency backing requirements – it is not predominantly a determinant of the balance of payments as is usually the case. This, in turn, serves to stabilize the exchange rate with far-reaching beneficial social and economic effects.

The central banks that developed in the English-speaking Caribbean were all products of their colonial heritage and, by design, modelled on the Bank of England at that time, where a primary characteristic was that it was subject to the dictates of the government. Right from the start, however, they developed along individual lines driven by national social and economic forces. The ECCB, arising out of the BCCB, as we have seen, retained much of its historical ties to the currency board and currency union aspects while developing as a central bank to its member states.

2.3 Central Bank Characteristics

2.3.1 The Eastern Caribbean Central Bank

The ECCB was established on 1 October 1983 to promote monetary stability and build a financial structure conducive to growth and development (Harris 1992). Unlike the ECCA, its predecessor, it was able to offer advice to governments. It was empowered to supervise the banking system, impose reserve requirements on financial institutions within its domain and encourage the pursuit of prudent and relevant credit policies (ECCB 1984). In these regards, the ECCB has features common with many central banks. The ECCB however, is a rare example of a multinational central bank in that it functions with considerable aspects of a currency board. It is noteworthy that while the regulatory minimum backing of the EC dollar remained at 60 per cent, the international assets held are often well in excess of that minimum. In March 2002, for example, the backing was 97 per cent (correspondence from the ECCB, 7 March 2002). Indeed, the international assets usually approximate 100 per cent backing of the money supply, rather than tend towards the legal 60 per cent minimum.

The effect of this currency board-based institutional structure is that monetary policy among the Eastern Caribbean states is effectively constrained by its regulatory framework. For example, this imposes notable constraints on fiscal policy in that fiscal deficits cannot be routinely financed through the issue of bills and bonds or increases in the money supply (Williams, Polius and Hazel 2005). These binding regulatory constraints thus served to enforce prudent, conservative monetary and fiscal policies that were not often observable among some of the other Caribbean economies, such as Guyana, Jamaica, and Trinidad and Tobago. The central banks of these countries, from the outset or soon thereafter, embarked on rapid increases in the money supply, due largely to financing government deficit expenditures. A notable exception was the case of Barbados. Although it was a stand-alone central bank, *and* although monetary policy was essentially discretionary, monetary policy was in the main distinctly conservative and, in this regard, can be seen as different from that of Guyana, Jamaica, and Trinidad and Tobago.

2.3.2 Central Bank of Barbados

Barbados left the ECCA (the predecessor of the ECCB) and formed its own central bank, the Bank of Barbados, in June 1972, again modelled along the lines as that of the Bank of England. However, from its inception, the Bank of Barbados not only exhibited a high regard for the goals of monetary stability, but also established a high degree of credibility as a monetary authority. The governor for the first fifteen years of its operations noted the following:

> Shortly after my appointment as Governor of the Central Bank of Barbados in 1972, I warned that the central bank was a "two-edged sword". A well-managed central bank can provide new credit to stimulate a depressed economy and restrain the expansion of money and credit during a boom. In particular, it can assist a prudent government in meeting its short-term liquidity needs more economically than by borrowing from commercial banks as in the old currency board days. On the other hand, excessive money creation in open economies, especially for the financing of fiscal deficits, will not only lead swiftly to inflation but also to balance of payments collapse, wreaking considerable economic and social havoc. (Blackman 1998, xvii)

This warning appears to have played a central role in the operations of the Central Bank of Barbados since then.

The Barbadian dollar (Bds$) was first issued in December 1973. From its introduction until 1975, the Barbadian dollar and the EC dollar maintained direct parity, and so had the same exchange rate tied to sterling. Circulation of the EC dollar in Barbados was, however, phased out over the first two years of circulation of the Barbadian dollar. Barbados later cut its ties with sterling in July 1975, as well as its parity with the EC dollar, and pegged the value of its dollar at Bds$2.00 = US$1.00.[7] That rate has remained constant over our sample period of 1980 / 81–2002/4,[8] and until the time of writing in 2008. Table 2.3 shows that over the period 1980 to 2002 the average annual rate of growth of broad money (8.4 per cent) was more in

---

[7] This revalued the BD$ upward relative to the EC$ that was pegged at US$ = EC$2.70 – an effective devaluation of the EC$.
[8] The dataset for table 2.3 is the same as that for the econometric analysis that follows so that the analytical contexts remain that same. The original download of the data was November 2007 and the publication revisions took place in August 2008.

line with the money growth of ECCB countries than with that of Jamaica, Guyana, or Trinidad and Tobago.

Although the essential institutional features of the stand-alone central banks were the same, monetary management in Barbados was considerably more prudent. An important aspect of the Barbados success seems to arise from the policy credibility that was rapidly established with the development of the Central Bank of Barbados. What we mean by "credibility" is that the private sector, both households and firms, soon established a relationship whereby the central bank, or rather, monetary policy pronouncements, could be taken seriously. They would be the basis on which expectations about the future could be formed.

Credibility, as a feature of monetary policy, is important in the literature. It is associated with the formation of expectations by the private sector and the follow-through of policy intentions by the monetary authority. The basic way that credibility is seen as working is as follows: A central bank announces the intention to follow a low inflation, stable exchange rate policy, and households and firms form their expectations and actions for the future based on this announcement. If then, monetary policy is expansionary and inflation is high and the exchange is devalued, the credibility of the central bank, or rather the credibility of monetary policy, is damaged and households and firms will not find it entirely rational to base their decisions about the future on policy announcements.

Consistency over time (referred to as time consistency) in policy announcement, implementation and outcome is important, therefore, in establishing institutional and policy credibility. Credibility is increasingly seen as crucial in the success of monetary policy (Clarida, Gali and Gertler 1999; Alesina and Summers, 1993). In this regard, the Central Bank of Barbados acquired an enviable record of credibility. A detailed look at that experience will show it to be not easily obtained in either personal, political or policy terms (Blackman 2006, 117–53; Blackman 1998). Prudent monetary policy, however, and the desirable policy outcomes served to secure monetary policy credibility in the case of Barbados (Downes 2004a).

2.3.3 Central Bank of the Bahamas

The Central Bank of the Bahamas (CBB) provides an interesting example of incorporating currency board aspects into the operations of a stand-alone central bank for a small open economy. The Bahamas, with a population of approximately 319,000, attained its independence from Britain in 1973, and the CBB started operations in 1974. Prior to the CBB, a currency board that was restricted to issuing currency operated in the Bahamas from 1919 to 1968. This functioned much the same way as the currency board that operated in the Eastern Caribbean described above, and was also, of course, historically linked to the sterling. In 1968, the Bahamas Monetary Authority replaced the currency board. Although the authority expanded its role as a monetary authority over that of the currency board, as was the case in the ECCA for example, the need for a wider role for the monetary authority was recognized, which led to the formation of the Central Bank of the Bahamas in 1974, six years after the Bahamas Monetary Authority.

Monetary stability was written into the CBB role as a primary duty. A major objective of this was to safeguard the 1:1 parity that was established between the Bahamian dollar and the US dollar at its inception. The CBB fulfils the traditional roles as issuer of legal tender, banker to both domestic banks and the government, and regulator and supervisor of the banking sector. However, in the administration of exchange, the CBB is required to ensure that external reserves are maintained to at least 50 per cent of the value of total notes and coins in circulation and demand liabilities of the bank. However, the CBB generally reports external reserves in excess of this minimum requirement. In addition to external reserves linked to the money supply, the CBB administers exchange rate controls. This combination of backing the domestic currency along with administrative exchange rate controls, harnessed elements of ECCB-type arrangements with the more usual widely found exchange controls, which are often common precursors to the devaluation of currencies. In the case of the Bahamas, however, this institutional arrangement has been associated with a currency that has been stable with respect to the US dollar since its introduction in 1974.

2.3.4 Central Bank of Jamaica

Jamaica was the first Caribbean country to gain its independence from Britain in 1962. As a part of that self-governing process, the Bank of Jamaica was established and began full operations in that year with a regulatory framework modelled on the Bank of England. The Bank of Jamaica was, in effect, a stand-alone central bank responsible for administering the national currency – the Jamaican dollar. Although the stated objectives included one of monetary stability, a dominant feature of its operations quickly became one of financing large government deficit expenditures, which resulted in a high rate of increase in the money supply year upon year.

Over the period of its operations, 1962–2003, the average annual increase in reserve money (notes and coins in circulation) was 18.4 per cent. During the decades of the 1960s, 1970s, 1980s and 1990s, the averages per annum were 10.8 per cent, 17.6 per cent, 25.4 per cent and 22.9 per cent, respectively (see table 2.2). The rate of growth in reserve money was above 20 per cent in 15 of the 43 years from 1962 to 2003. It was above 10 per cent 31 times over those years. All money supply aggregates showed similar increases whether M0, M1 or M2 (see table 2.2). The rate of growth in the Jamaican money supply, therefore, far exceeded the rate of growth of Jamaican real output over a long period of time. This, in turn, provided the basis for high inflation, balance of payments crises and foreign exchange shortages, in spite of the significant foreign investment inflows from bauxite/alumina exports, especially in the early years. In our sample of countries, Jamaica and Guyana consistently showed the highest increases in the money supply. As a consequence, they experienced the most severe inflation over the long run, along with long-term balance of payments difficulties, devaluations and output reductions.

2.3.5 Central Bank of Trinidad and Tobago

Trinidad and Tobago obtained its independence in 1962, as did Jamaica. Two years later, in 1964, Trinidad and Tobago left the BCCB and established the Central Bank of Trinidad and Tobago. Formally, the primary aims of the central bank covered both a monetary stabilization

Table 2.2 Jamaica: Annual Rate of Growth in Money Supply (%)

	M0 (Reserve Money: Notes and Coins in Circulation) IMF line (14)	M1 (Money) IMF line (34)	M2 (Money and Quasi Money) IMF line (35L)
1960s[a]	10.8	8.9	14.1
1970s	17.6	17.3	15.2
1980s	25.4	15.8	23.9
1990s	22.9	26.8	23.0
1962–2005	18.4	17.0	18.1

Source: IMF 2007.
[a]Comprises the years 1962–1969.

role and a developmental role, and there were regulatory limits on central bank public sector lending. However, as C.Y. Thomas notes, "in its first full year of operations the Bank of Trinidad and Tobago encountered a serious financial crisis which it attributed to the injudicious use of its capacity to grant credit to the public sector" (Thomas 1972, 28). This tension between deficit financing and monetary prudence was to be a feature of the bank's operations (Farrell 1990). Trinidad and Tobago had the good fortune of being an oil economy during the 1970s and 1980s. However, "even with massive foreign exchange inflows and, for a time, fiscal surpluses, the problem of stabilization and adjustment did not disappear" (Farrell 1989, 125–26). Overall, as we shall see below, the performance of Trinidad and Tobago in terms of inflation, exchange rate stability and growth has been poorer than that of the less resource endowed smaller island states, though better than that of the long-term crisis countries of Guyana and Jamaica.

2.3.6 Central Bank of Guyana

The Bank of Guyana represents the worst central banking record in our sample of countries. The Bank of Guyana was established in 1965 modelled on the Bank of England, as those of Jamaica and of Trinidad and Tobago. From the outset, the Bank of Guyana ran into crises centred on its inability to impose effective limits on public sector credit. Huge increases in government deficit expenditure financing led at first to huge increases in imports, foreign exchange demand, balance of payments crises and, later, domestic inflation (Thomas 1972, 20). These initial tendencies developed in the 1980s and 1990s. The resource rich Guyana experienced the highest inflation, largest devaluations, and most pronounced economic stagnation and decline over the decades. The economic performance of Guyana is the poorest among the sample group on almost every criterion.

2.3.7 Central Bank of Belize

Belize has a now familiar story in the development of current monetary institutional structure. From 1894 to 1976, monetary policy was implemented through the Belize Board of Commissioners of Currency and operated like the currency board familiar throughout the British colonies. It was succeeded by the Monetary Authority of Belize, which maintained the currency board functions, but which was limited in the services it could provide the government. The Monetary Authority of Belize was succeeded by the Central Bank of Belize, which began operations on 1 January 1982. The Belize dollar has been pegged at a value of Bel$2 to US$1 since it severed ties with sterling in 1976, following the break-up of the sterling area agreement, to the end of our sample period in 2003. Formally, exchange rate stability is a primary objective of the Central Bank of Belize. Although it does not operate a currency board, like the Central Bank of Barbados, the Central Bank of Belize follows conservative banking practices and effectively backs the currency with a significant holding of international reserves. The exchange rate has remained unchanged to the time of writing.

2.4 Comparative Country Performance

The money supply, inflation and growth indicators show clear differences between the ECCB group of countries and the non-ECCB countries. Some notable similarities exist, however, between ECCB countries and the Bahamas, Barbados and Belize. On the whole, the ECCB countries show a similar economic experience. In comparison to the entire sample, they have low money growth, low inflation, high incomes, high real growth rates and significant financial stability. Considerable differences exist between performance indicators of these countries and of Guyana, Jamaica, and Trinidad and Tobago.

Arguably, the differences in the annual rate of growth in the nominal money supply reported in table 2.3 provide an important basis for the exchange rate and real growth disparities observed. The M2 rate of growth for the ECCB countries ranges from 8.7 per cent to 11.6 per cent per annum. The rate of increase in the money supply of the Bahamas, Barbados and Belize also fall within this range.

On the other hand, Guyana and Jamaica, and to a certain extent Trinidad and Tobago, showed money supply growing at a considerably faster rate than in the other countries. Guyana and Jamaica showed average rate of growth of 21.4 per cent and 21.2 per cent per annum, respectively, over the twenty-three/twenty-four years 1980–2002/3. Table 2.3 reports the rates of growth of money supply from 1980 to facilitate same period cross-country comparisons. These countries were historically less prudent in their monetary policy and had difficulty constraining the financing of their public sector credit. The monetary and fiscal expansions resulted in their high-inflation, low-growth performance.

Among the stand-alone central banks in the sample, the experience of the Bahamas, Barbados and Belize accorded more with the ECCB example of relatively low inflation, high growth and financial stability. As noted above, the Bahamian increases in money were backed by foreign reserves at 50 per cent. Barbados and Belize followed conservative monetary policies, restricting the growth in money supply. Prudent policies and institutional arrangements gave rise to desirable policy effects and long-term financial stability in the face of considerable adversity by these very small non-mineral resource open economies.

Table 2.3 Rate of Growth in Money Supply (M2),[a] Prices and Output: Annual Average[b]

Countries	Sample Period	Average Rate of Money Growth (%, per annum)	Average Inflation Rate (%, per annum)	Average Rate of Growth (%, per annum)
ECCB				
Antigua and Barbuda	1980(1)–2003(4)	11.6	4.1	4.4
Dominica	1980(1)–2003(4)	8.7	3.3	2.2
Grenada	1980(1)–2002(4)	10.3	3.8	3.8
St Kitts and Nevis	1980(1)–2002(4)	10.1	3.3	4.3
St Lucia	1980(1)–2003(4)	9.7	3.4	4.0
St Vincent and the Grenadines	1980(1)–2003(4)	8.9	3.2	3.6
Non-ECCB				
The Bahamas	1980(1)–2001(4)	10.2	3.9	2.1
Barbados	1980(1)–2002(4)	8.4	4.0	1.0
Belize	1980(1)–2003(4)	10.0	1.9	5.4
Guyana	1980(1)–2003(4)	21.4	18.7	0.7
Jamaica	1980(1)–2002(4)	21.2 (18.2)[c]	17.0 (15.2)[c]	1.6 (1.5)[c]
Trinidad and Tobago	1980(1)–2003(4)	8.0 (12.1)[d]	7.5 (8.1)[d]	1.4 (2.6)[d]

Source: IMF 2007.
[a]M2 (l35L) = Money (l34) plus Quasi-Money (l35)
[b]Calculated as differences in the natural logarithmic values.
[c]The figures in the brackets are for a longer period 1965(1)–2003(4).
[d]The figures in the brackets are for a longer period 1965(1)–2002(4).

The rates of growth of money reported in table 2.3 and figure 2.1 show strong direct correlation with inflation. The correlation coefficient for the two series is 0.93. Inflation in the ECCB countries has been overall lower than in the other Caribbean countries, markedly so when compared to Guyana and Jamaica, which showed annualized inflation running at 150 per cent in 1991 q1 and 80 per cent in 1991 q4, respectively. The annualized inflation rate for the ECCB countries peaked at 30 per cent for Grenada in 1980 q3, and only seldom reached 15 per cent (annualized for any quarter) for the group over the 1980s and 1990s. The inflation rates of Barbados, Belize, and Trinidad and Tobago were not dissimilar to the ECCB over the 1980s and 1990s. Figure 2.1 shows that most of the countries had an average rate of growth in money around 10 per cent per annum. Associated inflation rates were below 5 per cent per annum. The cases of inflation rates above 5 per cent were Guyana, Jamaica, and Trinidad and Tobago.

The relatively low rate of money growth for the ECCB countries was also associated with relatively low and stable nominal interest rates. Measured as the short-term Treasury Bill Rate the ECCB rate was often stable for a long period and varied between 6.4 per cent and 7.0 per cent across all the member countries.

Among the non-ECCB economies, however, the rates varied considerably. For the Bahamas, Barbados and Belize, nominal rates were higher and less stable than those of the ECCB. The countries with the highest money growth (Guyana and Jamaica) show considerably higher nominal rates. These latter countries had nominal rates well in excess of 16 per cent – a level not reached by

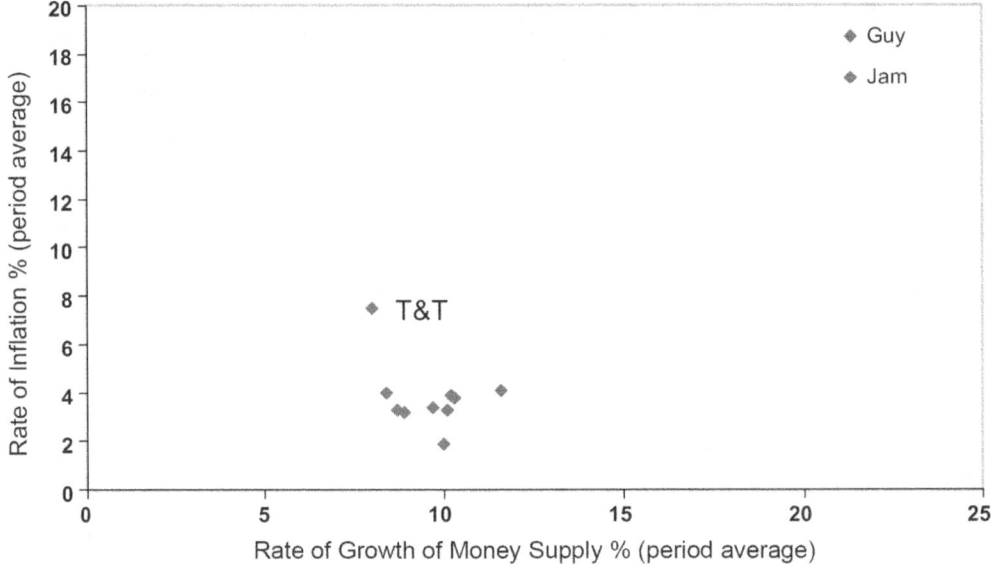

Figure 2.1 Money supply and inflation, 1980–2003

the other countries. The high rates in Guyana and Jamaica were sometimes a result of programmes supported by the International Monetary Fund (IMF) and the World Bank aimed at addressing extreme financial imbalances over long periods (Cornia 1988; Boyd 1988). As a consequence of their relatively low inflation, real interest rate for the ECCB was mainly positive over the period and averaged between 6.0 per cent and 8.8 per cent (see table 2.4) for the sample period.[9] The real interest rate is the nominal interest rate corrected for inflation. The relationship between the nominal interest rate, inflation, and the real interest rate is described by the Fisher Equation:

$$\text{Real Interest Rate} = \text{Nominal Interest Rate} - \text{Inflation}$$

In times of economic and financial stability, real interest rates are usually positive, reflecting an interest return on capital in excess of the rate of inflation.

The ECCB countries on the whole reported, at most, a single year of negative real interest rates, as did the Bahamas and Belize, which reported zero and one year of negative real rates, respectively. Barbados reported two years of negative real interest rates: 1981 and 1987.[10]

The Bahamas (3.7 per cent) and Belize (12.8 per cent) have the highest average real interest over the period. However, the remarkable feature is the difference in variation of real interest rates between the countries. Variation in real rates may be seen as an indication of the prevalence of monetary instability in a country. In this regard, Guyana shows a coefficient of variation of 29.0, which indicates severe financial instability. This is consistent with the record of seven

---
[9] As reported by the World Bank 2006 (http://www.esds.ac.uk).
[10] We should note however, that the available same-source comparable Barbados series is slightly shorter than the rest of the sample, covering only 1981 to 1996.

Table 2.4 Average and Variation in Real Interest Rates and GDP Growth Rates

Countries	Real Interest Rates		Rate of Output Growth[a]	
	Average (%, per annum)	Coefficient of Variation (σ_x / μ_x)	Average (%, per annum)	Coefficient of Variation (σ_x / μ_x)
ECCB				
Antigua and Barbuda	7.7	0.5	4.4	0.9
Dominica	6.4	0.6	2.2	1.6
Grenada	7.6	0.3	3.8	1.2
St Kitts and Nevis	6.0	0.6	4.3	1.0
St Lucia	8.8	0.3	4.0	2.6
St Vincent and the Grenadines	6.9	0.6	3.6	1.2
Non-ECCB				
The Bahamas	3.7	0.8	2.1	2.8
Barbados	6.0	0.6	1.0	4.7
Belize	12.8	0.3	5.4	0.9
Guyana	0.6	29.0	0.7	8.9
Jamaica	6.7	1.4	1.6	2.1
Trinidad and Tobago	6.9	1.0	1.4	4.1
World	N/A[b]	N/A[b]	2.8	0.4

Source: World Bank 2006.
[a] For the periods as reported in table 2.3.
[b] Not applicable.

years of negative real rates, the highest in the group. Jamaica, with six years of negative real rates, has the second highest measure of instability at 1.4. This is followed by Trinidad and Tobago with four years of negative interest rates and a coefficient of variation of 1.0. All other nine countries in the group have a coefficient of variation of 0.6 or below (except the Bahamas with 0.8), which indicates a level of stability not to be found in Guyana, Jamaica, or Trinidad and Tobago (see table 2.4).

Nominal exchange rate for the ECCB was stable at $2.70 per US dollar for the period of 1980–2003. This has been the rate since 1976, when the EC dollar was first pegged to the US dollar, preceding the establishment of the ECCB, which began operations in 1983. Over the same period, the Bahamas, Barbados and Belize have also had stable nominal exchange rates. In contrast, the US dollar rates for Guyana, Jamaica, and Trinidad and Tobago have showed considerable devaluations. For Guyana, the rate fell from G$2.55 to G$196.55. For Jamaica, the Jamaican dollar fell from J$1.78 to J$60.16. For Trinidad and Tobago, the rate fell from TT$2.40 to TT$6.30. These large devaluations were all associated with significant and prolonged foreign exchange crises, especially in the cases of Guyana and Jamaica. In the case of Trinidad and Tobago, the economic windfall associated with having an oil and gas economy served to mitigate some of the long-term adverse effects of the devaluation.

The graphs in figure 2.2 (A–C) show real GDP levels for all countries in the sample indexed to 1980 = 100. Figure 2.2A shows a clear distinction between the relatively high growth rate of the top seven countries (six ECCB countries and Belize) and five slower growing countries with the flatter profiles. The bottom group of five lines (those with the flattest slopes) belongs

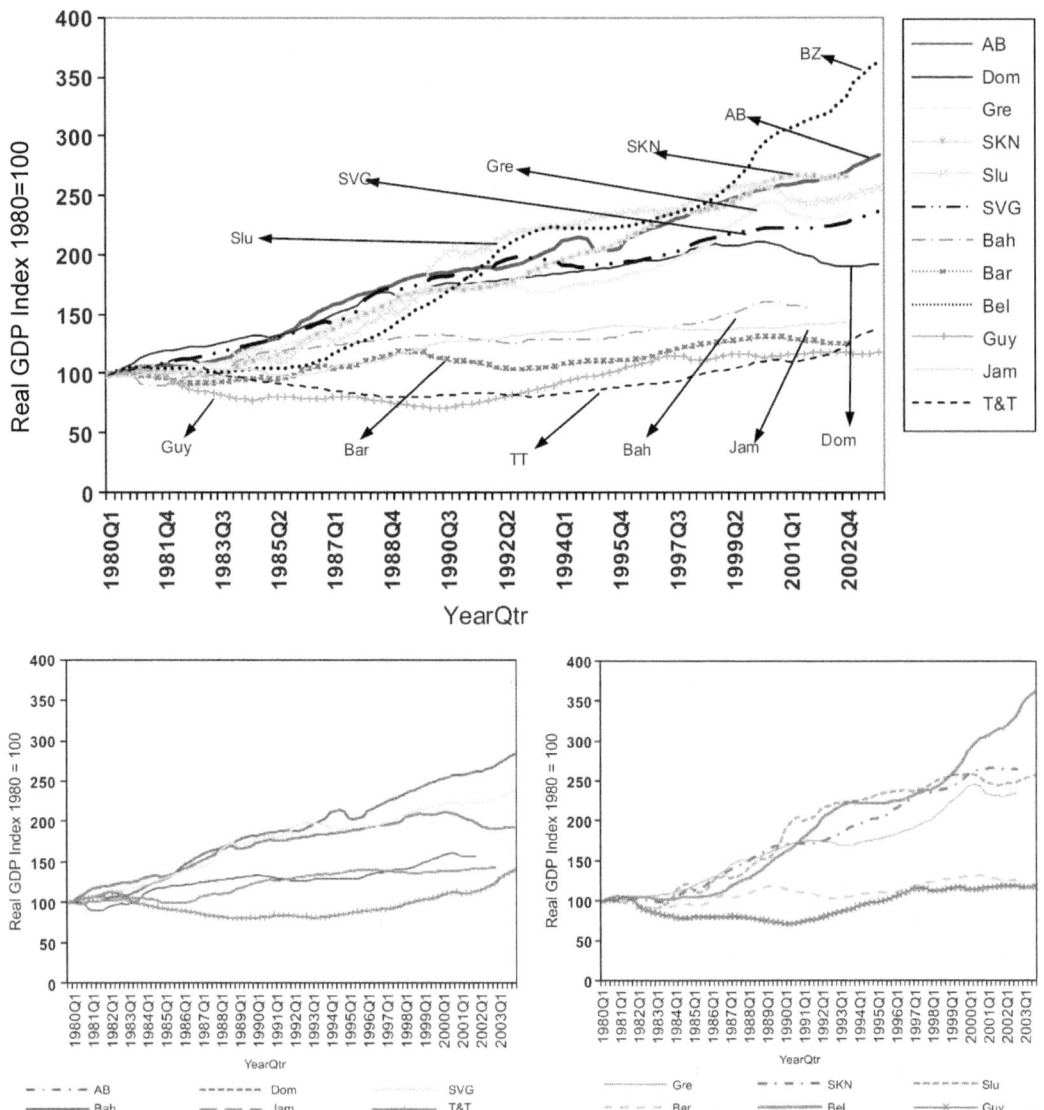

Figure 2.2 Real GDP: all countries, 1980–2003
Source: IMF International Financial Statistics 2006, www.esds.ac.uk download

to Guyana, Trinidad and Tobago, Barbados, Jamaica and the Bahamas. The graph indicates that output within the ECCB group grew relatively steadily over 1980–2003. This is in marked contrast to the experience of the three largest and more resource endowed countries (Guyana, Jamaica, and Trinidad and Tobago) that saw real output stagnate with significant decline in some years. In fact, the larger resource rich economies were the *only* ones to stagnate over the period. The three smaller non-ECCB economies (Barbados, Belize and the Bahamas), showed trend growth over the period. These growth features are even more pronounced when examined over a longer period (Boyd 1986). Figures 2.2B and 2.2C disaggregate figure 2.2A in order that the individual countries can be more easily tracked. Note that the vertical axes are the same in all the figures, so that the overall trends can be readily appreciated.

Real GDP growth in the ECCB countries was superior over the period to that of the other countries, with the exception of Belize. However, Belize is a special case because it started with a low level of absolute GDP, but has since shown high "catch up" growth rates. Real GDP in the ECCB countries showed a consistent increase over time with mean growth of 3.8 per cent per annum over 1980–2003. Note that for this period, world income averaged 2.8 per cent growth per annum. Note also that the coefficient of variations show that the growth was more stable in the ECCB countries than in the other countries. Among the ECCB countries, this measure of stability ranged from 0.9 to 1.6, with the exception of St Lucia with 2.6. Guyana showed an unstable 8.9 in this measure of growth instability. Considerable growth instability is also recorded by Barbados and Trinidad and Tobago at 4.7 and 4.1, respectively. The Bahamas and Jamaica recorded a less unstable 2.8 and 2.1, but it should be noted that the sample period just fell outside of one of Jamaica's most unstable growth periods in the late 1970s.

For the non-ECCB countries, excluding Belize, mean growth was highest in the Bahamas, which had a 2.1 per cent average per annum over the sample period, with a coefficient of variation of 2.8. That is, average growth is lower and growth instability is greater than any of the ECCB countries. Indeed, this relatively low and unstable growth experience demarcates the ECCB and non-ECCB country experience that is observable in figure 2.2A. The former group of countries shows higher trended growth with considerably less variation.

This relative superior performance of the ECCB countries is partly reflected in the per-capita incomes we saw earlier in table 2.1. The ECCB, along with the Bahamas and Barbados, showed per-capita incomes considerably higher than those of Jamaica, Guyana and Belize, which reported the three lowest per-capita incomes for 2004. The anomaly of Belize, in the group with low per-capita incomes while showing high growth rates, and Trinidad and Tobago, in the high per-capita group with lower growth rates, are easily explained. Belize has a low level of economic development, and although it shows high growth, the absolute level of its GDP is low. Trinidad and Tobago, on the other hand, is an oil and gas economy with a relatively well-developed economic (industrial and financial) infrastructure and high absolute level of GDP.

The growth in output has an interesting relationship with the inflation experience of the countries, shown in figure 2.3. Low inflation is associated with both high and low growth, but high inflation is only associated with low growth. Figure 2.3 confirms the intuitively appealing suggestion that low inflation appears to be a necessary, but not sufficient, condition for growth.

This analysis indicates clear differences in the money supply, inflation and growth experiences of this group of Caribbean countries. The ECCB group of countries showed the best performance with a record of low money growth, low inflation, and high and consistent real output growth rates.

On the other hand, Guyana, Jamaica, and Trinidad and Tobago recorded the worst performances. This group was characterized by high money growth, high inflation, and low and inconsistent real output growth rates.

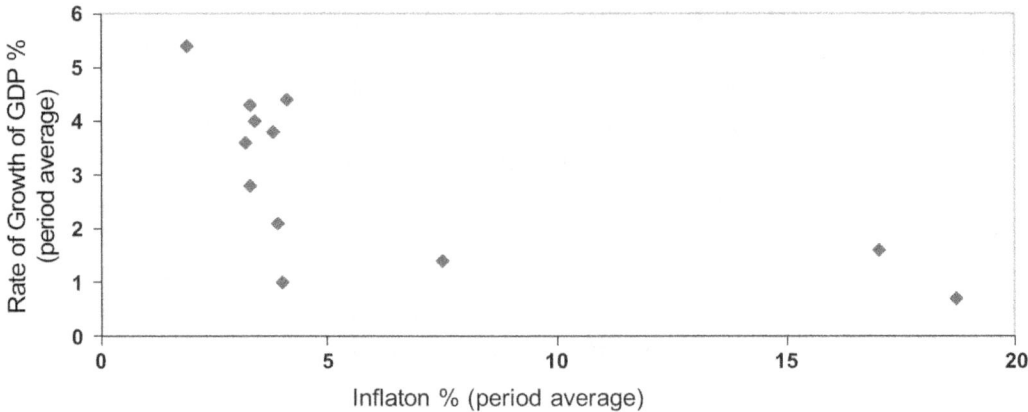

Figure 2.3 Rate of growth of GDP and inflation, 1980–2003

These results confirm the conclusions of Atkins and Boyd (1998):

> The pattern of growth between Caribbean sub groups seems to reflect differences in institutional constraints and policy regimes. The initially More Developed Countries – Barbados, Guyana, Jamaica and Trinidad and Tobago – (World Bank 1978), established central banks that allowed the individual governments autonomy over monetary and fiscal policies. This autonomy frequently resulted in fiscal and monetary expansions that ultimately created external imbalances and low growth (Cornia *et al.*, 1988; Sharpley, 1984). In contrast, the initially Less Developed Countries – St Vincent, Dominica – adopted a common currency and combined to establish the Eastern Caribbean Central Bank, which provided a framework for economic management. The shared framework constrained individual autonomy over monetary and fiscal policy and hence tended to force economies to make more rapid real adjustment to shocks. (Atkins and Boyd 1998)

2.5 Conclusions

In this chapter, we examined the primary policy aim, the economic principles and the institutional framework for monetary policy in the Caribbean. We analysed these aspects from the Caribbean's colonial background, tracing out the changes that gave rise to the contemporary Caribbean policy framework, policy and effects.

We saw that from the beginning of modern British monetary developments in 1597, a primary concern was to protect the economy from the *excessive printing of banknotes* by the authorized banks. Since that time, and for most of the time, the pound sterling was "specie backed", at first by silver (hence the term "sterling") and then by gold, which heralded the era of the "gold standard". The gold standard was important in providing stability for the currency, which was seen as crucial in providing the basis for economic growth, international trade and Britain's industrial development. Views may have differed as to how it was best achieved, but establishing a reliable measure and store of value and medium of exchange was long agreed upon as essential for economic development (New School 2006; Hollander 1910).

Asset backing and *convertibility* dominated monetary management in Britain from the time of the Tudors until the 1920s. A currency linked to specie and convertible from paper currency into silver or gold at a fixed rate at the issuing bank, provided its structural foundation. In this way, British governments through the centuries sought to ensure that the paper currency of the realm would hold its value in real terms. The outcome was that the currency maintained its value over long periods of time with respect to its reserve asset, silver or gold.

Asset backing and *convertibility* could be and were suspended during times of crises such as wars and financial crashes, but on the whole, they held until 1931, when Britain finally left the gold standard. From then on, the currency would be fiduciary issue.

The institutional background of monetary management in the Caribbean was founded on the principles underlying the aim of the British pound sterling. The robustness of the British sterling arrangements was imposed on British colonies – *all* of the British colonies in Asia and the Far East, Africa and the Americas (Clauson 1944).

Monetary management for British colonies took the form of currency boards administered by a Currency Authority, which was administered by the British civil service. Currency in the colonies had to be issued on the basis of sterling reserves held in London. This currency board framework brought to the colonial currencies the same constraints that protected sterling from the *excessive issuing of banknotes*. This arrangement ensured monetary stability through the administrative mechanism of the colonial currencies being fully backed by sterling deposits. As such, this arrangement ensured the colonial currency was a direct derivative of the gold standard British pound. The pound continued to be the colonial currencies' reserve assets after Britain left the gold standard in 1931.

The dominance of Keynesian demand management in economic policy, from the publication of the *General Theory* in 1936 until the stagflation of the 1970s, obscured the relationship between the rate of growth in the money supply and price inflation. Not until the seminal work of Friedman and Schwartz (1963), *A Monetary History of the United States, 1867–1960*, did the focus on the impact of the money supply return to centre stage. By the 1980s, the dominant view in macroeconomics was that the rate of growth in the money supply determined the rate of inflation. The time period of that function was open to some debate, but the direction and significance of that causality was generally accepted. This led some governments of leading industrial countries to use some form of monetary policy rule, such as setting the money supply targets. This monetarist approach has given way to "inflation targeting" in the 1980s approach. Inflation targeting maintains the causal link between money supply and inflation, but the policy instrument becomes a rate of interest. "Inflation targeting involves setting a target for inflation and changing interest rates from time to time to achieve that target" (Mankiw 2008, 430).

In our examination of this group of twelve Caribbean countries, the evidence supports the notion that the essential distinction between the countries' economic performance did not rest on the difference between the countries of the currency union and the non-currency union, ECCB and non-ECCB. Rather, the distinction lies between the nine countries that developed institutional arrangements – whether hardwired, in the case of currency board arrangements, or through consistent prudent policy approaches *that enforced certain policy rules aimed at monetary stability* – and those that did not. This was in stark contrast to the three countries in which monetary policy was largely discretionary *and* accommodating of large consistent fiscal deficits.

The important lesson here is that the institutional arrangements governing the implementation of monetary policy can be crucial in the determination of the economic outcomes (Mizen 2003; Blinder 1999; Rogoff 1985). As such, the prudency hardwired in the currency board arrangements of the ECCB, and to an extent the Bahamas, served to restrain monetary and fiscal expansion. Such restraints were noticeably absent in the cases of Guyana, Jamaica, and Trinidad and Tobago. This served to generate significant degrees of financial and real-side instability in these countries.

We saw that the micro-states of the Eastern Caribbean developed a joint monetary institution in the ECCB based closely on their historical monetary precedents. Their institutional arrangements evolved over time from a currency board, to a currency authority, through to a regional central bank that provided a wide range of services to the member states. Throughout the transition, however, the caution evident in the "reserve backing" of the currency and elements of that prudence were retained in the institutional and regulatory arrangements of succeeding institutions. This served to constrain fiscal deficit expenditure and limit the growth in money supply that served, in turn, to protect the value of the currency, and reduce the risk of generating inflation. This served to provide a relatively stable foundation on which to develop their fragile economies. These ECCB countries, in spite of their small size, absence of any significant mineral resources and high degree of openness, were able to achieve consistent growth and an absence of the balance of payments crises visited upon their larger more resource rich Caribbean neighbours.

In the economics literature, discretionary frameworks for monetary policy are often associated with excessive monetary expansion and stagflation. Indeed, this does appear to be the case in some of the countries in our sample. However, what is particularly remarkable in the cases of three of the countries in this sample (the Bahamas, Barbados and Belize) is that discretionary monetary policy frameworks were combined with prudent policies to deliver relatively good economic performances. The Bahamas adopted a primary currency board mechanism similar to ECCB, whereby its currency would have a minimum 50 per cent reserve backing of its currency. This, however, was combined with other administrative arrangements that also gave a high priority to the stability of the Bahamian dollar. In the cases of Barbados and Belize, institutional arrangements were similar to a traditional central bank, without the currency board type reserve arrangements. Nevertheless, the high priority given to prudency and monetary stability was effected through consistent conservative monetary policy since their establishment (Downes 2004a).

These countries provide interesting and fairly rare examples of prudent monetary policy within a discretionary framework, especially among small developing economies. The maintenance of a fixed exchange rate regime throughout the turbulent decades of the 1970s, 1980s and

1990s without any devaluation is a notable achievement for these micro-states with their small open economies. It is further evidence of the efficacy of their monetary policy approach. Such exemplary exchange rate achievement could not be achieved in the absence of consistently prudent monetary policies (Blackman 2006; Downes 2004a; Blackman 1982).

On the other hand, the stand-alone central banks of Guyana, Jamaica, and Trinidad and Tobago provided archetypical outcomes of inflationary prone discretionary frameworks. They largely accommodated the fiscal deficits of their central governments. This, as a consequence, generated significant increases in the money supply. Consequently, the ability of these central banks to pursue effective anti-inflationary monetary policy was inherently undermined. Within the fixed exchange rate regime that these economies adopted, especially in the earlier periods, this led to an overvaluation of the currency that resulted in prolonged balance of payments deficits and exchange rate instability (Downes 2004b). Indeed, internal and external financial imbalances characterized much of the economic experiences of these countries. Over the period of analysis, monetary policy failed to support long-term growth in these economies in spite of their relatively robust export resource base (agriculture and minerals in Guyana; bauxite/alumina in Jamaica; and gas/petroleum in Trinidad and Tobago). In the case of Trinidad and Tobago, the performance of the oil and gas industries internationally mitigated the adverse impact of the imprudent monetary policies (Watson 2003). However, neither Guyana nor Jamaica had export earning capacities to provide such mitigation. Therefore, the social and economic adverse impacts of their imprudent monetary policies are more discernible.

Chapter **3**

Monetary Policy Transmission Mechanisms in Developing Countries

Introduction

The focus of this book is on the process by which monetary policy affects economic growth and performance. This process is known in the literature as the *monetary transmission mechanism*. The monetary transmission mechanism literature examines the mechanisms through which monetary policy affects the real economy, that is, how monetary policy affects such things as output and employment. It does this through a variety of channels which we shall examine below in some detail.

The question of how monetary policies effects are transmitted to the real sector of the economy is fundamentally the same for industrial and developing economies. The answers tend to be different because of differences in economic structures, behavioural features, historical experience and institutions in economies. Indeed, even between advanced industrial countries (Canada, European Union, Japan, United States and the United Kingdom) the transmission mechanisms differ. Moreover, they do not remain constant over time for any particular country. Kamin, Turner and Van't Dack (1998) and Khan (1998) provide extensive surveys of the developing country literature, where its intersection with the literature of the developed countries is observable, as well as the areas of fundamental differences.

In the most basic explanation of the monetary transmission mechanism, a decrease in the money supply will bring about an increase in the interest rate. The increase in interest rate will, in turn, reduce the demand for investments and bring about, *ceteris paribus*, a decrease in output and employment (Mankiw 2003, 267–8). In this case, the transmission mechanism occurs through an investment function. The IS/LM model, for example, allows this transmission of changes in the money supply to changes in output to be theoretically examined through the derivation of the IS curve (Branson 1989, 81–83). In the standard IS/LM model, we are able to observe the monetary transmission mechanism through an examination of the money supply multipliers. Through these, we are able to inspect the direct and indirect money market effects via the mechanism through which they are transmitted into the goods market. In the standard simple case, the goods market effect is transmitted through the investment function via changes in interest rates.

It is especially on the empirical side that distinct differences become apparent, due mainly to the underdeveloped financial structures and lack of financial depth (Ramlogan 2004). In recent years, the focus in the major economies and in the literature has been on interest rates as the primary policy instrument, and the output gap and inflation as the primary target variables (Carlin and Soskice 2006; Carlin and Soskice 2005; Walsh 2002; Clarida, Gali and Gertler, 1999; Taylor 1993). In this regard, inflation targeting is increasingly adopted in industrial economies – New Zealand, Canada, United Kingdom, United States, Sweden, Israel, Australia and Switzerland – and emerging market economies including Chile, Brazil, Korea, Thailand and South Africa (Mishkin 2000).

Since at least Tinbergen (1952, 1964) and Theil (1956, 1964), economic policy has been analysed within a standard structure of five elements: objectives, instruments, model, forecasts and implementation (Acocella 1998, ch.8). The policymaker, whom we will call the central bank (CB), has certain objectives in terms of target variables that it wishes to influence, and certain instruments/variables that the CB can control. The CB has a model of the economy, of how the instruments influence the targeted variables. The CB and other agents make forecasts of each other's actions and exogenous shocks. The CB then implements what it considers the optimal setting of the instruments. Other agents respond and outcomes are observed. However, even if central banks can develop optimal policies, they may not be able to implement them due to political constraints on the CB's independence.

We will use this target – instruments structure. However, it is important to recognize that it operates within an institutional context, and that this institutional context shapes the choices available. In particular, within the three monetary frameworks we identified – classical, accommodating and inflation targeting – the instruments and targets are different. To understand the implications of this, it is worth beginning with the standard account of how monetary policy is set in industrialized countries. In section 3.1, we set out a New Keynesian analytical framework to analyse monetary policy. We establish the particular institutional context, policy instruments, objectives and transmission mechanisms. We set out the standard model to establish the main feature of the approach and the variations that seek to account for differences in economic behaviour. Section 3.2 argues that the primary objective of contemporary monetary policy is price stability, and that this is increasingly seen as a precondition for growth and development. As such, the monetary theory and policy focus on inflation targeting is relevant to industrial, emerging and developing economies. Section 3.3 examines the primary features of the monetary transmission mechanisms in developing countries in order that the link between policy instruments and development objectives may be established. The major constraints on development are identified via the Polak, McKinnon–Shaw and Structuralist models. Section 3.4 provides a theoretical discussion of the channels that give rise to the monetary transmission mechanism from the perspective of developing countries. The final section, 3.5, examines the evidence of these channels from developing countries empirical studies.

3.1 Monetary Policy in Industrialized Countries

We begin with an examination of how monetary policy – especially how real side impacts are generated from interest rates – is dominated in the research literature by what is often known as the New Keynesian approach (Carlin and Soskice 2005, 2006). Below, we follow this type of approach as set out in Clarida, Gali and Gertler (1999), which we will refer to as the CGG.

In this modelling, it is usually assumed that the CB's objective is a discounted sum of a function, which is usually quadratic, of current and expected future deviations of inflation π_t from its target, which is assumed to be zero, and from the output gap, which is x_t (the difference of log output from its natural rate). For example, it may minimize a loss function of the form:

$$L = E_t \sum_{i=0}^{\infty} \beta^i \left(\alpha x_{t+i}^2 + \beta \pi_{t+i}^2 \right)$$

where E_t denotes expectations formed at time t and β is the discount factor. A considerable amount of literature discusses why the objective function takes this form, and whether it imparts an inflationary bias to the economy (Svensson 2003; Walsh 2003; Woodford 1999; Barro and Gordon 1983). The policy instrument is usually assumed to be the short-term interest rate i_t. The transmission mechanism involves two equations. In the first equation, the interest rate influences, perhaps with a lag, the output gap (the difference between log output and its natural rate) through an aggregate demand (IS) curve. The CGG form of the relationship is

$$x_t = -\phi \left(i_t - E_t \pi_t \right) + E_t x_{t+1} + g_t$$

where g_t is a demand shock determined by government expenditure, for example. In the second equation, the output gap influences inflation, again perhaps with a lag, through an aggregate supply (Phillips) curve. The CGG form of the relationship is

$$\pi_t = \lambda x_t + \beta E_t \pi_{t+1} + u_t$$

where u_t is a cost – push shock.

Finally, the implementation of the optimal policy is often expressed in terms of a Taylor Rule, by which the short-term interest rate adjusts slowly to a desired value. This is a function of (expected or actual) deviations of inflation from target and the output gap. For example, assuming target inflation is zero and the rule is based on actual rather than expected values, the rule takes the following form:

$$r_t - r_{t-1} = \mu \left(r_t^* - r_{t-1} \right) + v_t$$

$$r_t^* = \gamma_0 + \gamma_1 \pi_t + \gamma_2 x_t$$

where v_t is a policy shock, and for stability, we require $\gamma_1 > 1$. Good accessible explanations of this type of New Keynesian modelling are to be found in Carlin and Soskice (2006; 2005).

An LM curve could be added to this model to determine real money demand as a function of output, interest rates and inflation. For example, it could take the form

$$M_t/P_t = AY_t^{\eta}(1+R_t)^{\kappa} e^{w_t}$$

where w_t is a money demand shock. Taking logarithms, represented by a lower case letter, and using the approximation $\ln(1+R) \approx R$, this can be written as

$$m_t - p_t = a + \eta y_t + \kappa R_t + w_t$$

Within the standard framework, it is not necessary to focus on this relationship, since money demand is driven by the other variables, and the interest rate rather than the money supply is the policy instrument. We will use relationships like this later in the text, because in a number of our countries, the money supply is controlled directly and the interest rate is not adjusted. The shift from treating money supply as the instrument to treating interest rates as the instrument reflects instability in money demand functions in many countries because of financial innovation, inflation or financial instability.

The standard account assumes that the CB, by shifting the short rate, can influence the long rate, which is what should appear in the aggregate demand, IS, curve. In the standard account with explicit expectations, both the CB and the private sector make forecasts using rational expectations, making use of information at time t. An important issue is whether the CB can influence the forecasts of the private sector, and thus the long rate of interest, through commitment to a target or a rule. It can do this if it has credibility with the private sector.

The institutional context of the standard account assumes floating exchange rates and fairly free movement of capital in and out of the country. The exchange rate is not a target, though it may play a role in the transmission mechanism from interest rates to output and inflation. Within the standard structure, it is impossible to have an independent monetary policy, fixed exchange rates and free movement of capital. At least one of the elements of this impossible trinity must be dropped. There can be fixed exchange rates and an independent monetary policy, as under Bretton Woods, if the exchange rate is protected by controls on capital movements. There can be free movements of capital and a fixed exchange rate, if monetary policy is devoted to maintaining the exchange rate target. It is often thought that this is difficult to achieve, since the monetary policies required may not be politically feasible. However, a number of our countries did follow such a policy. The institutional context of the standard approach also assumes fairly thick financial markets, in which interest rate changes have effects on the real economy. The structure of financial markets and the role of government debt within the financial system will influence objectives, instruments, transmission mechanism and implementation of policy. The institutional context also assumes a solvent public sector that does not need to print money to finance its deficit through seignorage, which a number of our countries did.

This is explicitly a short-run model, designed to analyse the impact of policy at cyclical frequencies. It abstracts from the long-run relationships, which operate at much lower frequencies. These would determine the growth of the natural rate of output, the equilibrium real interest rate and real exchange rate in the economy. In industrialized economies, these can be assumed to be close to their equilibrium values, and the analysis of growth and cycles can be disentangled to some extent.

Within developing countries, the institutional context and the channels through which monetary policy work are much more complex, because of the large differences between countries. The objective, then, will be to identify the differences in policy and the transmission mechanism, and use this to shed light on the qualitative differences in institutional context. These would determine the growth of the natural rate of output, the equilibrium real interest rate and real exchange rate in the economy. In developing countries, it is also much less plausible to assume that the long-run real variables are close to their equilibrium values, thus the analysis of growth and cycles cannot be as easily disentangled. To provide some background to this, we provide a brief review of the literature on objectives, instruments and transmission mechanism for monetary policy in developing countries, before surveying some empirical studies.

3.2 Objectives of Monetary Policy

Across the developing world, governments differ tremendously in their economic and political objectives, and in their economic competence. Monetary policy can play a role in meeting a large number of objectives including financing public deficits, stabilizing the economy, restraining inflation, attracting inward investment, managing the exchange rate and encouraging development of the financial system. In recent years, a growing consensus has emerged for price stability as the main long-run goal of monetary policy (Mishkin 1999a, 1999b) even in developing countries, where economic growth and development are cited as immediate objectives. The widespread financial crises following the shocks since 1973, the external and internal imbalances, and foreign exchange crises have convinced a growing number of developing country policymakers that macroeconomic financial stability is a worthwhile condition in support of – if not a necessary condition for – sustained economic growth and development (Bird 2001).

In the major industrial countries, price stability is increasingly identified as the single most important objective of monetary policy, and the developing countries have followed suit. Consequently, there is a growing consensus in the macroeconomics and development literature that an over-expansionary monetary policy cannot stimulate long-term growth of the economy, but rather that such actions lead largely to inflation and to an adverse impact on growth, inter alia. To the extent that monetary policy is used to encourage financial developments, it may help growth by increasing investment, as savings are better mobilized, and increasing the efficiency of investment by improving the allocation of funds to projects. However, the quantitative importance of this effect is a matter of debate.

Some argue that preconditions for adopting a framework of inflation targeting, such as the necessary degree of central bank independence and political concern about the negative effects of inflation, are not present in most developing countries (Bird 2001; Masson, Savastano and Sharma 1998). However, nine countries of our sample have independent, conservative central banks who were concerned about the negative effects of inflation. Furthermore, the experiences of many developing countries that have seen the high social and economic costs of hyperinflation have encouraged an awareness of the negative effects of inflation. Consequently, a growing number of non-OECD countries are adopting low inflation as the primary economic policy objective, including Chile and Brazil (Carare and Stone 2003; Loayza and Soto 2002).

3.3 Policy Instruments

The choice of instruments for monetary policy is constrained by the nature of the financial system and the channels through which monetary policy measures are deemed to work through the system. These have also been changing radically over time in many emerging or developing market economies. Over the last thirty years, for example, there have been significant changes in the macroeconomic background of developing countries. Liberalization and internationalization have characterized many developing countries over recent decades. For many countries, therefore, the external balance sheet has been critical in policymaking and economic performance, and as a consequence, foreign exchange and exchange rate effects have been important.

The possible instruments of monetary policy are quite large. The monetary authorities may try to influence interest rates, and there are a number of different interest rates they may try to influence. They may try to control the money supply: either directly through the provision of notes and coins; or indirectly, through the banking system, via open market operations or reserve requirements. There are a number of different measures of the money supply they may try to control. They may operate a variety of financial restrictions, such as credit controls, capital controls on foreign exchange movements and multiple exchange rate systems. They may try to influence the banking system through moral suasion. Which combination of techniques a particular government will use will depend on the institutional context, in particular the relation between the central bank and the Ministry of Finance. This can make the detailed analysis of monetary policy quite complex and country dependent. However, a number of more approaches of general applicability have been developed.

An important early foundation for analysing monetary policy developed from the work of Polak (1957). This played an important role in the development of the International Monetary Fund approach to macroeconomic management, and so has been important in many developing countries. In this model, the financial imbalances, both internal and external, give rise to the need for planned, orderly and consistent financial stabilization policies. What the Polak (1957) model does is to focus attention on the link between domestic credit expansion, in the main, and external imbalance. The Polak Model and other contributions from the IMF formed the basis for the development of the Monetary Approach to the Balance of Payment (Frenkel and Johnson 1976). If there is an imbalance between absorption and domestic output (reflected in a balance of payment deficit), this must correspond to too-liberal credit expansion in the "Chicago" model, especially to the public sector. From this model, the exchange rate also developed as an important policy instrument (Tarp 1993).

A key issue of the transmission mechanism in developing countries is the extent to which the short interest rates most directly under control of the central bank can affect long rates through the term structure of interest rates, which, in turn, lead to changes in demand for investment and consumption of goods and services. During the 1970s and 1980s, analyses of financial repression in developing countries tended to fall into two camps: the McKinnon–Shaw tradition (McKinnon 1973; Shaw 1973) and a neo-structuralist approach (Taylor 1981, 1983; Van Wijnbergen 1982, 1983).

Adherents of the McKinnon–Shaw view maintain that raising controlled bank interest rates need not be contractionary, because in a rationed regime, the induced increase in saving would result in an increased supply of credit to facilitate the financing of private investment, working capital or both. The process of financial deepening that builds the financial superstructure is regarded as a binding constraint on growth and development. This intermediation between savers and investors is viewed, therefore, as playing a crucial role in this type of model. The McKinnon–Shaw model has been considerably extended over the years since its inception. The initial *financial repression* (low or negative real interest rates) focus of the model has been extended to cover other constraints on growth and development that may be posed by the financial sector (Gemech and Struthers 2003).

The structuralist approach, on the other hand, argues that the impact of economic structure on policy outcome tends to be under-recognized. The thrust, therefore, of the structuralist approach is to see inflation and balance of payments problems as part and parcel of underdevelopment – not as primarily due to monetary phenomena (Taylor 1981). Monetary policy, in this approach, is mediated through the heterogeneous institutional characteristics (Van Wijnbergen 1982; 1983) of the economy. A one-size-fits-all monetary policy approach is seen as doomed to failure. Lance Taylor's paper "IS/LM in the Tropics" presents the classic exposition of this approach (Taylor 1981).

Fry (1988) presents a useful survey of the early literature of the transmission mechanism in developing countries. In a study of 14 Asian developing countries over 1961–1983, Fry (1988, 155–57) presents evidence that the sensitivity of M3 money demand to real deposit rate of interest is relatively high. He reports that, on average, for the 14 countries, a 1.0 percentage point change in the real deposit interest rate changes demand for financial deposits by 0.8 per cent in the short run and 1.4 per cent in the long run. This implies that an increase in real deposit rates increases the proportion of saving routed to investment through the financial intermediation channel. Fry (1988, 140) estimated statistically significant effects of real deposit rates on savings, but on average, the effects are low. He writes that, on average, across the countries in his study, the national saving rate would be increased by about 0.1 percentage point for each one percentage point rise in the real deposit rate of interest. He notes that since the magnitude is not large enough to warrant much policy significance, only in countries where the real deposit rate is negative by a considerable margin can there be much scope for increasing saving directly by raising the deposit rate.

Fry reports an early contribution by Mikesell and Zinser (1973, 17) that concluded "it seems likely that interest rates are more significant in determining the channels into which savings will flow in the developed and developing countries than in altering saving propensities". Lanyi and

Saracoglu (1983) analysed the effect of interest rate policies on financial deepening, as measured by the rate of growth in real M2 money balances and concluded that positive real interest rate policies stimulate output growth, and that this stimulus is transmitted mainly through the intermediation of financial asset accumulation. Jung (1986) used Granger causality tests to provide support for Lanyi and Saracoglu (1983) and showed that the predominant direction of causality is from financial conditions to the rate of economic growth.

On the other hand, the neo-structuralists argue for the importance of informal loan markets when bank rates are subject to legal ceilings. They emphasize that increases in bank interest rates will draw funds away from informal markets (Van Wijnbergen 1982). Structural conditions are at the centre of the Krugman and Taylor (1978) model of deflationary devaluation effects.

The different models provide varying views as to the nature of the binding constraints on development and the relative or temporal importance of policy approaches at different times. This dictates the policy approach and policy instruments that should be given priority.

3.4 Short-Run Transmission Mechanisms in Developing Countries

Interest in the monetary transmission mechanism in developing countries resides in how changes in the monetary instruments available to policymakers connect to changes in the real variables in the economy – how they connect to changes in the aggregate demand and supply of goods and services. The transmission mechanisms in industrial economies have long been a focus in the macroeconomics literature (Vinals and Valles 1999; Morsink and Bayoumi 1999; Gertler 1988; Mishkin 1995). For developing countries, however, the process through which monetary policy decisions are transmitted into changes in real GDP and inflation is not as well examined, although there is a growing body of literature (Shabbir 2008; Watson 2003; Kamin, Turner and Van't Dack 1998; Bennett 1995; Montiel 1990).

The absence of well-organized and integrated securities markets in developing countries is one of the main factors giving rise to the difference between the monetary transmission mechanisms of the industrial countries and those of developing countries. The financial structures of the industrial economies show a relatively high degree of convergence when compared to the financial structures to be found in the developing economies, see Worrell et al. (2001) comparative analysis of the financial structure in Caribbean economies. The limitations of the transmission mechanisms will be as widespread and varied as the differences in the institutional and historical economic experiences and financial structures (Birchwood and Matthias 2007; Watson 2003; Baksh and Craigwell 1997; Cottarelli and Kourelis 1994).

In the presence of rudimentary financial systems, in some cases, and given particular historical experiences and institutional structures, some channels will be more important than others (Diaz 1998). The historical experience of hyperinflation, for example, generally affects the post hyperinflation instruments, as shown by the prominent role indexation plays in Chile and Brazil, for example (Eyzaguirre 1998; Lopes 1998). Understanding the transmission mechanism in the context of developing countries that are often undergoing stabilization policies is made more difficult because stabilization policies are often aimed at producing important structural and behavioural changes in the economy. That is, changing the structural characteristics that give rise to the behavioural mechanisms we wish to examine.

The conclusion reached from a recent Bank of International Settlement study of emerging market economies is that the channels of transmission continue to evolve, often in unexpected ways (Kamin, Turner and Van't Dack 1998). In the literature on monetary transmission mechanisms, however, four channels are generally identified as important in the transmission of monetary policy effects in the modern financial systems (Loayza and Schmidt-Hebbel 2002; Mishkin 1995). The four channels are interest rate channel, exchange rate channel, domestic asset price channel and credit channel. These are briefly examined below from a theoretical standpoint. The section that follows examines the empirical evidence of these channels for developing countries.

3.4.1 Interest Rate Channel

The interest rate channel has a long history. From the dawn of modern economics in classical theory, it has played the role of bringing about equality between aggregate savings and investment in the *Loanable Funds Theory of Savings and Investment*. The investment function was recognized as the transmission mechanism for the interest rate monetary instrument having an effect on output and employment – real side effects. In 1936, *The General Theory* saw the investment function being developed into ISLM analysis. In the most basic format, nominal interest rates are derived through changes in the money supply, for given prices, since it is the real rate of interest that determines investment and consumption demand.

From the 1980s, increases in nominal interest rates, in the presence of sticky prices and rational expectations, may be seen as increasing real long-term interest rates as well, at least for a time (Mishkin 1995) and Taylor (1995, 18) argues that durable consumption, business fixed investment, residential investment and even inventory investment are negatively related to the real interest rate in many countries.

The interest rate channel, therefore, has a long and distinguished history. Contemporary macroeconomic policy, with its focus on inflation targeting, and the use of short-term nominal interest rates as primary monetary policy instruments give considerable priority to the interest rate channel. Microeconomic theory on the profit maximizing activity of firms, both industrial and financial, also accords an important role to interest rates in the determination of economic activity. Hence, there can be little doubt as to the fundamental importance of this channel in theoretical and policy terms for economies – industrial, emerging and developing.

3.4.2 Exchange Rate Channel

For the open economies of many developing countries, monetary policy shocks may induce output fluctuations via the exchange rate channel through net exports and balance sheet effects. A standard explanation of the exchange rate channel would suggest that a rise in domestic interest rate may cause an inflow of foreign capital, the theoretical impact of which will depend on the *exchange rate regime* that is in place. Under a floating exchange rate regime, the inflow of capital will cause an appreciation in the domestic currency. This will cause a fall in net exports and output. However, if the country is following a fixed exchange rate regime, the inflow of capital will be sterilized by an increase in the money supply to maintain the exchange rate at its fixed value. Therefore, the monetary policy response will not allow the foreign capital inflows to transmit effects into the exchange rate under the fixed exchange rate regime. In developing countries, foreign capital inflows are not generally responsive to interest changes since they do not have significant foreign capital markets. However, in the presence of black market or parallel market, pulses of the policy will be transmitted into the economy via black market trade (Shabbir 2008; Seerattan 2006; Taylor 1995).

The exchange rate channel is essentially linked to interest changes inducing an increase in currency deposits (Mishkin 1995). The central objective is to induce changes in the demand for money. To do this, a flexible exchange rate regime is necessary (Diaz 1998; Obstfeld and Rogoff 1995). Under such an arrangement, a monetary expansion can be brought about through the various channels that influence the nominal exchange rate. One is for the central bank to engage in non-sterilized purchases of foreign currency. As it purchases foreign currency, the central bank will induce an increase in the monetary and financial assets held by commercial banks on their central bank accounts. As banks withdraw these non-interest-bearing assets and try to place them among borrowers, lending rates will fall and banks will also be compelled to lower the interest rates paid to depositors as well (Diaz 1998). In this case, the decline in interest rates may be associated with a depreciation, the exchange rate, and an increase in net exports and output.

3.4.3 Domestic Asset Price Channel

The main arguments for this channel come from a more monetarist approach that gives more importance to the effects induced by a broad range of assets and wealth effects. The main aim in this channel is to link monetary policy with changes in a broad set of asset prices, usually proxied by equity prices (Mishkin 1995). There are two main explanations of the transmission mechanisms in this regard: one focusing on the firms; the other on households' behaviour.

A primary mechanism to link changes in monetary policy with a broad range of assets and the real economy is through explanations based on Tobin's q theory. Tobin (1969) defines q as the market value of firms divided by the replacement cost of capital. This means that if q is high, the market price of firms is high relative to the replacement cost of capital. Companies can issue equity and get a high price for it, relative to the cost of the plant and equipment they are buying. A high q, therefore, encourages investment. On the other hand, if q is low, firms will be more encouraged to buy another firm, since it is relatively cheaper to acquire old capital than to invest in new plant and machinery. Investment spending will be low, as a consequence. This assumes a stock market, which was once less relevant in the context of developing countries. However, stock markets are becoming increasingly common, and there are markets in a number of our countries.

Some writers also see household balance sheet effects as providing another set of mechanisms for the transmission of monetary policy through a broad range of assets (Mishkin 1995; Meltzer 1995). In this regard, the Modigliani MIT-Penn-SSRC (MPS) model provides an important basis for such explanations. In this model, consumption spending is positively determined in part by financial wealth, which is determined by equity and other asset prices.

3.4.4 Credit Channel

Bernanke and Gertler (1995) noted that the credit channel is not a distinct and free-standing alternative to traditional monetary transmission mechanism, but rather a set of factors that amplify and propagate conventional interest rate effects. According to the credit channel theory, the direct effects of monetary policy on interest rates are amplified by endogenous changes in the *external finance premium*, which is the difference in cost between funds raised externally (by issuing equity or debt) and funds generated internally (by retaining earnings). In the credit channel explanations, two basic sets of mechanisms arise as a result of agency problems in credit markets: the *balance sheet* mechanism and the *bank lending mechanism*.[1]

The balance sheet mechanism operates through the net worth of firms and through households' consumer spending. Bernanke and Gertler (1995) and Mishkin (1995) provide extensive reviews of these mechanisms. A monetary contraction that reduces firms' equity prices and lowers their net worth may lead to a decrease in lending (adverse selection problem) to finance investment spending. Also, a decline in net worth that lowers owners' equity stake in their firm, may give them more incentive to engage in risky investments (moral hazard) that, in turn, reduces investment lending, and hence investment spending. Note here that it is the lending (a supply response to either adverse selection or moral hazard problems) that is reduced.

Contractionary policies that raise interest rates may also cause deteriorations in firms' balance sheets, because they reduce cash flow. This, in turn, may lead to adverse selection and moral hazard problems, and the mechanisms noted above. The monetary contraction operating through a cash flow effect in the balance sheets of firms may give rise in turn to a decline in investment and output (Mishkin 1995, 8).

Bernanke and Gertler (1995) also suggest a household balance sheet mechanism arising from supply-side sources of credit whereby, a decline in bank lending induced by a monetary contraction may cause a decline in durables and housing expenditure by consumers who do not have access to other sources of credit. In the liquidity-effect view, balance-sheet effects work through their impact on consumers' desire to spend, rather than on the lenders' desire to lend. Mishkin (1995, 9) proposes a liquidity effect on consumer expenditures working on the demand side. Another transmission mechanism for monetary policy working through consumer expenditure is explained through falling equity prices reducing the value of financial

---

[1] In general, agency problems arise when a principal hires an agent to perform tasks, yet the agent does not share the principal's objective. The common example of principal–agent relations arising between the owners and managers of firms give rise to the cases in which we are interested.

assets. Because consumers have less secure financial positions, this gives rise to a reduction in expenditure on consumer durables and housing (Mishkin 1995).

Introducing a liquidity effect, Palley (1997) augmented the Poole (1970) model to provide a direct link between the money supply and aggregate demand. This mechanism works by additional liquidity relaxing the demand side liquidity constraints on agents' spending. Poole (1970) argues that monetary authorities should target interest rates if LM disturbances dominate, and target the money supply if IS disturbances dominate.

Bank lending may play an important role in the credit channel, since banks are especially well suited to deal with certain types of borrowers, especially small firms, where the problems of asymmetric information can be especially pronounced. In general, increasing financial innovation has given rise to criticism of this channel (Kakes 2000). However, there is evidence that, especially in some developing countries, this channel may be of significant importance (Bank of Korea 1998; Van Wijnbergen 1982).

3.5 Recent Empirical Developing Country Studies

Although the evidence cannot be definitive, this literature suggests that there are strong reasons to link interest rates and the real side impact through the IS curve demand and supply side mechanisms. We noted earlier that in the theoretical macroeconomics literature, an expansionary monetary shock can lead to a decline in interest rates, which may affect the demand for investments on the supply side and the consumer demand on the demand side, through the availability of cheaper credit via the interest rate channel. This is the fundamental mechanism of the monetary transmission mechanism in macroeconomics.

Interest rates can have a measurable impact on real variables through a wide range of mechanisms, as we discussed when describing the four channels. We noted, for example, that the credit channel is not a distinct freestanding channel (Bernanke and Gertler 1995). This channel, however, may well be identified as giving rise to real side effects, especially through balance sheet and bank lending mechanisms for households and firms. Although firms in industrial and developing countries obtain finance very differently, the cost of financing economic activity is expected to be fundamental in all economies. There is strong evidence of a relationship between interest rates and output in developing countries. The nature and significance of the link may vary. There is strong evidence from the empirical literature that the relationship may vary between countries and over time. The cost of capital effect on investment financing comes through different social and institutional contexts in many instances. The case of Korea (Bank of Korea 1998; Van Wijnbergen 1982) is different from that of Brazil (Lopes 1998), and different from the experience in Chile (Eyzaguirre 1998), and in Trinidad and Tobago (Watson 2003), which shows its characteristic response via these channels. In an important study, Kamin, Turner and Van't Dack (1998) provide an interesting set of eight empirical assessments of attempts to measure the impact of monetary policy in developing countries.

Various forms of VARs, impulse response functions and different forms of decompositions provide the econometric method to carry out many of these empirical analyses. In the remainder of this section, we comment briefly on the nature of the empirical study and on the main conclusions reached by studies of the monetary transmission mechanism channels in developing economies.

A Bank of Korea (1998) study of the bank's lending channel, in the transmission of monetary policy in Korea, used VAR and impulse response functions applied to monthly time-series for four variables. The policy instrument was the monetary base, industrial production, the consumer price index and primary assets (bank loans, cash and securities holding) for 1987–94. The study found that a reduction in the monetary reserve base had a significant impact on the lending volume and securities holdings of small and medium size banks. However, it did not have an impact on the larger banks. The smaller banks in Korea appear to rely more heavily on deposits for fund-raising and face higher borrowing costs compared to larger banks. As a consequence, they seem to cut their lending volume to a relatively greater extent than large banks do, in the wake of a monetary contraction. So there is an asymmetric effect across banks of different sizes.

A study by Eyzaguirre (1998) in Chile found that monetary policy transmission effects focus mainly on the traditional interest rate/aggregate demand mechanism and on the exchange rate channel. Credit aggregates and asset prices receive less emphasis. Chile has a relatively free and developed financial system, compared to most developing countries. Chile has also seen considerable structural change in the financial sector, such as the ending of restrictions on foreign currency holding, for example. A high degree of indexation, however, notably in the labour and financial markets and tax system, has prevented a rapid fall in inflation. Monetary policy uses the real interest rate as its instrument. The exchange rate band is indexed to the consumer price index. Chile was among the early implementers of inflation targeting. Since 1991, the central bank has operated with explicit annual inflation targets. The bank aims to achieve a level of interest rates, expenditure and output consistent with the stated inflation targets. Most financial instruments (government and private sector) are denominated in terms of a unit of account known as the development unit or "unidad de formento" (UF), which indexed credit contracts to the consumer price index with a one-month lag. The central bank operates an overnight UF interest rate that in turn affects longer-term UF rates through the term structure. These rates approximate real rates and are expected to impact on expenditure activities. Error correction estimates by Eyzaguirre (1998, 78) indicate that market rates significantly affect aggregate demand. A decline in aggregate demand is also estimated to bring about a reduction in inflation, although this effect seems to be small. In an earlier study, Mendoza and Fernandez (1994) found no clear evidence of such a link. However, during a period of large rate hikes, a reduction in inflation and output was observable after nine months (1994, 20–21). Eyzaguirre (1998, 79) found no significant impact when the impact of changes in interest rates on the real exchange rates was estimated.

Monetary and exchange rate policy in Colombia is implemented by an independent central bank in the context of rapidly evolving, though relatively underdeveloped, financial markets (Carrasquilla 1998). The bank operates an exchange rate zone where interventions take place at the margins. On the interest rate side, the bank acts in the overnight money market. The market for equities is underdeveloped. Carrasquilla (1998, 93) presents some graphical evidence in support of the exchange rate and interest rate channels. The credit channel showed some evidence of responding to a monetary expansion in 1990–92, but no evidence on a contraction over 1980–84. Carrasquilla offers an explanation of what could be a structural asymmetry between the effects of a monetary expansion and those of a contraction.

Since 1983, the Bank of Indonesia has sought to achieve the multiple objectives of inflation and monetary growth targets primarily through control of monetary aggregates M1 and M2 through open market operations (Iljas 1998). This framework requires a stable money demand function. The error correction model estimates used by Iljas (1998, 109) show some evidence of a stable function. Reserve requirement, credit management and moral suasion are also employed in support of open market operations. There is some question about the extent to which financial factors such as cash flows and financial leverage influence firms' investment behaviour. Agung's (2000) panel examination of 219 non-financial firms over 1993–97, of this balance sheet effect, estimated a Tobin's q model of investment and found evidence to support the credit channel mechanism. Agung's estimates imply that the response of the real sector to a monetary policy shock in Indonesia depends upon the financial structure of firms, the segmentation of the financial market between large and small firms, and the degree of financial/credit friction in the capital/credit market. Accordingly, there could be distributional effects arising from monetary policy shock if this transmission mechanism is relatively important.

Diaz (1998) reports that in Mexico the central bank intervenes through its provision of liquidity. Interest rates are then determined by the market. Tightening or loosening monetary restrictions is done by daily announcements by the central bank for the cumulative balance of commercial bank accounts at the central bank, which has a zero reserve requirement. Diaz (1998, 171) writes that prices and wages in Mexico have a long history of sensitivity to the exchange rate, and that the exchange rate and the interest channels are important. The operational framework would, in addition, tend to suggest that the credit channel through its control of liquidity may also be relevant.

As a country with considerable experience of hyperinflation, Brazil has for a long time produced a series of adaptations that tended to reduce the power of monetary policy (Lopes 1998). Like Chile, there is a developed and sophisticated financial indexation mechanism. In a high inflation economy, where banks are dependent on deposits and assume minimum credit risk, the credit channel is not important. The interest rate channel is also dependent on the absence of hyperinflation for an effective mechanism to develop. In a narrative exposition, Lopes (1998, 71) notes that the exchange rate channel has probably been the key transmission mechanism of monetary policy in recent Brazilian experience. The nominal exchange rate was indexed to the consumer price index. From 1995, a "very dirty float" has been used with almost weekly interventions, aimed at avoiding exchange rate appreciations, supported by real interest rates of 17 to 33 per cent.

Since 1990, financial stabilization policies have brought about structural changes, which have changed the way monetary policy affects the Peruvian economy (de la Rocha 1998). Under the reforms, price stability was the sole objective of the central bank. As de la Rocha (1998, 191) notes, in this liberalized financial system, with its high degree of dollarization, monetary policy has two sets of instruments: intervention in the foreign exchange market through sales and purchases to/from financial institutions; and intervention in the money market through open market operations using central bank certificates of deposit which are auctioned. Three channels are deemed important in this study: the interest rate channel, the credit channel and the exchange rate channel.

By controlling base money growth via the interest rate channel (which de la Rocha calls the money channel), there is graphical evidence that the central bank can influence interest rates, and thus, aggregate demand and inflation. Monetary policy is transmitted via the credit channel, mainly through that part of the money stock denominated in foreign currency. As in the case of Brazil, a history of high inflation preludes the functioning of this channel with respect to local domestic currency. Foreign currency reserve requirements are used to limit credit growth for any given increase in deposits. The exchange rate channel is also important. As long as domestic and foreign currency assets are not perfect substitutes, central bank intervention in the foreign exchange market will have an impact on the exchange rate. The goal of the central bank's intervention is to reduce exchange rate variability.

The Bank of Thailand has the multiple objectives of economic growth, price stability and external stability, though price stability is of particular concern (Sirivedhin 1998). Post the liberalization, the main instruments used by the bank have been inter-bank lending rates and money market liquidity through open market operations. Sirivedhin (1998) uses VAR and impulse response functions to examine the interest rate channel and credit channel mechanisms in Thailand. The four variables included in the VAR were, the inter-bank rate, domestic credit, private investment index and the consumer price index. Estimation of pre- and post-liberalization indicated that monetary policy has been more effective in the post-liberalization period, since 1990. The impulse responses suggested that the interest rate channel most effectively transmitted monetary policy shocks.

In their study of the CFA Zone, East African Currency Board and Rand Monetary Area, Guillaume and Stasavage (2000) compare periods of compliance with the monetary rules with periods of non-compliance. They argue that most African countries lack the institutions necessary for credible monetary policy at the national level but that those that participated in the monetary unions were able to do so within a union for a time. Success of monetary unions depends crucially on the design of monetary rules and on the member states willing to oppose attempts to break the monetary rules. Guillaume and Stasavage argue that African countries that have participated in regional monetary agreements have often been characterized by sound and credible monetary policies, and that this has been particularly so when exiting from unions has been costly.

In the cases of the CFA Zone and Rand Monetary Area, financial and economic assistance from France and South Africa, respectively, were important benefits to member countries of the union. Exiting the unions could be made costly, therefore, by having to forgo such benefits. However, they caution that even in the presence of costly exits, the willingness of participating states to veto attempts to break policy rules remains critical.

In a study of oil and gas rich Trinidad and Tobago, Watson (2003) employed VAR and generalized impulse response functions, applied to quarterly data spanning the period 1971–1998, to measure the impact of monetary policy on real activity. He found that exchange rate is the most important transmission mechanism of monetary policy to the real sector.

Khan (1998) estimated a common VAR across five countries (the Bahamas, Belize, Guyana, Jamaica and Suriname) with interest rates, M2, unemployment, output and the consumer price index. Impulse response functions and variance decomposition averages were used to trace monetary to real side impacts. For the Bahamas, he did not observe any link between the financial variables and output. The Guyana estimates showed a link going from the Treasury Bill rate, money supply and output, but he suggested that this may be due to measurement problems in the data, since it is counter to his expectations (Khan 1998, 66). For Jamaica, some evidence of a link between loan rates and output was found. For Suriname, no significant link between the monetary policy variable and the real side variable was found.

The cost of liquidity and capital is a fundamental determinant of economic activity at all levels of economic development. There is strong evidence of this in the empirical literature reviewed above. Overall, interest rates remain a primary variable in the transmission mechanism in developing countries as in industrial countries. Arestis and Sawyer (2002) noted that in the case of the euro area, that interest rates affect output substantially through changes in the rate of investment. This means that interest rate changes can have long-lasting effect through changes in the size of the capital stock. If, in LDCs, capital is financed through borrowing (Friedman 1981; Taylor 1981), there is some scope for interest rates to have some impact on the long-run supply curve, as well as in the short run.

The studies by Kamin, Turner and Van't Dack (1998) showed evidence of asymmetric impact of monetary policy across banks of different sizes. Different historical experience and institutional framework gave rise to a variety of ways of defining an appropriate interest rate instrument, for example. Its impact was mediated through the financial structure in different ways.

3.6 Conclusions

In this chapter, we have seen that the monetary transmission mechanism literature examines how monetary policy affects the real side of the economy – such things as output and employment. The issue of how monetary policies effects are transmitted to the real sector of the economy is fundamentally the same for industrial and developing economies. The explanations of how the mechanisms work tend to be different because of the differences in economic structures, behavioural features, historical experience and institutions in economies. However, this is not a difference between developed and developing economies. These are differences between economies and for an economy over time. Differences arise between economies because fundamental characteristics of economies are not identical, and for a single economy because the factors determining the behaviour of the economy will change over time.

Within industrial economies, the institutional contexts and the channels through which monetary policy work are complex because of the complicated financial superstructures that exists. Nevertheless, the financial structures of the industrial economies tend to show a relatively higher degree of convergence when compared to the financial structures to be found in the developing economies. If monetary policy effects are transmitted through the financial structure, then it stands to reason that the sometimes rudimentary financial systems found in developing countries should affect the way in which the monetary transmission mechanisms in these countries function.

We have also seen that the character of the transmission mechanisms will be as widespread and varied as the differences in the institutional and historical economic experiences and financial structures. The varied experiences of Brazil and Trinidad and Tobago come to mind. The former, with its history of hyperinflation, and the latter, with its oil and gas bonanza, give rise to distinct experiences (Watson 2003; Lopes 1998; Kamin, Turner and Van't Dack 1998).

In the transmission of monetary policy effects, four channels are generally identified as important: the interest rate channel; the exchange rate channel; the domestic asset prices channel; and the credit channel.

The choice of monetary policy design depends on the nature of the financial system and the channels through which policy measures are deemed to work. These have also been changing radically over time in many emerging and developing market economies. For example, liberalization and internationalization have characterized many developing countries over recent decades. Consequently, balance, payments and exchange rate effects have been important in policymaking and economic performance. Different models have provided different views of the nature of the binding constraints on economic growth and development, which dictate the policy approach and policy instruments that should be given priority (Fry 1988; Van Wijnbergen 1982, 1983; Taylor 1981, 1983; McKinnon 1973; Shaw 1973).

There is a growing consensus in macroeconomics that an over-expansionary monetary policy cannot stimulate long-term growth of the economy, but rather, that such actions lead largely to inflation with an adverse impact on growth and development, among other things. Consequently, price stability is increasingly identified as the single most important objective of monetary policy in developing countries. Price stability, however, is not an end in itself, but the means to economic growth and development. Hence, monetary policy has an important role to play in laying the foundation for a sustainable growth in output.

The cost and availability of capital is among the fundamental determinants of economic activity at all levels of economic development. There is strong evidence of this in the empirical literature reviewed above. Overall, interest rates remain a primary variable in the transmission mechanism in developing countries as in industrial countries. We have seen from the empirical studies surveyed that different historical experiences and institutional frameworks across a wide range of countries, give rise to a variety of ways in which monetary policy, via interest rates, has an impact on economic activity.

Chapter **4**

The Data

Introduction

It should be noted right from the outset that this chapter is not intended to be read from beginning to end, as one would normally read the text of a book. It is designed to provide detailed and accurate information about the data used throughout the book, so that readers are able to accurately identify variables and replicate the results, should they wish to do so. This is an important part of the role we hope the book will play for the study of applied econometrics. As such, the primary aim is to accurately describe the data sources, definitions, salient characteristics, and any patches or transformations carried out.

In general, there were three limitations in building the dataset that are worth pointing out.

1. Some time-series were available on a quarterly basis, whereas others were only available annually. The analysis of the monetary transmission mechanism in chapter 6, for example, uses quarterly data, but the crucial variable GDP was only available on an annual basis. Therefore, we interpolated GDP to deal with the difference in frequency. We describe the interpolation method below.
2. The analysis of the external balance in chapter 8 uses annual data since most of the variables were not available on a quarterly basis. However, even on an annual basis we had to drop St Lucia and the Bahamas from this analysis because exports and imports time-series were not available for these two countries.
3. For some countries, certain series show no variation. In particular, interest rates and exchange rates were, in some cases, fixed. This raised major issues in estimating comparable models across all the countries at some times.

In section 4.1, we describe the sources and variables used in the quarterly dataset. We define the variables and provide the IMF *line codes* where these are available, to accurately identify the series. The definitions in this section provide the default definitions of the variables used.

In section 4.2, we provide a detailed description of the data for each of the countries in the study. We hope that the methods employed here may encourage some students and researchers to apply these and other econometric techniques to individual country data to carry out more detailed examination of their economic behaviour. This could, we think, be a useful way of developing postgraduate econometric projects. We describe each of the country datasets separately so as to facilitate this single country study process. In section 4.3 we describe the process we used to convert the annual data series into quarterly data series. Section 4.4 describes the annual data series used in, notably, the external balance estimations.

4.1 Data Sources and Variables

To carry out comparative analyses, it is desirable that the variables are defined and measured in the same way across the countries in the study. Consequently, we have sought to build the dataset from two common sources and confine the variables to consistent definitions. In this subsection, we describe the variables that were common across the countries in the study.

All the data used in this study were obtained from two sources: the IMF, *International Financial Statistics* (*IFS*), and the World Bank, *World Development Indicators* (*WDI*). The single exception, the oil price series, is explained below. Not all the countries have data series of the same length. We built the maximum length available for any particular country since estimation will, in general, take place on the basis of a single country.

The nominal exchange rate S is taken from the IFS (line *rf*), which refers to period averages of the market or official exchange rates for the countries quoted in units of national currency.

The money variables are derived from *Money* (line *34*) – currency and demand deposit (M1) – and *Quasi-Money* (line *35*) – time, savings and foreign currency deposits of resident sectors, excluding central government. The summation of the two provides a broad definition of money (M2) in some definitions, which is used throughout the study.

The interest rate R, for the various countries, used throughout the study is the average for the period short-term *Treasury Bill Rate* (line *60c*).

Domestic prices are the *Consumer Price Index* (line *64*), or the GDP deflator from the *WDI*, where the CPI is unavailable, as in the cases of Antigua and Barbuda and Guyana. In these latter cases, quarterly price series were interpolated from the annual *WDI* series. The interpolated quarterly series were annualized to be compatible with the CPI series derived from the IMF source and the other variables of the study.

Exports and imports are in most cases *Exports of Goods and Services Constant 1995 US$* and *Imports of Goods and Services Constant 1995 US$* from the *WDI*.

Domestic real output Y is in most cases *GDP a factor cost in local currency units* sourced from the *WDI*, except in the cases of the Bahamas and Jamaica, where *GDP at market prices in local currency units* were used due to the unavailability of the former.

The foreign variables are all proxied by the counterpart US variables and obtained from the IMF, *International Financial Statistics*.

The foreign interest rate R* is the short-term US Treasury Bill rate (line *60c*).

The foreign price index P* is the US Consumer Price Index (line *64*). The foreign real output series Y* is the US GDP Volume Index (1995 = 100) (line *99bvp*).

The observations on the price of oil were obtained from the data used by Garratt, Lee, Pesaran and Shin (2000) in their long-run structural macro econometric model of the United Kingdom.

4.2 The Country Data

The data for Antigua and Barbuda cover 1980(1) to 2004(4). Quarterly series on S, M and R variables were obtained from the IMF *International Financial Statistics (IFS)*. Quarterly P and Y were not available from the *IFS*. Annual series for P and Y were obtained from the *WDI* for 1977–2004, and were interpolated to obtain quarterly series covering the period 1977(1) to 2003(4). In the case of P, the CPI series was unavailable, so annual series of the *GDP deflator (1990 = 100)* was used. For Y, we used *GDP (constant 2000 US$)*. The series were annualized by multiplying the interpolated series by four.

Data for Dominica covered 1980(1) to 2003(4). Quarterly series for the S, M and R, and P were obtained from the *IFS*. The Y used was *GDP (constant 2000 US$)*, obtained from the *WDI* and interpolated to obtain a quarterly series and annualized.

Data for Grenada covered 1980(1) to 2002(4). Quarterly series for the S, M and R, and P were obtained from the *IFS*. The Y used was the annual *GDP (constant 2000 US$)*, obtained from the *WDI* and interpolated to obtain a quarterly series and annualized.

Data for St Kitts and Nevis are for 1980(1) to 2002(4). Quarterly series for the S, M and R were obtained from the *IFS*. Annual series for P and Y were obtained from the *WDI* and were interpolated to obtain quarterly series and annualized.

Data for St Lucia are for 1980(1) to 2003(4). Quarterly series for the S, M and R, and P were obtained from the *IFS*. The Y used was the annual *GDP (constant 2000 US$)* obtained from the *WDI* and interpolated to obtain a quarterly series. IMF data show that the 1979 GDP volume was 1.021 of the 1980 volume (46.9041/45.933) = 1.021 (IMF 2002 for GDP volume [1995=100], line reference *99bvp*). With this, an annual figure for Y for 1979 was estimated and spliced onto the longer series so that the interpolation could generate quarterly series from 1980(1).

Data for St Vincent and the Grenadines are for 1980(1) to 2003(4). Quarterly series for the S, M and R, and P were obtained from the *IFS*. The Y used was the annual *GDP (constant 2000 US$)*, obtained from the *WDI* and interpolated to obtain a quarterly series and annualized.

Data for the Bahamas are for 1971(2) to 2001(4). Quarterly series for the S, M and R, and P were obtained from the *IFS* (line *rf* for the Bah's nominal exchange rate was not available, so line *ae* was used instead) and annual series for Y (1964–2002) obtained from the annual *GDP (constant 2000 US$)* from the *WDI* and interpolated to obtain a quarterly series for Y to 2001(4) and annualized.

Data for Barbados are available over the period 1968(1) to 2002(4). Quarterly series for the S, M and R, and P were obtained from the *IFS* and annual series for Y (1960–2003) obtained from the annual *GDP (constant 2000 US$)* from the *WDI* and interpolated to obtain a quarterly series for Y to 2002(4) and annualized.

Data for Guyana are available over the period 1972(1) to 2003(4). Quarterly series for the S, M and R were obtained from the *IFS*. For P we used the GDP deflator (1970–2004) from the *WDI*. For Y, we used the annual *GDP (constant 2000 US$)* from the *WDI*. Both series were interpolated to obtain quarterly the series and annualized.

Data for Belize are available over the period 1979(1) to 2003(4). Quarterly series for the S, M and R were obtained from the *IFS*. For P, we used the GDP deflator (1978–2004) from the *WDI*. For Y, we used the annual *GDP (constant 2000 US$)* from the *WDI*. Both series were interpolated to obtain quarterly the series and annualized.

Data for Jamaica are available over the period 1965(1) to 2002(4). Quarterly series for S, M and R, and P were obtained from the *IFS*. The annual series for Y (1964–2003) was obtained from the same source as GDP volume, 2000 = 100 (*99bvp*). This allowed an interpolated quarterly series for Y to 2002(4). Multiplying by four, annualized the interpolated quarterly Y series.

Data for Trinidad and Tobago are available over the period 1965(1) to 2003(4). Quarterly series for the S, M and R, and P were obtained from the *IFS*. Annual series for Y (1960–2004) was obtained from the annual *GDP (constant 2000 US$)* from the *WDI* and interpolated to obtain a quarterly series for Y to 2003(4) and annualized.

4.3 Interpolation

We sought to carry out this exercise using quarterly data, but some of the required data series were unobtainable in quarters. Therefore, we constructed quarterly series from the reported annual series. In general, the series obtained from the IMF downloads were quarterly, but the GDP Volume Indices (*99bvp*) were in the Caribbean cases annual series, as were those from the World Bank. The method of interpolation used to derive quarterly figures from the annual *WDI* series is that of Goldstein and Khan (1976), as reported in Weliwita and Ekanayake (1998) as follows:

Let x_{t-1}, x_t and x_{t+1} be three successive annual observations of variable x. If the quadratic function that passes through the three points is such that

$$\int_0^1 (as^2 + bs + s)ds = x_{t-1}$$

$$\int_1^2 (as^2 + bs + s)ds = x_t$$

$$\int_2^3 (as^2 + bs + s)ds = x_{t+1}$$

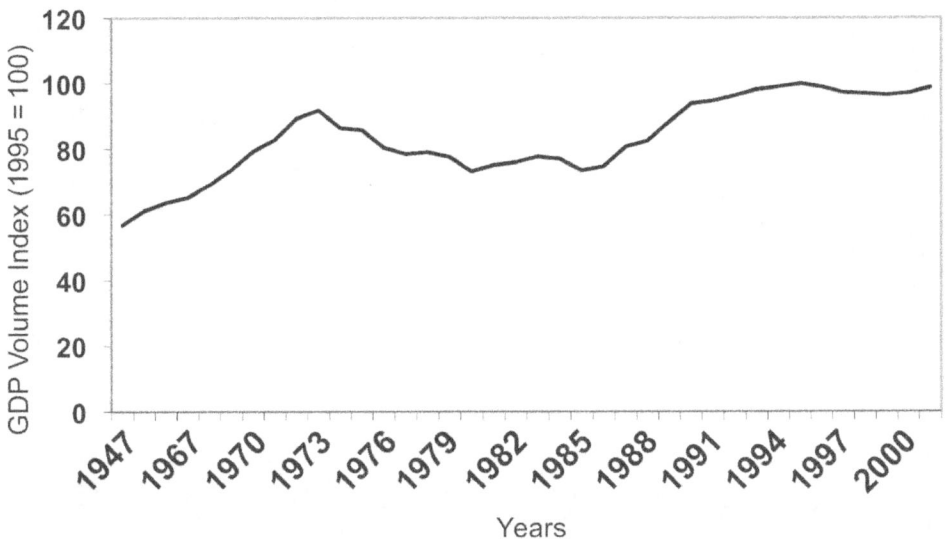

Figure 4.1 Jamaica: GDP volume index, annual (1995 = 100)
Source: International Monetary Fund, *International Financial Statistics June 2002 cd.*

then, integrating and solving for *a*, *b* and *c* gives:

$$a = 0.5x_{t-1} - x_t + 0.5x_{t+1}$$
$$b = -2x_{t-1} + 3x_t - x_{t+1}$$
$$c = 1.8333x_{t-1} - 1.1666x_t + 0.333x_{t+1}$$

The four quarterly figures within a given year can now be interpolated, respectively, using

$$\int_{1}^{1.25} (as^2 + bs + s)ds = 0.05468x_{t-1} + 0.23438x_t - 0.039067x_{t+1}$$

$$\int_{1.25}^{1.50} (as^2 + bs + s)ds = 0.00781x_{t-1} + 0.26563x_t - 0.02344x_{t+1}$$

$$\int_{1.50}^{1.75} (as^2 + bs + s)ds = -0.02344x_{t-1} + 0.26562x_t + 0.00781x_{t+1}$$

$$\int_{1.75}^{2.0} (as^2 + bs + s)ds = -0.0391x_{t-1} + 0.23437x_t + 0.05469x_{t+1}$$

The interpolated series can be expressed at annual rates by multiplying by four.

For example, let us examine a Jamaican series that was unavailable quarterly. Figure 4.1 shows the annual real GDP volume index (*99bvp*) obtained from the IFS for Jamaica 1964–2001. We transformed this annual series to obtain an interpolated series *in quarterly rates*

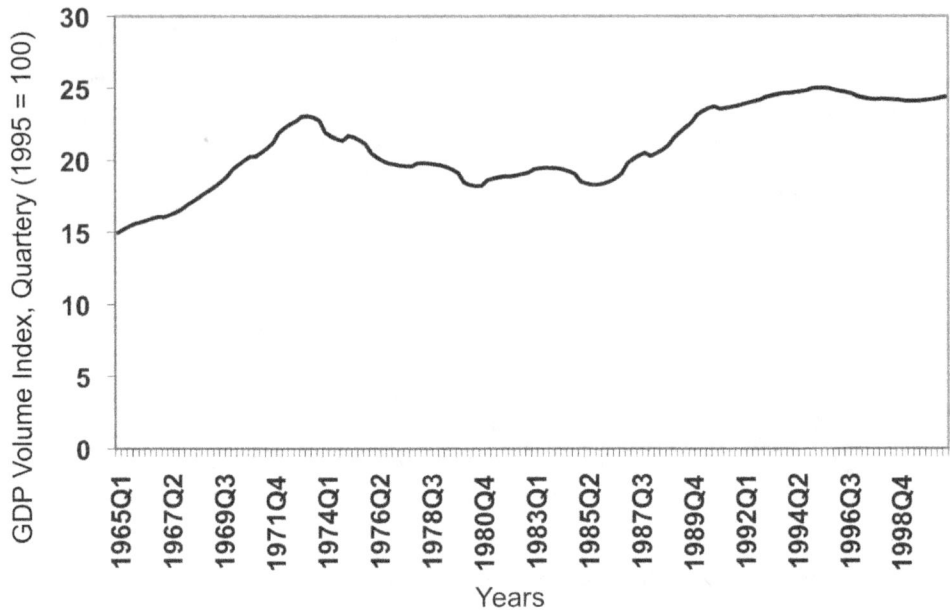

Figure 4.2 Jamaica: GDP volume index, quarterly (1995 = 100)
Source: International Monetary Fund, *International Financial Statistics June 2002 cd*.

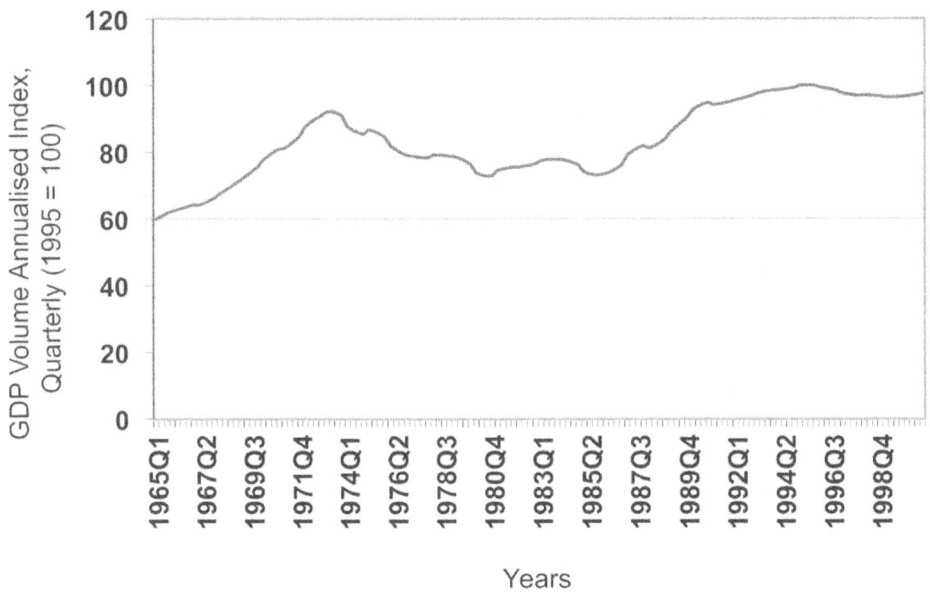

Figure 4.3 Jamaica: GDP volume index, quarterly (1995 = 100) annualized
Source: International Monetary Fund, *International Financial Statistics June 2002 cd*.

Table 4.1 Annual Data Series Used in Open Economy Estimations

Country (Abbreviation)	Period
Antigua and Barbuda (AB)	1978–2002
Dominica (DOM)	1978–2003
Grenada (GRE)	1978–2003
St Kitts and Nevis (SKN)	1981–2003
St Lucia (SLU)	1980–2003
St Vincent and the Grenadines (SVG)	1977–2003
The Bahamas (BAH)	1976–2002
Barbados (BAR)	1981–2003
Guyana (GUY)	1974–2002
Belize (BEL)	1986–2003
Jamaica (JAM)	1976–2004
Trinidad and Tobago (TT)	1980–2004

shown in figure 4.2 using the procedure explained above. Figure 4.3, on the other hand, shows the interpolated quarterly series, but this time the series is annualized. Note that the vertical axis values are the same for the annualized series, but the values are less for the quarterly rates in figure 4.2. The consistent profiles in all three figures confirm the appropriateness of the interpolation.

The interpolated series that were originally indices were multiplied by four to annualize them so that series, such as the CPI and GDP volume indices, could relate more directly to their base year and annual counterparts.

4.4 Annual Data for External Balance Estimates

The open economy estimations were carried out with annual data series, not quarterly series, because balance of payments and trade data are only available annually. For S, M, PF and YF, we used the IMF series from the IMF *International Financial Statistics* (*IFS*), downloaded from http://www.esds.ac.uk. The variable definitions are described below. For P, Y, R, X, M, and RF we used World Bank series from the *World Development Indicators*, also downloaded from http://www.esds.ac.uk. These variable definitions are described below. We used the series downloaded from the World Bank as the default series, and filled in as necessary with other variables from the IMF's *International Financial Statistics* and from the World Bank's *World Development Indicators* (*WDI*). The default series were as follows:

- S = nominal exchange rate (line *rf*)
- M = *the summation of money and quasi money* (line *35l*)
- P = GDP deflator
- Y = GDP constant lcu (local currency units)
- R = lending interest rate (%)
- X = exports of goods and services (constant 2000 US$)

- M = *imports of goods and services (constant 2000 US$)*
- PF = foreign prices is the US *consumer price index* (line *64*)
- YF = foreign income is the US *real GDP at 2000 prices, in local currency US$* (line *99br*)
- RF = foreign income is the US *lending interest rate (%)*

For BAH, BAR, JAM and SLU, the *WDI* series for X and M were either not available or short, so we used IMF sources. X represented *exports FOB US$m* (line *70D*), and M were *imports CIF US$m* (line *71D*). The annual time-series for all other countries were constructed as described above. The series for each country varied in length and all are described in table 4.1.

Chapter 5

Econometric Methods and Issues

Introduction

In chapters 5 to 8, we will estimate small models for these countries and calculate impulse response functions that measure how these economies respond to certain types of shocks. This chapter sets out the econometric techniques that we shall use, such as vector autoregressions (VARs) and cointegrating vector error correction models (VECMs), and explains how the impulse response functions are calculated.

We intend to analyse a vector of m variables w_t, observed over time periods $t = 1, 2... $ T. Choice of m is a central issue. There are about a dozen domestic and foreign variables that we have data on. These include real money, the real exchange rate, domestic prices, interest rate, output, trade-balance foreign prices interest rate and output, and the oil price. All variables except the interest rates are in logarithms. However, given our short time-series, it would be impossible to estimate a VAR for all of them together. In practice, we will work with subsets of the variables, starting with a single variable, inflation, and then including more variables. Under certain assumptions we can partition w_t into a set of domestic endogenous variables and a set of foreign exogenous variables. For the moment, however, we will treat them together. The basic statistical model that we will use to describe the data is a vector autoregression. This can be regarded as the reduced form of a dynamic structural economic model. To give an economic interpretation to the estimates, we need to identify this structural model. We will discuss the issues involved in this chapter. We examine the dynamic behaviour of the system by considering how the time profile of the variables responds to shocks. These time profiles are called impulse response functions. We will discuss their estimation. We use a small monetary model to provide an example of these issues.

5.1 Unit Roots and Cointegration

A variable is said to be stationary if its mean, variance and covariances are not functions of time. It is said to be trend stationary if its mean is a deterministic function of time. If a variable is trend stationary, it is said to be integrated of order zero, $I(0)$. If it is stationary after being differenced once, it is said to be integrated of order one, $I(1)$, and has a stochastic trend, as distinct from a deterministic trend. If it is stationary after being differenced twice, it is said to be $I(2)$. If it is $I(1)$, it is also said to have a unit root. Consider an autoregression for a scalar variable y_t:

$$y_t = \rho y_{t-1} + \varepsilon_t$$

where ε_t is a white noise process, with expected value or mean zero, constant variance and independent through time. This can be written as follows:

$$\Delta y_t = (\rho - 1) y_{t-1} + \varepsilon_t = \beta y_{t-1} + \varepsilon_t$$

If $\rho = 1$, or equivalently $\beta = 0$, the variable is just a random walk, there is a unit root in y_t. The unit root hypothesis can be tested by running a regression of Δy_t on y_{t-1} and calculating the t ratio for the estimate of β. This ratio does not have a standard t distribution, but a non-standard Dickey-Fuller distribution, for which critical values are available. In practice, we allow for deterministic elements, constant and trend, and allow up to p lagged changes in Δy_t to remove any serial correlation, and to ensure that ε_t is white noise. This gives the augmented Dickey-Fuller (ADF) equation:

$$\Delta y_t = \alpha + \beta y_{t-1} + \sum_{i=1}^{p} \gamma_i \Delta y_{t-i} + \delta t + \varepsilon_t$$

Again, we can test the hypothesis $\beta = 0$ using the t ratio and non-standard critical values. We will use ADF type tests, but there are a variety of other tests available which differ in a number of ways. Rather than using the null of a unit root, $\beta = 0$, the null hypothesis can be that y_t is stationary, as in the KPSS test. Rather than removing serial correlation parametrically by including lagged changes in Δy_t, we can allow it for non-parametrically, as in the Phillips-Perron and the KPSS test. In many cases, the decision about whether the variable is $I(0)$ or $I(1)$ is not clear cut. The results are sensitive to the treatment of the deterministic elements, whether a constant and trend are included; the allowance for serial correlation: the number of lags in ADF-type tests; and the window size in non-parametric tests. They tend to have low power because it is very difficult to distinguish between a value of ρ that is close to one and a value that is exactly one. They are sensitive to structural shifts, which can make I(0) series with a break look I(1). When in doubt, for many purposes it is safer to treat the series as $I(1)$.

If the data are non-stationary, $I(1)$, but there are some long-run relationships between the variables, linear combinations, which are $I(0)$, stationary, they are said to cointegrate. The linear combinations are called cointegrating vectors. If the m series in w_t have r cointegrating vectors, they have $m - r$ stochastic trends driving them. There are many methods available for estimating cointegrating vectors, including the original Engle-Granger method, the Dynamic OLS and Fully Modified estimators. Like unit root tests, they differ in the way that they model serial correlation, parametric or non-parametric, and also in how they handle endogeneity. The method we use is due to Johansen, which uses a parametric VAR, reparameterized to a VECM. The Johansen method is attractive because it integrates testing for the number of cointegrating vectors with estimation of them; it handles multiple cointegrating vectors easily, which some of the other methods do not; and the VECM gives us crucial economic information about the process of adjustment to equilibrium. Treating the cointegrating vectors as equilibrium relations may allow us to impose sensible long-run properties on the system. We discuss estimation of VARs and VECMs in more detail below to motivate the econometric methodology that we will adopt in the following chapters.

5.2 Vector Autoregressions (VARs)

For estimation, we will start from a VAR of order p in the $m \times 1$ vector of variables w_t. This takes the following form:

$$w_t = a_0 + A_1 w_{t-1} + \ldots + A_p w_{t-p} + u_t$$

Each of the variables in the vector w_t is regressed on p lags of itself and the other variables. The A_i are $m \times m$ matrices. For estimation, we assume that the errors are independent normal with expected value zero and variance covariance matrix Σ, an $m \times m$ symmetric positive definite matrix:

$$u_t \sim IN(0, \Sigma)$$

Each equation of the VAR can be efficiently estimated by ordinary least squares (OLS), giving estimates of the residuals $\hat{u}_{it}$. The elements of the covariance matrix Σ can be estimated as

$$\hat{\sigma}_{ij}^2 = \sum_{t=1}^{T} \hat{u}_{it} \hat{u}_{jt} / T$$

This has $m(m+1)/2$ independent elements, because the matrix is symmetric.

There are statistical procedures for determining the order of the system, the number of lags to include in the VAR. The most common are two model selection criteria: the Akaike Information Criterion (AIC) and the Schwartz Bayesian Criterion (SBC). The AIC tends to include more parameters in the model than the SBC. If the correct model is among the set of models considered, the SBC will consistently estimate it as the sample gets large. If none of the models considered are correctly specified, the AIC may better approximate the true model, by having more parameters. For exposition, we will work with a first order VAR:

$$w_t = a_0 + A_1 w_{t-1} + u_t$$

5.3 Identification

The VAR is suitable for forecasting (as long as the parameters remain constant over time). However, it is difficult to give the estimates an economic interpretation, and thus it is not suitable for structural analysis, for answering questions such as, "What is the effect of a shock to monetary policy?" For this, we require the structural form, which allows for the contemporaneous feedbacks between the variables. We first go through the model in matrix form and use a monetary model as an example in the next section. The structural form is:

$$B_0 w_t = b_0 + B_1 w_{t-1} + \varepsilon_t$$

where

$$\varepsilon_t \sim IN(0, \Omega)$$

The VAR is the reduced form of this system:

$$w_t = B_0^{-1} b_0 + B_0^{-1} B_1 w_{t-1} + B_0^{-1} \varepsilon_t$$
$$a_0 = B_0^{-1} b_0;$$
$$A_1 = B_0^{-1} B_1;$$
$$u_t = B_0^{-1} \varepsilon_t$$

where $\Sigma = B_0^{-1} \Omega B_0^{-1\prime}$. The reduced form, which we can estimate, gives us estimates of the $m \times 1$ intercepts a_0; the $m \times m$ regression coefficients in A_1 and the $m(m+1)/2$ estimates of the reduced form covariance matrix Σ. The structural form has $m \times 1$ intercepts b_0; $2(m \times m)$ matrices of regression coefficients in B_0 and B_1 and the $m(m+1)/2$ estimates of the covariance matrix Ω.

The identification problem involves deriving estimates of the structural parameters from the estimates of the reduced form coefficients. Just by counting the number of known reduced form estimates and comparing them with the number of unknown structural parameters, it is clear that we are m^2 coefficients short. To estimate the structural parameters we need m^2 extra pieces of information, m on each equation. These are called "just-identifying restrictions" and should be provided from a priori economic theory – they cannot be tested. The choice of these just-identifying restrictions can make a lot of difference to the answers to such questions as, "What is the effect of a monetary policy shock?" However, there is no way of deciding from the data which are the correct set of just-identifying restrictions. Alternative just-identifying restrictions are observationally equivalent. They are all consistent with the same estimated VAR. This can be seen above since

$$A_1 = B_0^{-1} B_1 = (B_0^{-1} P^{-1})(P B_1)$$
$$\Sigma = (B_0^{-1} P^{-1}) \Omega (B_0^{-1} P^{-1})'$$

for any non-singular $m \times m$ matrix P. Therefore, we cannot distinguish between the alternative sets of structural parameters, for example, B_1 or PB_1. We can think of the identification problem as specifying the $m \times m$ matrix P, which embodies the restrictions from economic theory. These restrictions can be put either on the regression matrices B_0 and B_1 or on the covariance matrix Ω. For example, with the restrictions that B_0 is triangular and Ω is diagonal, the system becomes recursive and can be efficiently estimated by OLS. An example of this will be used below. The restrictions can be expressed in terms of relationships between the variables or relationships between the unobserved shocks to the equations, or the errors. When it is done in the latter form, it is often referred to as a structural VAR. This distinction will play an important role in our later discussion of impulse response functions. The choice of just-identifying restrictions is a major controversy in the empirical economics of monetary policy. We will call this the "short-run identification problem", since a different long-run identification problem arises below.

5.4 An Example

Consider a simplified version, without expectations, of the three-equation model of monetary policy in industrialized countries discussed in chapter 3, which determines output, inflation and interest rates. Suppose the output gap is determined through an IS curve by lagged real interest rates and the lagged output gap; inflation is determined through a Phillips Curve by the output gap and lagged inflation; and interest rates are determined through a Taylor Rule by output gap, inflation and lagged interest rates. The structural form can be written as follows:

$$x_t = b_{10} + b_{12}^1(r_{t-1} - \pi_{t-1}) + b_{13}^1 x_{t-1} + \varepsilon_{1t}$$
$$\pi_t = b_{20} - b_{21}^0 x_t + b_{22}^1 \pi_{t-1} + \varepsilon_{2t}$$
$$r_t = b_{30} - b_{31}^0 x_t - b_{32}^0 \pi_t + b_{33}^1 r_{t-1} + \varepsilon_{3t}$$

We use the superscript zero to indicate the coefficients of current values, and superscript one to indicate the coefficients of lagged values. We can stack this structural system in matrix form as follows:

$$B^0 w_t = b + B^1 w_{t-1} + \varepsilon_t$$

$$\begin{bmatrix} 1 & 0 & 0 \\ b_{21}^0 & 1 & 0 \\ b_{31}^0 & b_{32}^0 & 1 \end{bmatrix} \begin{bmatrix} x_t \\ \pi_t \\ r_t \end{bmatrix} = \begin{bmatrix} b_{10} \\ b_{20} \\ b_{30} \end{bmatrix} + \begin{bmatrix} b_{13}^1 & -b_{12}^1 & b_{12}^1 \\ 0 & b_{22}^1 & 0 \\ 0 & 0 & b_{33}^1 \end{bmatrix} \begin{bmatrix} x_{t-1} \\ \pi_{t-1} \\ r_{t-1} \end{bmatrix} + \begin{bmatrix} \varepsilon_{1t} \\ \varepsilon_{2t} \\ \varepsilon_{3t} \end{bmatrix}$$

The restriction $b_{13}^1 = -b_{12}^1$, in the first row arises because it is the lagged real interest rate that appears in the output equation. Zeros appear when a variable does not appear in an equation.

Since $m = 3$ in this case, to identify the system, we need $3^2 = 9$ restrictions on the parameters of the structural form, 3 on each equation. This system has the equality restriction $b_{12}^1 = -b_{13}^1$, seven zero restrictions, such as of the form $b_{12}^0 = 0$, and three normalization restrictions, $b_{11}^0 = b_{22}^0 = b_{33}^0 = 1$, which specify which is the dependent variable in each equation. Together, there are eleven restrictions, so there are more than enough restrictions, and the system is over-identified. It could be estimated by two-stage or three-stage least squares. "Cowles Commission" type structural models were often very large, identified by equality and zero restrictions of this sort. Typically, these were heavily over-identified.

Notice that this particular system, unlike most Cowles Commission type models, has the structure of a causal chain, which makes the B_0 matrix lower triangular, zeros above the diagonal. This is because output is not influenced by current inflation or interest rates, and inflation is not influenced by current interest rates. Identification is achieved by the causal chain structure and by restrictions on the dynamics. For example, lagged output and interest rates do not influence current inflation. As Sims 1980 emphasized in his critique of Cowles Commission type models, it is difficult to justify the restrictions on the dynamics. Suppose that we had added to the inflation equation another explanatory variable, the expectation of inflation in t based on information in period $t-1$. Output and interest rates in $t-1$ would influence the next period forecast of inflation made in $t-1$, so it would appear in the inflation equation. Thus, the dynamic zero restrictions would not be appropriate. Without these four dynamic restrictions, there are only seven restrictions, and the system as a whole is not identified, since we need nine. In fact, without the dynamic restrictions, the first and second equations are identified, but the third is not.

Another source of identification restrictions is restrictions on the covariance matrix. Assume that Ω is diagonal with the following form:

$$\begin{bmatrix} \omega_{11} & 0 & 0 \\ 0 & \omega_{22} & 0 \\ 0 & 0 & \omega_{22} \end{bmatrix}$$

This involves three restrictions: $\omega_{12} = \omega_{13} = \omega_{23} = 0$, since the covariance matrix is symmetric. With the restrictions that B_0 is triangular (three zero restrictions and three normalization restrictions) and Ω is diagonal (three restrictions), the system is identified. Such systems are known as recursive systems and can be efficiently estimated by OLS. In general, there is no reason to expect the structural shocks in this system to be uncorrelated. For example, an increased oil price shock might influence the errors in all three equations reducing output, increasing inflation and prompting some monetary response. The errors in aggregate equations such as this will typically aggregate a large number of more fundamental shocks.

The unrestricted reduced form for the system is as follows:

$$x_t = a_{10} + a_{11}x_{t-1} + a_{12}\pi_{t-1} + a_{13}r_{t-1} + u_{1t}$$
$$\pi_t = a_{20} + a_{21}x_{t-1} + a_{22}\pi_{t-1} + a_{23}r_{t-1} + u_{2t}$$
$$r_t = a_{30} + a_{31}x_{t-1} + a_{32}\pi_{t-1} + a_{33}r_{t-1} + u_{3t}$$

The causal chain structure of the model is given as follows:

$$u_{1t} = \varepsilon_{1t}$$
$$u_{2t} = -b_{21}^{0}\varepsilon_{1t} + \varepsilon_{2t}$$
$$u_{3t} = -(b_{31}^{0} + b_{32}b_{21}^{0})\varepsilon_{1t} - b_{32}\varepsilon_{2t} + \varepsilon_{3t}$$

If Ω is diagonal, we can estimate the b_{ij}^{0} and recover the structural errors.

$$\varepsilon_{1t} = u_{1t}$$
$$\varepsilon_{2t} = u_{2t} + b_{21}^{0}\varepsilon_{1t}$$
$$\varepsilon_{3t} = u_{3t} + (b_{31}^{0} + b_{32}b_{21}^{0})\varepsilon_{1t} + b_{32}\varepsilon_{2t}$$

This is the procedure adopted by orthogonalized impulse response functions with the variables ordered x_t, π_t, r_t. Implicitly, this imposes the assumptions that there is a causal chain structure and the structural errors are uncorrelated. This is a strong identifying assumption. The impulse response function for a 1 standard error (SE) shock in the first variable, $\delta = \sqrt{\omega_{11}}$ in period zero is therefore,

$\tau =$	x_t	π_t	r_t
0	δ	$-b_{21}^{0}\delta$	$-(b_{31}^{0} + b_{32}^{0}b_{21}^{0})\delta$
1	$b_{13}^{1}\delta$	$-b_{22}^{1}b_{21}^{0}\delta$	$-b_{33}^{1}(b_{31}^{0} + b_{32}^{0}b_{21}^{0})\delta$

and so on.

The generalized impulse response function allows for the covariance between the shocks. This can be applied to the structural shocks if the model is identified without covariance restrictions, as in our first example, or it can be applied to the reduced form shocks. Suppose we estimate the reduced form and obtain estimates of the coefficients a_{ij} and of the variances and covariances σ_{ij}. Suppose that there is a 1 standard error shock to the first equation, which we can write as follows:

$$\delta_{11} = \sqrt{\sigma_{11}} = \sigma_{11}/\sqrt{\sigma_{11}}$$
$$\delta_{11} = \sqrt{\sigma_{11}}$$

The effect on the error in the second equation of a 1 standard error shock to the first equation will be as follows:

$$\delta_{21} = (\sigma_{12}/\sigma_{11})\delta_{11}$$
$$= (\sigma_{12}/\sigma_{11})\sqrt{\sigma_{11}} = \sigma_{12}/\sqrt{\sigma_{11}}$$

The term $(\sigma_{12}/\sigma_{11})$ is just the regression coefficient, in the regression of the second error on the first error. Therefore, δ_{21} is the predicted change in the second error of a 1 standard error shock in the first error. In general,

$$\delta_{ij} = \sigma_{ij} / \sqrt{\sigma_{jj}}$$

Thus, the reduced form generalized impulse response function is as follows:

t	x_t	π_t	r_t
0	δ_{11}	δ_{21}	δ_{31}
1	$a_{11}\delta_{11} + a_{12}\delta_{21} + a_{13}\delta_{31}$	$a_{21}\delta_{11} + a_{22}\delta_{21} + a_{23}\delta_{31}$	$a_{31}\delta_{11} + a_{32}\delta_{21} + a_{33}\delta_{31}$

The effects of shocks to other equations can also be calculated.

5.5 Impulse Response Functions

To analyse the dynamic interaction between variables, we use impulse response functions. For linear systems, which we will focus on, the impulse response function starting at some period τ measures the expected value of the time profile of the future values of a variable in response to a shock to one of the errors. For example, the effect on variable i of a shock to the error in the equation for variable j is given by the difference in the conditional expectations:

$$\psi_{ij,\tau+n} = E(w_{i,\tau+n} / \varepsilon_{j\tau} = \delta_{j,\tau+n}) - E(w_{i,\tau+n} / \varepsilon_{j\tau} = 0)$$

For a linear model, the impulse response function is independent of the initial conditions in period τ. In a non-linear model, this is not the case. For example, one might expect that the effect of a monetary stimulus might be quite different when the economy is near full capacity from when there is substantial excess capacity. This is an example of a non-linear effect. There are various ways that one can specify the intervention. It could be a transitory innovation (for example, $\varepsilon_{j\tau} = \delta, \varepsilon_{j,\tau+n} = 0, n > 0$) or it could be permanent (for example, $\varepsilon_{j,\tau+n} = \delta$) for all n. We will focus on transitory shocks. There is an issue as to how big to make the shock. It is conventional to analyse a 1 standard error shock. What is crucial is the assumption about how other errors change in response to a shock to the error of one equation. Orthogonal impulse response functions impose identifying assumptions that make the structural errors uncorrelated. Therefore, there is no change in the other errors when one is shocked. Generalized impulse response functions allow for correlation between the errors.

5.6 Cointegration

We can write the first order VAR as a vector error correction model:

$$w_t - w_{t-1} = a_0 + (A_1 - I)w_{t-1} + u_t$$
$$\Delta w_t = a_0 + \Pi w_{t-1} + u_t$$

This is just another way to write the same reduced form.

As noted above, a variable is said to be integrated of order zero – $I(0)$ – if it is stationary and has means, variances and covariances that are constant through time. It is said to be integrated of order one – $I(1)$ – if it is stationary after being differenced once. There are tests for the null hypothesis that a variable is $I(1)$ against the alternative that it is $I(0)$. This hypothesis is called the hypothesis of a unit root. However, these tests are not powerful. In practice, it is difficult to determine whether a variable is $I(1)$ or $I(0)$. If the set of variables in w_t are each $I(1)$, but there are linear combinations of them that are $I(0)$, they are said to be cointegrated. If there are r linear combinations, such as:

$$z_t = \beta' w_t$$

that are $I(0)$, where β' is a $m \times r$ matrix, then the VECM can be written as follows:

$$\Delta w_t = a_0 + \alpha z_{t-1} + u_t$$
$$\Delta w_t = a_0 + \alpha \beta' w_{t-1} + u_t$$

Since w_t are $I(1)$, then Δw_t are $I(0)$, and the left sides of the above equations are $I(0)$. The right side is also $I(0)$, since z_t are also $I(0)$. The two sides balance. In terms of interpretation, the z_t are interpreted as deviations from equilibrium and the α are interpreted as adjustment coefficients, which measure how deviations from equilibrium feed back onto the variables to bring them back into equilibrium.

This structure of cointegration implies $\Pi = \alpha \beta'$.

Of course, we can estimate Π from the reduced form VECM. The number of cointegrating vectors has implications for the structure of Π. If $r = 0$, there are no cointegrating vectors, $\Pi = 0$ and a first difference model is appropriate without levels terms. For $0<r<m$, the rank of $\Pi = r$ is the number of cointegrating variables. If $r = m$, contrary to what we assumed, all the variables must be $I(0)$, and this is a standard levels VAR in stationary variables. There are statistical methods available to test for how many cointegrating vectors there are, that is, what value r takes, and conditional on r to estimate α and β. But a long-run identification problem arises here. For any non-singular $r \times r$ matrix Q, we can always write:

$$\Pi = \alpha\beta' = \alpha Q Q^{-1} \beta'$$

giving us new adjustment coefficients, αQ, and new cointegrating vectors $Q^{-1}\beta$. The matrix Q plays the same role at the matrix P in 5.3, on identification above. Thus, we need to specify the $r \times r$ matrix Q, which will embody any restrictions from economic theory, to obtain long-run identification. These restrictions will be of the same form as those in section 5.3. For example, where certain variables do not appear in certain equations, their coefficients take the value zero, or certain variables are the dependent variable and their coefficients take the value one. As before, the just-identifying restrictions are not testable. However, if we have over-identifying restrictions, these can be tested.

Since we want the models to have coherent long-run equilibrium properties consistent with arbitrage and solvency constraints, we will use the cointegrating VAR framework discussed above. In many cases, the economic interpretation of these constraints suggests ways of identifying these cointegrating vectors. Some object to this approach of using cointegrating VARs and argue that it is better to use unrestricted VARs, either in levels or first differences, or use prior theory to specify Bayesian VARs. They emphasize the difficulty of estimating the order of integration and the number of cointegrating vectors, as well as the adverse consequences of imposing possibly false restrictions based on pre-testing hypotheses. Like identification, this is a major source of controversy within the empirical analysis of monetary policy. Although we do not underestimate the difficult choices involved in cointegration analysis, we feel that the benefits of a coherent long-run model, if it can be obtained, outweigh these difficulties.

Chapter **6**

Estimating the Monetary Policy Effects on Inflation and Output: Closed Economy Unrestricted Vector Autoregression Modelling

Introduction

In chapters 6 to 8, we develop an econometric analysis of the monetary transmission mechanism in our sample of twelve Caribbean countries. A central choice in macro-econometric modelling is the number of variables considered. If the set of variables is too small, the equations are misspecified because they omit relevant variables. If the set of variables is too large, the estimates are likely to be very inefficient, with large variances, because there are not enough degrees of freedom. We try to deal with this issue by starting small and steadily enlarging the set of variables. We start with a simple univariate model in prices to describe the inflation process. We go on to an unrestricted VAR in the three central macroeconomic variables: prices, money and output. We use money rather than interest rates because in many of these countries interest rates are not the policy instrument and show almost no variation. We then extend the model to allow for long-run relationships using a cointegrating vector error correction model. At each stage, we use impulse response function to examine the impact of money supply and price shocks. There are two structural features of these economies that are of primary interest:

1. The dynamic process by which the economies responded to shocks, which will be analysed using impulse response functions
2. The nature of the long-run relations that characterize the economies, which will be analysed in terms of cointegrating relations

In this chapter, we begin with an examination of the time-series properties of the price variable using a univariate modelling procedure in prices (section 6.1). This enables us to examine features of a country's inflation in terms of the steady state rate of inflation, the persistence of inflation and the volatility of inflation. We consider whether there are any patterns across countries between these three features, the monetary policy approaches and institutional framework. In section 6.2, we consider the causal relationship between money, prices and output using a Granger non-causality procedure. This provides us with our first parametric procedure for considering monetary policy effects, albeit in a highly aggregated and simple estimation. In section 6.3, we use a closed economy unrestricted vector autoregression model and impulse response functions to examine the impact of money supply and price shocks on the economy. In general, the money shock showed some evidence of increasing real output over the medium term, which may be due to sticky price effects. Increases in prices tended to reduce real incomes in general (in eight of the twelve cases).

The next step will be to use an open economy model, but we leave this until the next chapter, where we develop an open economy cointegration modelling procedure. We will use these systems to examine if there are any differences in the structure of the economies that followed currency board and conservative monetary policies within a fixed exchange rate system, and those that allowed their exchange rates to adjust and follow a more discretionary and accommodating approach.

6.1 Inflation Dynamics

The dynamics of inflation play a central role in monetary policy. However, the time-series properties of inflation are controversial, therefore, we begin with those. The objective here is to see if this univariate analysis can identify differences in the time-series properties of price over the countries. We know that prices are determined by monetary, demand, supply and other factors. In this analysis, however, we limit ourselves to examine if our univariate econometric specification allows us to discern differences in time-series properties experiences of the country prices that may inform us about their comparative determination.

If p_t is the log of the price level, then, Δp_t is the rate of inflation, and we will have the following three possibilities:

1. The price level may be considered as trend stationary following a partial adjustment process:

$$\Delta p_t = \alpha + \lambda(\pi t - p_{t-1}) + \varepsilon_t \tag{6.1}$$

where ε_t is a white noise process, and the steady state rate of inflation is π. This is the ADF equation that would be used to test for a unit root in p_t, that is, $\lambda = 0$. If p_t is $I(1)$, the standard way of representing p_t as a unit root variable is to define it as a random walk with drift variable:

$$p_t = \alpha + p_{t-1} + \varepsilon_t \tag{6.2}$$

with ε_t as a white noise process and α, the drift is the steady state rate of inflation. Here, p_t is $I(1)$ and inflation Δp_t is $I(0)$.

However, assuming ε_t as white noise is likely to be too strong, and there may be persistence in the rate of inflation.

2. In the second case, then, we would have the process,

$$\Delta p_t = \mu + \rho \Delta p_{t-1} + \varepsilon_t \quad (6.3)$$

where ρ is the persistence of inflation, and the steady state rate of inflation is $\pi = \mu/(1-\rho)$.

3. The price level may be $I(2)$ and the rate of inflation $I(1)$ and changes in the rate of inflation is $I(0)$. This is the intuitive case where inflation is non-stationary but the rate of change in inflation (the acceleration) is stationary. To test for this, we would run the ADF equation for two unit roots:

$$\Delta^2 p_t = \nu + \beta \Delta p_{t-1} + \delta \Delta^2 p_{t-1} + \varepsilon_t \quad (6.4)$$

and test $\beta = 0$. If $\beta < 0$, the steady state rate of inflation is $-\nu/\beta$. If $\beta = 0$, there is no steady state rate of inflation.

Notice that since $\Delta^2 p_t = \Delta p_t - \Delta p_{t-1}$, we can write equation 6.4 as follows:

$$\Delta p_t = \nu + (\beta - 1)\Delta p_{t-1} + \delta \Delta^2 p_{t-1} + \varepsilon_t \quad (6.5)$$

which is of the same form as equation 6.3 with $\rho = \beta - 1$ and the addition of a lagged term in the second difference. To also nest equation 6.1, we can add the trend stationary term to get:

$$\Delta p_t = \nu + \lambda(\pi t - p_{t-1}) + (\beta - 1)\Delta p_{t-1} + \delta \Delta^2 p_{t-1} + \varepsilon_t \quad (6.6)$$

By putting various restrictions on equation 6.6, we can obtain, equation 6.2, the trend-stationary representation used to test for a unit root; equation 6.3 the inflation persistence equation; and equation 6.4, the equation used to test for two unit roots.

Equation 6.6 can also be written as follows:

$$\Delta p_t = a + b p_{t-1} + c \Delta p_{t-1} + d \Delta^2 p_{t-1} + et + \varepsilon_t \quad (6.7)$$

As noted above, this nests a number of interesting cases. If $b = 0$, there is a unit root in the price level. If $b = 0$ and $e = 0$, then c is a measure of the persistence of inflation, and the steady state inflation rate is $a/(1-c)$, which is likely to be close to the mean inflation, since the mean of $\Delta^2 p_{t-1}$, the average acceleration in inflation, is likely to be close to zero. The persistence of inflation is of some interest because it has often been argued that it is a function of monetary policy or exchange rate regime. For example, Alogoskoufis and Smith (1991) argue that inflation persistence will be lower under fixed exchange rates. There are a number of ways to define persistence, but we will treat it as the sum of the autoregressive coefficients.

Table 6.1 reports the average inflation rate in per cent per annum, calculated for a common period (1980Q2 to 2001Q4) for the following categories:

- cross country comparisons
- estimates of b, the coefficient on lagged prices
- the t statistic for b, the test for a unit root, which has the non standard Dickey-Fuller distribution
- the estimate of persistence, c
- the standard error of persistence
- the standard error of regression, which measures the volatility of inflation

The hypothesis of a unit root can be rejected only in the case of Grenada (GRE). Rejection of a unit root depends both on the size of b and its standard error. The estimates suggest that we should treat eleven of the twelve prices as having a unit root, which implies that the effect of any shock to the price level will persist indefinitely. In the single case (GRE) where rejection of the null implies the price is trend stationary, this implies that the effect of a shock will die away to zero. However, if we use these estimates more generally, the effects of shocks will die away to zero in all of the countries, though relatively slowly, since the estimates show high persistence for the majority of the countries ($c > 0.5$).

These results raise a modelling issue that will recur. The ADF tests suggest we should use different models for different countries, treating the variables as $I(0)$ in one case (GRE) and $I(1)$ in the rest. However, if we have different models for different countries, we lose comparability. Therefore, as a general strategy, where different specifications appear appropriate in different countries, we will estimate the alternative models for all countries. In this case, the alternatives are the trend-stationary model, which we estimated above, and the unit root model. With just one variable suggested to be $I(0)$ the case for the alternative specification is overwhelming.

The unit root restriction was imposed to give a second order autoregression in the inflation rate:

$$\Delta p_t = \alpha + \rho \Delta p_{t-1} + \gamma \Delta^2 p_{t-1} + \varepsilon_t \qquad (6.8)$$

This was estimated for all twelve countries. The results, shown in table 6.2, give the following results:

- the mean inflation calculated over the entire sample series for each country
- the persistence of inflation ρ and its standard error
- the estimate of the standard error of the regression (σ), which measures the average size of the inflation shocks
- the t statistic for $\rho = 1$ and the t statistic for $\rho = 0$
- the γ statistic, which was not significant in ten cases and is not reported, and was negative and significant in the two cases reported (BAR and TT)

Table 6.1 Unrestricted ADF Estimates from Equation 6.7

Countries	Average[a] Inflation 1980q2–2001q4 (%, per annum)	Unit Root Coefficient $b = (1-\rho)$	t: ADF $I(1)$[b] 5% critical value = –3.44	Measure of Persistence c	Standard Error of c	Standard Error of Regression (%)
ECCB						
AB	4.5	–0.01	–1.27	0.662	0.09	0.5
DOM	3.4	–0.05	–2.14	–0.018	–0.13	1.1
GRE	3.9	–0.10	–4.11	0.248	2.59	0.8
SKN	3.4	–0.06	–2.99	0.703	9.77	0.4
SLU	3.7	–0.15	–3.16	0.237	1.83	1.4
SVG	3.4	–0.08	–2.80	0.098	0.70	1.2
Non-ECCB						
BAH	3.9	–0.002	–0.35	0.553	6.02	0.7
BAR	4.1	–0.005	–0.80	0.442	4.55	1.8
GUY	20.0	–0.01	–1.47	0.631	7.39	6.3
BEL	2.1	–0.07	–2.81	0.677	6.98	1.1
JAM	17.5	–0.02	–2.63	0.699	11.91	2.4
TT	7.8	0.0002	0.03	0.600	7.30	1.3

Source: IMF 2006, 2007; World Bank 2006, 2007.
[a] To facilitate cross country comparisons, we used the common period (1980Q2–2001Q4) to calculate these average annual inflation rates. The estimates reported in the other columns, however, use the full available dataset for each country.
[b] The ADF 5%. The critical value used was –3.44 based on MacKinnon (1991) one-sided p-values, as referenced in the EViews 5 Users Manual.

Table 6.2 Restricted ADF Estimates from Equation 6.8

Countries	Period	Average[a] Inflation (%, per annum)	Measure of persistence ρ	Standard Error of ρ	Standard Error of Regression (%)	ADF t $\rho = 1$ Statistics	Standard t $\rho = 0$ Statistics
ECCB							
AB	1980–2003	4.1	0.845	0.06	0.5	–2.58	13.6
DOM	1980–2003	3.3	0.190	0.13	1.2	–6.92	1.5
GRE	1980–2002	3.8	0.550	0.07	0.8	–6.43	7.5
SKN	1980–2002	3.3	0.694	0.07	0.5	–4.37	9.5
SLU	1980–2003	3.4	0.259	0.13	1.4	–5.70	2.0
SVG	1980–2003	3.2	0.290	0.13	1.3	–5.46	2.2
Non-ECCB							
BAH	1971–2001	4.9	0.717	0.07	0.7	–4.04	9.9
BAR	1968–2002	6.8	0.593	0.08	1.9	–5.09	7.0
GUY	1972–2003	16.5	0.616	0.08	6.3	–4.80	7.3
BEL	1979–2003	2.3	0.614	0.09	1.1	–4.29	6.6
JAM	1965–2002	15.2	0.713	0.06	2.4	–4.78	12.1
TT	1965–2003	8.1	0.627	0.08	1.3	–4.66	8.1

[a] The average inflation rates reported are calculated for the entire period available for each country.

Imposing the unit root did not change the acceleration effect. It was there in the previous estimates, insignificant in all cases except TT, when it was negative and significant, indicating a significant deceleration in prices.

The ADF t statistics in table 6.2 indicate that inflation in eleven of the twelve countries may be treated as stationary. That is, Δp_t is $I(0)$. The single exception is Antigua and Barbuda (AB), where the unit root null could not be rejected with a t test statistic of –2.58. Note, however, that the unit root null was not rejected in eleven of the twelve cases reported in table 6.1. The exception is Grenada, which reported ADF t statistics of –4.11. The evidence overall, therefore, indicates that, for the majority of countries (10 of 12), the inflation rate may be regarded as stationary. This also excludes the Grenada case, which was $I(0)$ in p_t.

The average mean inflation rates are relatively low (below 5 per cent per annum) in all of the ECCB countries and in the Bahamas and Belize. These make up two-thirds of the sample countries. The remaining third (BAR, GUY, JAM and TT), had relatively high inflation, with two countries (GUY and JAM) showing particularly high average inflation rates.

Persistence is measured by the proportion of the previous years' inflation carried over into the current year – the first order autocorrelation coefficient ρ. There is evidence from table 6.2 that it is high (greater than 0.5) and significant in nine of the twelve countries. It is not significant in DOM, SLU and SVG, three of the common currency area countries. The volatility of inflation, measured by the standard error of the regression σ, is high (above 2 per cent) in GUY and JAM, with GUY being very high.

Figure 6.1 shows the relationship between mean inflation and persistence. It should be noted that persistence is not an undesirable property in itself. Low inflation, associated with high persistence, measured by the autocorrelation coefficient is not necessarily an indication of poor monetary policies. We can see from figure 6.1 that among two-thirds of the sample counties that show low mean inflation, there is both low and high persistence.

High inflation accompanied by high persistence is a clear indication of a monetary policy problem. There is some evidence of this, to varying degree in the cases of GUY, JAM, TT and BAR, over the long run. Over a shorter period, 1980–2001, the evidence of this problem for BAR was less, but it remained the case for the other three countries (see the second column of table 6.1).

The variation of inflation measured by the standard error of the regression σ, is a measure of the average size to the inflation shocks to the economy. Figure 6.2 shows a positive relationship between the mean inflation and the variation in inflation rates. The eight countries with low mean inflation are grouped together toward the origin of the axes, whereas the high and varying experiences of BAR, TT, JAM and GUY show considerably higher inflation variation, especially in the case of the latter two. The positive trend line can be observed to be a good fit even in the presence of the two outliers.

From these estimates, we are able to show that the inflation experiences of the ECCB countries with low mean inflation, low persistence and low variation (BEL, BAR and BAH) stand in contrast to that of GUY and JAM, with TT falling somewhere between and AB, which is considered an anomaly. This can, in important part, be attributable to the institutional framework within which the monetary policies are developed.

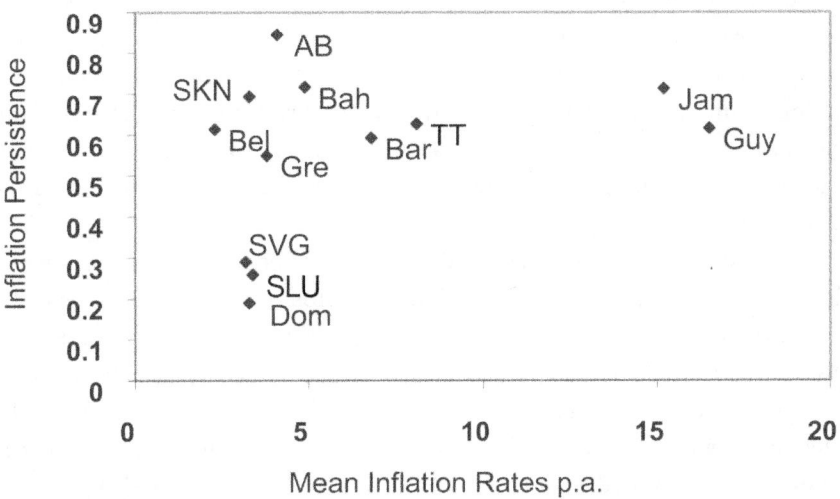

Figure 6.1   Mean inflation and inflation persistence

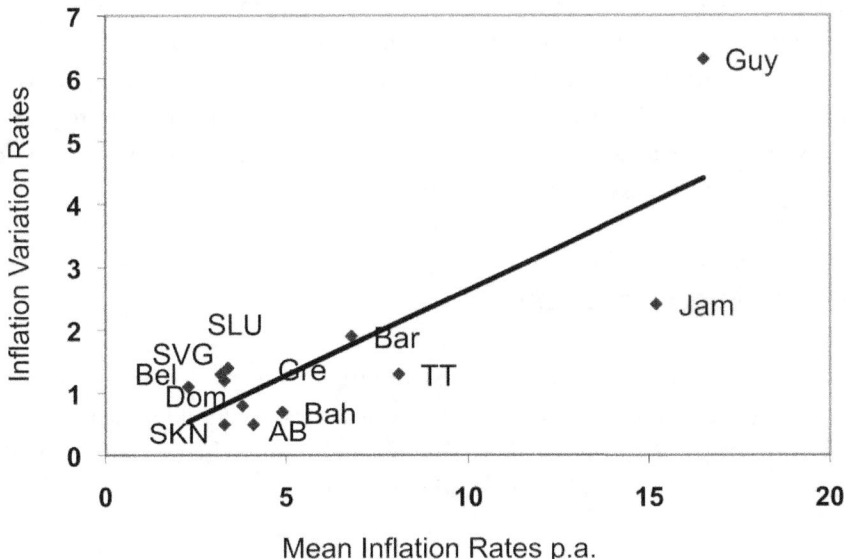

Figure 6.2   Mean inflation and inflation variation

The currency union countries of the ECCB with a currency board framework for monetary policy consistently produced low inflation relative to the other countries, because such a framework is hardwired to constrain monetary expansion in the face of external imbalances and government deficit financing. Inflation persistence was high across the countries, but with the currency union countries showing low inflation rates and low variation in the rate of inflation, this does not necessarily indicate a monetary policy problem. Low inflation, low variation and high persistence could be consistent with acceptable monetary policy performance. This appears to be the case with these countries.

Barbados and Belize followed conservative discretionary policy rules and the Bahamas has distinct elements of a currency board. These countries produce performances generally in line with those of the ECCB countries. Overall, in this group of nine countries, the institutional frameworks did not allow fiscal dominance, either institutionally or through the discretionary approach adopted. This resulted in consistently low rate of growth in the money supply that, in turn, resulted in a low rate of inflation. In contrast, Guyana and Jamaica followed discretionary monetary policies that resulted in high mean rates, high persistence and high variations in inflation. This was also largely true of Trinidad and Tobago. In this case, however, the monetary policy performance was less problematic due, no doubt, to its oil and gas resource endowments. Fiscal dominance was a feature of this group of three to a greater or lesser extent. This was reflected in the group's relatively high growth of money supply over long periods, which led to high inflation and low rate of growth in real output.

Our use of a standard autoregression equation for inflation, to see whether the estimates allow us to discern differences in policy performance between the countries, has enabled us to discern differences between the countries' inflation performances, which may be attributed to policy responses conditioned by institutional structure. In general, the results provided evidence in support of the argument of a relationship between the monetary policy framework and the inflation performance of these Caribbean countries.

6.2 Vector Autoregression

The univariate representation will reflect feedbacks through other variables. To investigate these feedbacks, we will use vector autoregressions. To see how these feedbacks influence the univariate inflation persistence process, suppose that the feedbacks come through money growth and are described by a first order VAR in inflation and money growth:

$$\Delta p_t = a_{10} + a_{11}\Delta p_{t-1} + a_{12}\Delta m_{t-1} + u_{1t}$$
$$\Delta m_t = a_{20} + a_{21}\Delta p_{t-1} + a_{22}\Delta m_{t-1} + u_{2t}$$

Solving for Δm_{t-1} in terms of lagged values of Δp_t and the errors gives an ARMA (2,1) representation for inflation:

$$\Delta p_t = [a_{10}(1-a_{22}) + a_{12}a_{20}] + (a_{11}+a_{22})\Delta p_{t-1} + (a_{12}a_{21} - a_{11}a_{22})\Delta p_{t-2} + u_{1t} - a_{22}u_{1,t-1} + a_{12}u_{2,t-1}$$

with the persistence of inflation being as follows:

$$\rho = (a_{11} + a_{22}) + (a_{12}a_{21} - a_{11}a_{22})$$

reflecting both the direct and indirect feedbacks.

When developing systems of this sort, a large number of choices need to be made, including the following:

- choice of endogenous variables
- the treatment of exogenous variables, if any
- choice of lag length
- short-run identification
- calculation of the impulse response functions

6.3 Money, Income and Prices

The choice of the set of variables is the crucial issue. We will experiment with various combinations. We consider a set of domestic variables (money, spot exchange rate, prices, interest rate and output) and a set of foreign variables (output, interest rates, prices and the price of oil: $m_t, s_t, p_t, R_t, y_t, y_t^*, R_t^*, p_t^*$ and p_t^o). With the exception of R and R_t^*, all the variables used are in natural logarithms, indicated by lower case letters. There is a trade-off between having a common specification versus getting the right specification for each country. Between the two choices is having one specification for fixed and one for flexible exchange rate countries. Since we want to compare transmission mechanisms between the two groups, it is worth starting with a common specification. The major problem is that for nine of the countries, the exchange rate does not vary and the interest rate does not show much variation. In most theoretical models, these variables play a major role in the adjustment process. Clearly, however, this is not the case for the majority of our sample. Therefore, we will begin with a small standard monetary model in 3 variables (y_t, p_t, m_t) and a trend. The VARs in these three variables have been estimated for many countries. This system is consistent with an IS or aggregate demand curve determining output; a Phillips curve determining inflation in terms of deviation of output from its trend; and a money demand curve, with inflation being taken as a measure of the opportunity cost of holding money. However, in the unrestricted VAR, such theoretical structure is not imposed, and it is not clear that one would expect a traditional Phillips curve type relationship in these small developing country economies. In this case, the VAR takes the following form:

$$y_t = a_{10} + b_1 t + \sum_{i=1}^{p} a_{11i} y_{t-i} + \sum_{i=1}^{p} a_{12i} p_{t-i} + \sum_{i=1}^{p} a_{13i} m_{t-i} + u_{1t}$$

$$p_t = a_{20} + b_2 t + \sum_{i=1}^{p} a_{21i} y_{t-i} + \sum_{i=1}^{p} a_{22i} p_{t-i} + \sum_{i=1}^{p} a_{23i} m_{t-i} + u_{2t}$$

$$m_t = a_{30} + b_3 t + \sum_{i=1}^{p} a_{31i} y_{t-i} + \sum_{i=1}^{p} a_{32i} p_{t-i} + \sum_{i=1}^{p} a_{33i} m_{t-i} + u_{3t} \qquad (6.9)$$

where trends are included. The first stage is to take the unrestricted VAR, with a maximum lag of four, and use the AIC to determine lag length. This suggests p = 2, which we use below. We can also investigate whether a particular variable is Granger non-causal for the other variables. Granger causality measures whether one variable helps to predict another, and need not be related to the usual interpretation of economic causality. If prices were Granger non-causal with respect to output, then all $a_{12i} = 0$, because past values of inflation do not help explain current values of output. We test whether each variable is Granger non-causal with respect to the other two variables. Therefore, the test for prices being Granger non-causal with respect to output and money tests both $a_{12i} = 0$ and $a_{32i} = 0$. With two lags, this is four restrictions. Table 6.3 gives the p values of the tests for Granger non-causality for each variable. A p value below 0.05 indicates that the column variable is a significant predictor of the other two variables at the 5 per cent level. The reported probability statistic is for testing the null hypothesis that the coefficients of the lagged values of a variable (for example, y_t) in the block of equations explaining the variables p_t and m_t are zero. In this case, a p value of 0.012 would mean the non-causality null would be rejected at the 5 per cent significant level. Therefore, for AB, income is a significant predictor of prices and output. However, price is not a significant predictor for money and output, nor is money a significant predictor of output and prices.

Output is significantly Granger causal for the other two variables in all cases but DOM, SVG, BEL and JAM. In the case where the variables are $I(1)$, the distributions of the test statistics are non-standard, so the tests can only be indicative. The true critical values will be different from the usual asymptotic values. Also, the interpretation of the Granger causality of output is complicated by the fact that output is an interpolated variable. The other two variables are only marginally less important for prediction. In table 6.3, output is Granger causal in eight cases, whereas price and money are each Granger causal in seven cases. Overall, therefore, in almost two-thirds (22 out of 36) of the cases, the variables are Granger causal and subject to the conditions noted. They show evidence of being significant predictors of the other variables in the small estimated system in equation 6.9. There is no obvious pattern to the Granger non-causality tests, so we are unable to interpret these results as indicating the dominance of one or the other of these variables as a deterministic factor.

For many purposes (for example, forecasting), the VAR is all we need. However, for other purposes, we need a structural model as discussed in chapter 5. In our three equation system, we need nine restrictions to identify B_0. This is the short-run identification problem. There are three pieces of information in the fact that the diagonal elements of B_0 are all one. A common identifying assumption (implicit in the Choleski decomposition used to construct the orthogonal impulse response functions below) is that the variables are ordered in such a way that B_0 is lower triangular. In addition, Ω, the covariance matrix of the structural errors, is diagonal. The structural errors are orthogonal, there are no correlations between them. The ordering we assume is based on how fast the variables are able to adjust. We assume that output is the slowest and cannot adjust to current prices and money; that prices adjust faster and can respond to current output, but not to current money shocks; and that current money holdings can adjust the fastest and respond immediately to current output and prices. With these assumptions, and the ordering, y_t, p_t, m_t, the system then becomes:

Table 6.3 Unrestricted Second Order VAR (y_t, p_t, m_t): Granger Non-Causality p Values

Countries	AIC Lag	y	p	m
ECCB				
AB	2	*0.012*[a]	0.066[b]	0.488
DOM	2	0.130	0.370	*0.001*
GRE	2	*0.037*	0.189	0.658
SKN	2	*0.000*	*0.020*	0.116
SLU	2	*0.025*	*0.009*	*0.001*
SVG	2	0.064	0.371	0.118
Non-ECCB				
BAH	2	*0.000*	*0.016*	*0.006*
BAR	2	*0.000*	*0.004*	*0.007*
GUY	2	*0.000*	*0.000*	0.546
BEL	3	0.265	*0.020*	*0.007*
JAM	2	0.185	*0.000*	*0.016*
TT	3	*0.013*	0.058	*0.010*

[a] Figures in ***bold italics*** are significantly Granger causal at 5 per cent.
[b] Figures in regular text do not reject the Granger non-causal null hypothesis.

$$y_t = b_{10} + \sum_{i=1}^{2} b_{11i} y_{t-i} + \sum_{i=1}^{2} b_{12i} p_{t-i} + \sum_{i=1}^{2} b_{13i} m_{t-i} + v_{1t}$$

$$p_t = b_{20} + b_{21,0} y_t + \sum_{i=1}^{2} b_{21i} y_{t-i} + \sum_{i=1}^{2} b_{22i} p_{t-i} + \sum_{i=1}^{2} b_{23i} m_{t-i} + v_{2t}$$

$$m_t = b_{30} + b_{31,0} y_t + b_{32,0} p_t + \sum_{i=1}^{2} b_{31i} y_{t-i} + \sum_{i=1}^{2} a_{31i} p_{t-i} + \sum_{i=1}^{2} a_{33i} m_{t-i} + v_{3t}$$

In this case, the B_0 matrix is:

$$\begin{bmatrix} 1 & 0 & 0 \\ -b_{21,0} & 1 & 0 \\ -b_{31,0} & -b_{32,0} & 1 \end{bmatrix}$$

which imposes six restrictions, three normalization and three zeros. In addition, we have the three zero covariance restrictions that $\omega_{12} = \omega_{13} = \omega_{23} = 0$. This makes nine in total, as required. With these just-identifying restrictions, which cannot be tested, we can calculate the effects of shocks to the system. This uses the structural moving average representation, obtained by solving for lagged values of the endogenous variables in terms of the errors that determine them:

$$w_t = B_0^{-1} \varepsilon_t + B_0^{-1} B_1 B_0^{-1} \varepsilon_{t-1} + \ldots$$

Since the structural errors, ε_t, are by construction uncorrelated under the just-identifying assumptions, the effect of a shock to one of the errors is well defined. If they were correlated, when one error changed, the others would also change. With this ordering, which is common in the literature, the money shock, ε_{3t}, is a pure monetary shock, often treated as a money supply surprise. The effects of contemporaneous output and inflation have already been allowed for in the system. However, these estimates are only as reliable as the just-identifying assumptions that are made. The 1 standard error impact of money, and the long-run impact from the impulse response function, is given in table 6.4, which will be discussed after we have considered an alternative approach.

An alternative approach is to use generalized impulse response functions (GIRFs). As discussed in chapter 5, GIRFs use the information from the VAR, although they could also be used for a structural model when the model is identified and Ω is not diagonal. Supposing there is a 1 standard error shock to one variable, we will examine the effect of a shock to inflation. The GIRF uses the estimate of Σ to work out by how much each of the other errors will change. Thus, we get the effect of a typical shock to the system, associated with a 1 standard error shock to the focus variable. Supposing the elements of Σ are denoted σ_{ij}, then a 1 standard error shock to inflation will be $\delta_2 = \sqrt{\sigma_{22}}$. The shock to the output equation will be given by $\delta_1 = (\sigma_{12}/\sigma_{22})\delta_2$, where $(\sigma_{12}/\sigma_{22})$ is the coefficient obtained by regressing u_{1t} on u_{2t}. The shock to the money equation would be calculated similarly. The dynamic effects of these shocks are then calculated from the moving average representation of the VAR. The GIRF for a 1 standard error shock to inflation is given in table 6.5. In this unrestricted VAR case, the shocks occur once and are shocks by construction.

This ordering of the variables is consistent with the standard view. For example, output may respond with a lag to a monetary shock (due to sticky prices). When prices adjust fully in the long run (flexible prices), output will return to its initial position. To examine this aspect, we report the initial impact and the response after 4 quarters and after 50 quarters for the orthogonalized impulse responses. Overall, if the above argument holds, we expect the output responses from a positive money shock to be positive in the fourth quarter and to be zero in the fiftieth. Prices should show a low level of response in the fourth quarter, but should be fully adjusted by the fiftieth.

Table 6.4 indicates that a 1 standard error shock to money in AB raises it by 3.5 per cent. In the fourth quarter, income is unaffected; prices are also virtually unaffected with a 0.1 per cent increase; and money grows by 1.1 per cent. In the 50th quarter, output and prices move by –0.1 per cent and money by –0.2 per cent. Figure 6.3 shows the impulse response graphs for the orthogonalized and the generalized impulse responses. The graphs indicate that nine of the twelve countries showed no notable positive income response from the money shock. The exceptions are SLU, BEL and JAM. In figure 6.3, the cumulative effects are the areas under the curves.

To obtain an assessment of the overall effect of each money and price shock, we calculated the cumulative effect over eight quarters (the medium term) for each country along with its overall average. These are reported in tables 6.6 and 6.7, respectively.

Table 6.4 Unrestricted VAR: Orthogonalized Impulse Response Functions

	1SE Shock to Money (%)								
	On Impact			After 4 Quarters			After 50 Quarters		
	Y	p	m	Y	p	M	Y	p	m
ECCB									
AB	0.0	0.0	3.5	0.0	0.1	1.1	−0.1	−0.1	−0.2
DOM	0.0	0.0	4.6	0.2	0.5	2.5	0.3	0.2	0.5
GRE	0.0	0.0	3.4	0.2	0.0	1.7	0.0	0.0	0.0
SKN	0.0	0.0	6.1	0.2	−0.1	1.5	0.0	0.0	0.0
SLU	0.0	0.0	2.5	1.1	0.0	2.3	0.4	0.1	0.4
SVG	0.0	0.0	5.6	−0.6	0.3	1.6	−0.1	−0.1	−0.1
Non-ECCB									
BAH	0.0	0.0	2.9	0.4	−0.5	0.8	−0.4	−0.5	0.0
BAR	0.0	0.0	3.1	0.4	−0.6	1.4	0.0	−0.4	−0.2
GUY	0.0	0.0	4.0	−0.1	0.0	1.8	0.2	−0.5	−0.3
BEL	0.0	0.0	2.9	0.8	0.7	0.9	−0.1	0.0	0.0
JAM	0.0	0.0	3.4	0.6	0.6	3.0	0.3	0.7	0.9
TT	0.0	0.0	3.2	0.0	0.7	3.3	−2.0	1.6	−0.9

Table 6.5 Unrestricted VAR: Generalized Impulse Response Functions

	1SE Shock to Prices (%)								
	On Impact			After 4 Quarters			After 50 Quarters		
	Y	p	m	y	p	M	Y	p	m
ECCB									
AB	−0.1	0.5	0.3	0.2	0.9	0.2	0.2	0.4	0.4
DOM	0.0	1.0	−0.1	0.2	0.4	0.7	0.2	0.1	0.3
GRE	0.0	0.8	−0.5	0.2	0.6	−0.4	0.0	0.0	0.0
SKN	0.0	0.5	0.0	−0.7	0.9	0.4	0.0	0.0	0.0
SLU	−0.2	1.3	−0.1	−0.6	0.3	−1.1	−0.3	−0.1	−0.3
SVG	−0.1	1.2	−0.4	−0.4	0.7	−1.0	0.0	0.0	0.0
Non–ECCB									
BAH	−0.3	0.6	−0.4	−1.7	0.9	−0.5	0.4	0.5	0.0
BAR	0.0	1.8	0.1	−0.2	2.6	0.3	0.1	1.7	0.9
GUY	0.2	6.0	0.1	0.4	8.9	2.3	−0.2	−5.0	−3.6
BEL	0.2	1.1	0.4	0.2	1.8	1.2	−0.1	0.0	0.0
JAM	0.0	2.4	0.0	0.2	6.2	3.2	0.2	0.5	0.8
TT	−0.1	1.2	0.2	0.0	1.8	0.9	−1.1	−0.1	−2.2

AB
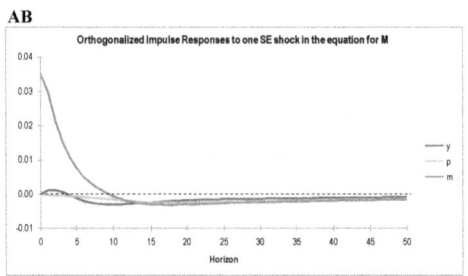

AB
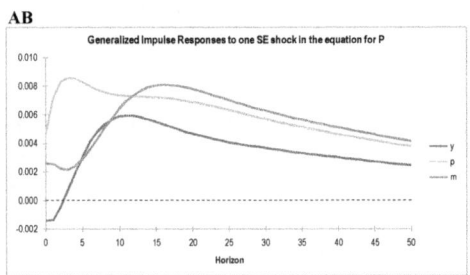

DOM
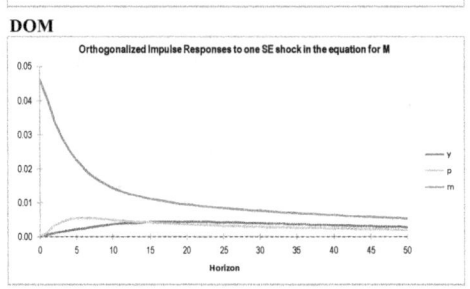

DOM
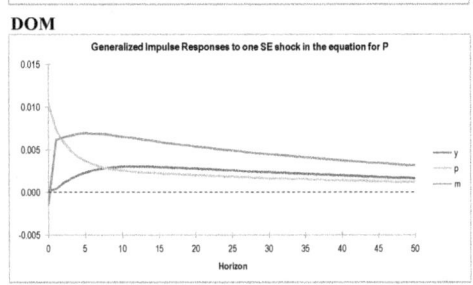

GRE
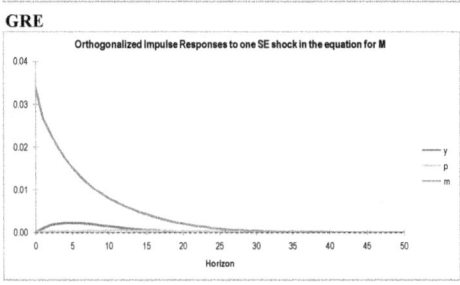

GRE
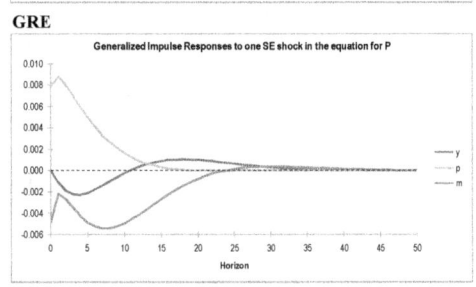

SKN
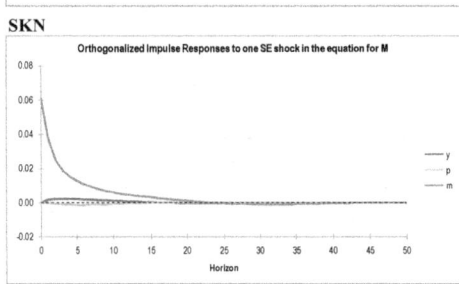

SKN
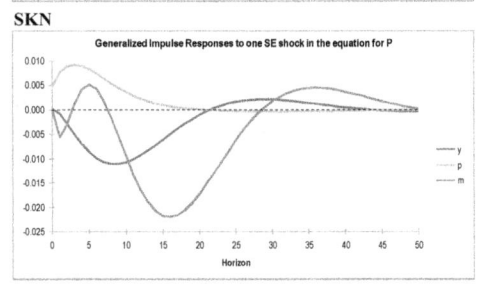

SLU
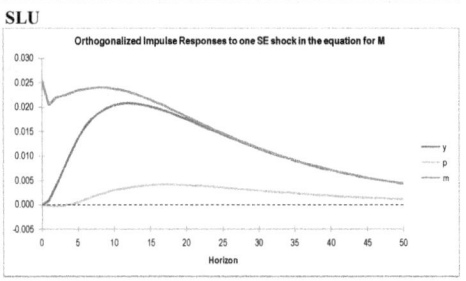

SLU
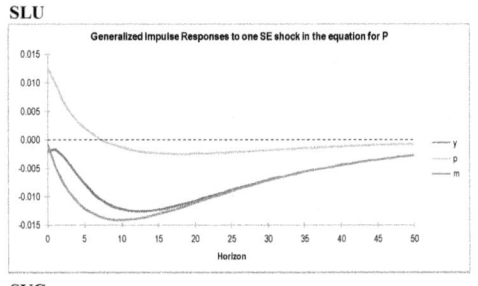

SVG
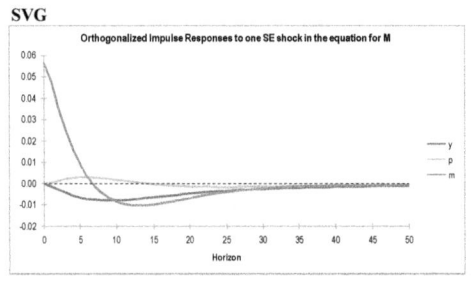

SVG
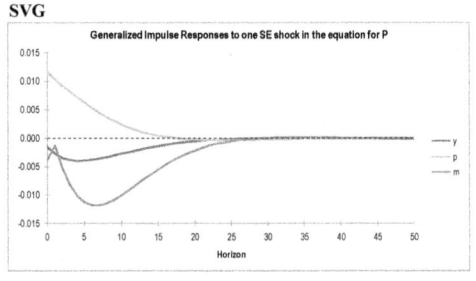

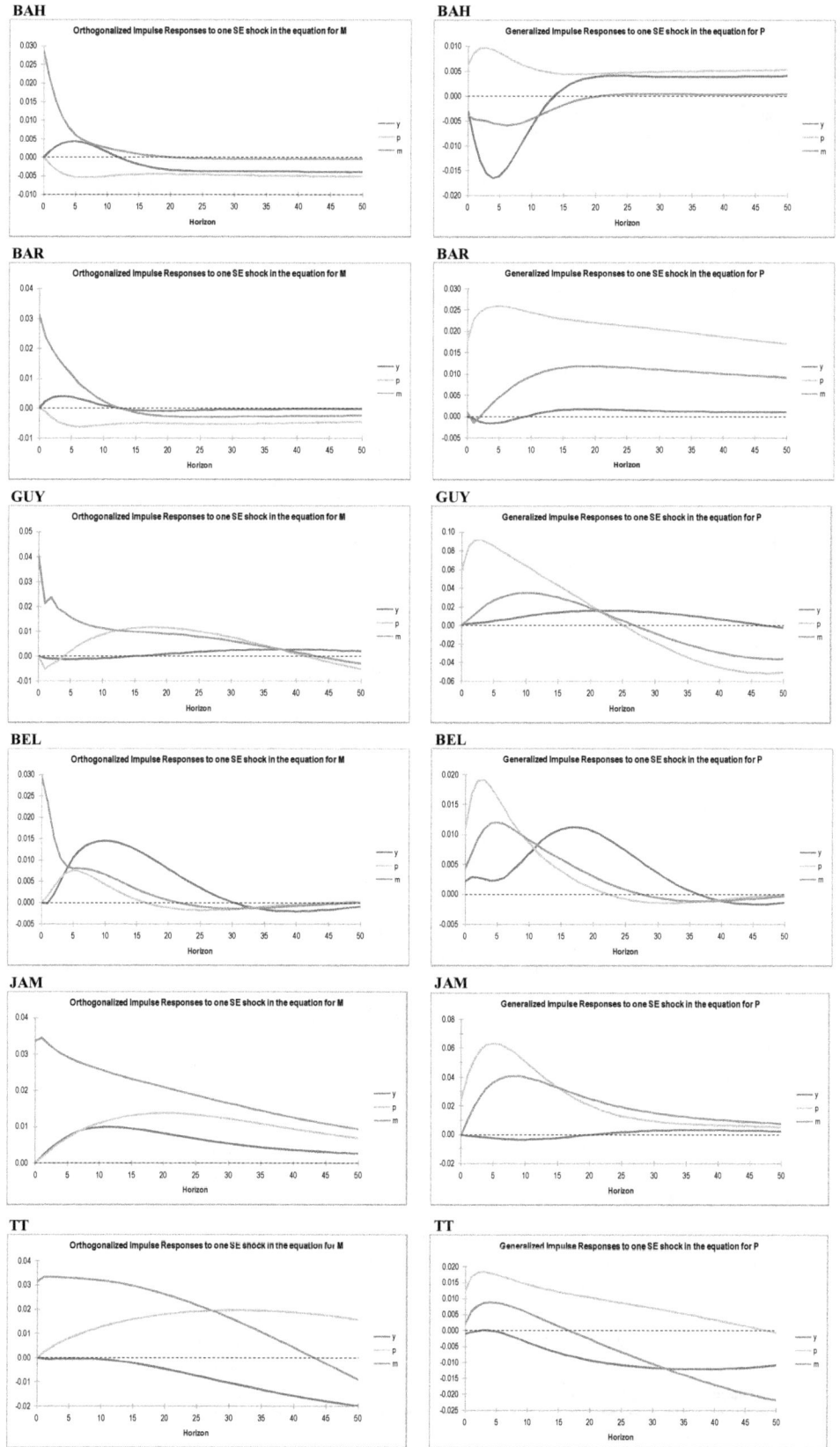

Figure 6.3 Impact effect of a one standard error money and price shock: unrestricted VAR

Table 6.6 Cumulative Orthogonalized Impulse Response

| | 1SE Shock to Money (%) | | |
| | Cumulative Impact After 8 Quarters | | |
	Y	P	m
ECCB	(Impact Quarter Index = 100)		
AB	99.3	99.4	113.7
DOM	101.6	103.6	128.2
GRE	101.7	100.3	119.6
SKN	101.5	99.2	121.4
SLU	109.2	100.5	122.8
SVG	95.7	101.9	119.9
Non-ECCB			
BAH	102.8	96.5	110.7
BAR	102.6	96.2	114.5
GUY	99.1	100.7	119.2
BEL	106.6	104.7	112.5
JAM	105.1	104.9	131.1
TT	99.6	105.9	133.8
Average	**102.1**	**101.2**	**120.6**

Table 6.7 Cumulative Generalized Impulse Response

| | 1SE Shock to Prices (%) | | |
| | Cumulative Impact After 8 Quarters | | |
	Y	P	m
ECCB	(Impact Quarter Index = 100)		
AB	101.7	107.1	102.8
DOM	101.6	104.7	105.4
GRE	98.6	105.4	96.2
SKN	94.5	106.9	100.7
SLU	94.6	104.1	91.8
SVG	97.0	106.8	92.7
Non-ECCB			
BAH	89.4	107.7	95.4
BAR	99.1	124.1	103.0
GUY	104.0	201.8	119.8
BEL	102.6	114.7	109.2
JAM	98.3	159.7	127.0
TT	99.4	116.0	106.7
Average	98.4	121.6	104.2

Table 6.6 shows that an orthogonalized response from a 1 standard error money supply increase will, on average, increase output by 2.1 per cent cumulatively over eight quarters. This average will obscure the fact that some negative output growth responses are recorded, as the fourth quarter responses in table 6.4 shows in two cases. Overall, nine of the twelve cases show no significant increase in y over the eight quarters. The exceptions are SLU, BEL and JAM, where y grew by more than 5 per cent over eight quarters (see table 6.6).

The 1 standard error increase in money shock averaged a 3.8 per cent increase in the money supply across the twelve economies and led to a 1.2 per cent increase in prices. The money supply impact on prices is averaged. Therefore, it is less than proportional at 1.2 per cent increase over eight quarters. The relatively small price response may be seen as consistent with the sticky price effect, which is a standard explanation of monetary induced real-side effect in the macroeconomics literature. From a Quantity of Money Theory perspective ($MV = Py$), this could also imply that the income velocity of money circulation is not constant. The sticky prices imply that velocity and real output adjust. This is interesting since there is evidence of a 2.1 per cent growth in output across the countries, on average, where eight of the twelve showed an increase simultaneous with the less than proportionate increase in prices from the money supply shock. We have to be cautious in drawing out implications. Nevertheless, the results offer some basis for theoretical interpretations.

Table 6.5 reports the generalized impulse responses from a price shock. It indicates that for AB, a 1 standard error shock to prices raises them by 0.5 per cent. In the same period, this lowers output by 0.1 per cent and increases the money supply by 0.3 per cent. In the fiftieth quarter, the impact of this composite shock is to make output 0.2 per cent higher and prices and output 0.4 per cent higher. It also indicates that the short-run correlation between an inflation shock and output shock is negative or zero in all the cases, except for GUY and BEL, where they are positive at 0.2 in each case. The short-run correlation between an inflation shock and money is positive or zero in six cases (AB, SKN, BAR, GUY, BEL and TT) and negative in the other six cases. The negative association is one that standard economic theory would not suggest.

Table 6.7 reports that on average across all the countries the cumulative impact of a 1 standard error increase in prices (prices increase by 1.5 per cent on average) will decrease output to 98.4 per cent of its former value (a 1.6 per cent fall) over eight quarters. Eight of the twelve cases show a cumulative decline in output over eight quarters. Table 6.5 reported that after four quarters, six of the twelve output responses are negative or zero. On the whole, therefore, the results suggest an overall output decline in response to a general price increase, which accords with economic theory.

6.4 Conclusions

In this chapter, we introduced the econometric analyses by first considering the time-series properties of the inflation. This comparative univariate analysis showed that high inflation was associated across countries with monetary frameworks that facilitated excessive money growth. This is consistent with standard monetary theory, which suggests that changes in money supply may determine price inflation, which in turn may influence the growth in real output, through sticky price effects in the short-run incomes, although money may be neutral in the long run. These findings are consistent with evidence produced in chapter 2 that showed low inflation associated with both high and low real income growth, but high inflation only associated with low growth. Overall, the use of a standard autoregression equation for inflation, to examine differences in policy performance between the countries, enabled us to discern differences between the countries' inflation performances, which may be attributed to policy responses conditioned by institutional structure. In general, therefore, the univariate results provided evidence in support of the argument of a relationship between the monetary policy framework and the inflation performance of these Caribbean countries.

The Granger block non-causality null hypothesis tests did not provide evidence of the endogeneity of output and prices relative to the other two variables. Evidence of causality was spread fairly evenly across the output, prices and money. Therefore, all of the variables appear to influence the others to a similar extent.

The y_t, p_t, m_t unrestricted VAR closed economy specification allowed us to examine the behaviour of these variables for the twelve Caribbean economies. This small system allows us to investigate the extent to which this specification can provide evidence of a monetary transmission mechanism between a monetary policy shock and real output effects. From the estimates of the responses reported in tables 6.4 to 6.7 and figures 6.3, there is little evidence that a monetary shock will lead to a notable increase in real income across the twelve economies – only SLU, BEL and JAM showed evidence of this from the orthogonalized impulse responses. Interestingly, there was also little evidence of a proportional increase in price from a money shock. The relatively small price response may be seen as consistent with the sticky price effect arising from an Expectation Augmented Phillips Curve Analysis explanation. From a Quantity Theory of Money perspective $(MV = PY)$, this could also imply that the income velocity of money circulation is not constant. We have estimated a small closed system and have to be cautious in drawing out implications. Nevertheless, it is interesting, especially since there is evidence of an increase in income across the countries on average (2.1 per cent growth in output), where eight of the twelve countries showed some increase (see table 6.6). At the same time, there is a less than proportionate increase in prices from a money supply shock.

A comparative analysis of the ADF and the VAR results of a price shock indicates the following: The ADF tests suggests that a price shock will die out (prices are mean reverting) only in the single case of GRE, where $p \sim I(0)$. Inflation in eleven of the twelve countries may be treated as stationary: Δp_t is $I(0)$. The VAR results suggest that after fifty quarters, the long-run impact of a price shock is zero for GRE, SKN and SVG. Therefore, the VAR list of where the shocks die out does not match the ADF tests, which suggested that they should die out in only GRE. We still have the issue of whether to treat the variables as $I(1)$, shocks persist; or $I(0)$, shocks die out. The results of the VAR would indicate that in three cases, prices should be treated as stationary, that is, $p \sim I(0)$. However, the rather large change in prices over eight quarters, reported in table 6.7, suggests an overall non-mean reverting property of prices.

In general, the money shock showed some evidence of increasing real output over the medium term, which may be due to lagging price expectations and increases in prices, tended to reduce real incomes across the board (in eight of the twelve cases). The money shock increased output by 2.1 per cent on average across the twelve countries and the price shock decreased output to 98.4 per cent of its initial value. However, table 6.6 and 6.7 show that, for the two countries with a history of high inflation (GUY and JAM), the output responses were different. After eight quarters, the money shock decreased GUY's output to 99.1 per cent of its initial level, but increased output in JAM by 5.5 per cent. The price shock decreased the JAM output to 98.3 per cent of its initial value, but increased the output in GUY by 4.0 per cent.

The VAR estimates showed little evidence of the money shock having an impact on prices. Prices increased by only 1.2 per cent over the eight quarters. As mentioned earlier, in terms of standard theory, this could indicate that, in the presence of virtually no income effect, the velocity of circulation of money is not constant, or that velocity and real output between them adjust. Similarly, the price shock had little effect on the money supply over eight quarters. Money increased by 4.2 per cent.

Chapter 7

The Monetary Transmission Mechanism: Vector Error Correction Modelling and Cointegration

Introduction

In chapter 6, we treated the variables as $I(1)$, that is, we assumed that shocks are persistent and estimated an unrestricted VAR. In this chapter, we examine the extent to which the variables in the VAR cointegrate to give a long-run money demand relationship. In addition to the choices for the unrestricted VAR, the number of variables and lag lengths, when estimating cointegrating VARs, we must also make choices about the following:

- the treatment of intercepts and trends
- the number of cointegrating vectors
- just-identifying long-run restrictions
- over-identifying long-run restrictions
- interpretation of the cointegrating vectors (for example, whether they have the right signs); and
- interpretation of the feedbacks (long-run forcing)

The Johansen procedure allows us to make these choices within a consistent framework.

7.1 Cointegration Modelling

As discussed in chapter 5, to conduct the cointegration analysis, we can write a second order VAR as a vector error correction model:

$$w_t = a_0 + A_1 w_{t-1} + A_2 w_{t-2} + u_t$$
$$w_t - w_{t-1} = a_0 + (A_1 + A_2 - I)w_{t-1} - A_2 \Delta w_{t-1} + u_t$$
$$\Delta w_t = \mu + \Pi w_{t-1} + \Gamma_1 \Delta w_{t-1} + u_t$$

If there are $r < m$ cointegrating vectors, the $m \times m$ matrix Π will have rank r and the system can be written as follows:

$$\Delta w_t = \mu + \alpha \beta z_{t-1} + \Gamma_1 \Delta w_{t-1} + u_t$$

where α is an $m \times m$ matrix of feedback coefficients and β is an $r \times m$ matrix of cointegrating vectors. The r cointegrating relationships are $z_t = \beta w_t$, often interpreted as deviations from equilibrium. The identification problem arises because, for any non-singular matrix Q, we cannot distinguish $\Pi = \alpha\beta$ from $\Pi = (\alpha Q^{-1})(Q\beta)$ with new feedback coefficients $\alpha^* = (\alpha Q^{-1})$ and cointegrating vectors $\beta^* = (Q\beta)$. To identify the models we need to specify the $r \times r$ matrix Q, which gives the cointegrating vectors an economic interpretation. As with short-run identification, r of the restrictions will come from normalization restrictions.

We will assume that our three variables are $I(1)$ and have a single cointegrating vector, which we will interpret as a demand for money function, where z_t is trend adjusted velocity:

$$z_t = y_t + p_t + \beta_3 t - m_t$$
$$m_t = y_t + p_t + \beta t - z_t$$

Since $r = 1$, the single just-identifying restriction that we need is to normalize the logarithm of real money to have a coefficient of -1. However, we will also impose the over-identifying restrictions that y_t and p_t have unit coefficients. We have restricted the trend to enter the cointegrating vector, but we have allowed the intercept to be unrestricted. This allows for linear trends in the data, but precludes quadratic trends. Assuming a VAR (2), the system is then as follows:

$$\Delta y_t = \mu_1 + \alpha_1 z_{t-1} + \gamma_{11}\Delta y_{t-1} + \gamma_{12}\Delta p_{t-1} + \gamma_{11}\Delta m_{t-1} + u_{1t}$$
$$\Delta p_t = \mu_2 + \alpha_2 z_{t-1} + \gamma_{21}\Delta y_{t-1} + \gamma_{22}\Delta p_{t-1} + \gamma_{21}\Delta m_{t-1} + u_{2t} \quad (7.1)$$
$$\Delta m_t = \mu_3 + \alpha_3 z_{t-1} + \gamma_{31}\Delta y_{t-1} + \gamma_{32}\Delta p_{t-1} + \gamma_{31}\Delta m_{t-1} + u_{3t}$$

Notice that the trend is restricted because it appears within the cointegrating vector. The intercept is unrestricted; it appears outside. The feedback coefficients α_i tell us how disequilibrium in the money demand feeds back on the three variables in the system. We would expect the lagged value of each variable to have a negative effect on its change, so that $\alpha_1 < 0$; $\alpha_2 < 0$; $\alpha_3 > 0$. In systems with more cointegrating vectors, it is not simple to sign the adjustment coefficients. In this case there is a simple way to interpret the adjustment, since ignoring the dynamics and errors:

$$\Delta z_t = (\mu_1 + \mu_2 - \mu_3) + (\alpha_1 + \alpha_2 - \alpha_3) z_{t-1} + \ldots$$

and the system is stable if $0 > \alpha_1 + \alpha_2 - \alpha_3 > -1$.

The α_i are reduced form adjustment coefficients. Let us suppose that the structural VECM was $B_0 \Delta w_t = b + \lambda \beta w_{t-1} + C_1 \Delta w_{t-1} + \varepsilon_t$, with structural adjustment coefficients λ_i. The reduced form would then be $\Delta w_t = B_0^{-1} b + (B_0^{-1} \lambda) \beta w_{t-1} + B_0^{-1} C_1 \Delta w_{t-1} + B_0^{-1} \varepsilon_t$, and $\alpha = (B_0^{-1} \lambda)$ might have a much more complicated structure than λ.

Johansen provided two tests for the number of cointegrating vectors, which differ in their alternative hypothesis. The Johansen trace 10 per cent test has the alternative that the number of cointegrating vectors is greater than the hypothesized value. This test seems more appropriate and is used as our default. The number of cointegrating vectors is reported in column CV in table 7.1. The test identified a single cointegrating vector in eight of the twelve cases. JAM showed no cointegrating vectors, whereas SLU, BAH and BAR showed two cointegrating vectors. From this set of variables, standard economic theory would lead us to expect that the most likely relationship between them is described by a money demand function. Therefore, a single cointegrating vector could fit with that expectation.

On this basis, it was assumed that there was a single cointegrating vector in each economy. Imposing a single just-identifying restriction allowed us to identify the cointegrating vector as a money demand function. We further imposed the over-identifying restrictions of unit income and price elasticity, but these restrictions were rejected in all but three cases – SVG, JAM and TT (see column OIR in table 7.1). However, since the asymptotic critical values are likely to cause over-rejection in small samples, and the restrictions allow a simple economic interpretation, they were maintained.

Table 7.1 also reports the estimates of the adjustment coefficients. Cointegration requires significant feedbacks. Significant adjustment coefficients are shown in bold, using standard significance levels ($t > 2$), although these test statistics have non-standard distributions. There may be cointegration and no significant adjustment if the restricted cointegrating vector that we are using is not the right one. There is at least one significant adjustment coefficient, everywhere except BAH and BAR (where there is evidence for two cointegrating vectors, although this is also the case in SLU). Nine of the feedbacks to output have the correct (negative) sign. The exceptions are AB, GUY and TT, but only in the case of TT was the wrong sign significant. Ten of the feedbacks to prices also have the correct (negative) sign. The exceptions are AB and BAH, and in neither case was the sign wrong and significant. The ECM term in the money equation had the correct (positive) sign in ten cases. Of these, six were statistically significant. SLU and TT had negative coefficients, which was significant for SLU. Only JAM came close to having all the feedback coefficients with correct and statistically significant signs. Overall, most of the adjustment coefficients (29 out of 36) had the correct sign. Of these, fourteen were statistically significant.

Only two of the seven feedbacks with incorrect signs were statistically significant. The last column of figure 7.1 gives the estimates of α_i and of $a = \alpha_1 + \alpha_2 - \alpha_3$, where stability in the system requires $(-1 < a < 0)$. The condition for stability in the system was met in eleven of the twelve cases. The single exception was TT.

This cointegrating modelling provided reasonable results. Of the thirty-six feedback coefficients the VECM system estimated, 40 per cent were of statistically significant feedback coefficients. A further 40 per cent had the correct sign, but were statistically insignificant. The remaining 20 per cent had incorrect feedback coefficient signs, of which two were statistically significant.

Orthogonalized impulse responses are analysed for pure money shocks. Generalized impulse responses are analysed for price shocks. By construction, shocks are permanent in this cointegrated system where the system is shocked every quarter, unlike the unrestricted

Table 7.1 Cointegration and Adjustment Coefficients[a]

Countries	Period	CV	OIR	α_y	α_p	α_m	α
ECCB							
AB	1980(1)–2003(4)	1	0.00	0.000	0.007	**0.103**	−0.096
DOM	1980(1)–2003(4)	1	0.00	−0.011	**−0.051**	**0.155**	−0.217
GRE	1980(1)–2002(4)	1	0.02	−0.011	**−0.033**	**0.084**	−0.128
SKN	1980(1)–2002(4)	1	0.01	−0.002	−0.002	**0.274**	−0.278
SLU	1980(1)–2003(4)	2	0.00	**−0.108**	−0.003	**−0.065**	−0.046
SVG	1980(1)–2003(4)	1	0.22	−0.005	**−0.033**	**0.077**	−0.115
Non-ECCB							
BAH	1971(2)–2001(4)	2	0.00	−0.004	0.002	0.024	−0.026
BAR	1968(1)–2002(4)	2	0.00	−0.001	−0.003	0.027	−0.031
GUY	1972(1)–2003(4)	1	0.00	0.005	**−0.053**	0.006	−0.054
BEL	1979(1)–2003(4)	1	0.00	**−0.037**	**−0.035**	0.049	−0.121
JAM	1965(1)–2002(4)	0	0.63	−0.013[b]	−0.049	**0.090**	−0.152
TT	1965(1)–2003(4)	1	0.78	**0.008**	−0.022	−0.020	0.006

[a] Significant values for the feedback coefficients are shown in **bold** for Johansen trace test carried out at the 10% significance level.
[b] Coefficient significant at the 5% level.

VAR we examined earlier, where the system is given a once-and-for-all shock. Theoretically, the sizes of the shocks are likely to be different because the standard errors in the restricted cointegrating system may be larger than those in the unrestricted VAR. In this case, however, an examination of figures 7.1 and 7.2 for the orthogonalized and the generalized impulse

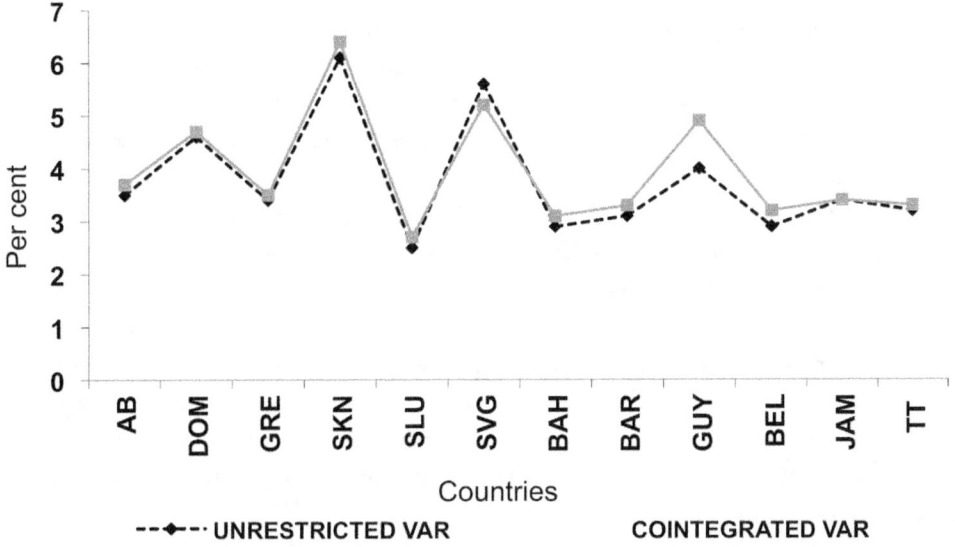

Figure 7.1 Othogonalized impulse response to one standard error money supply shock

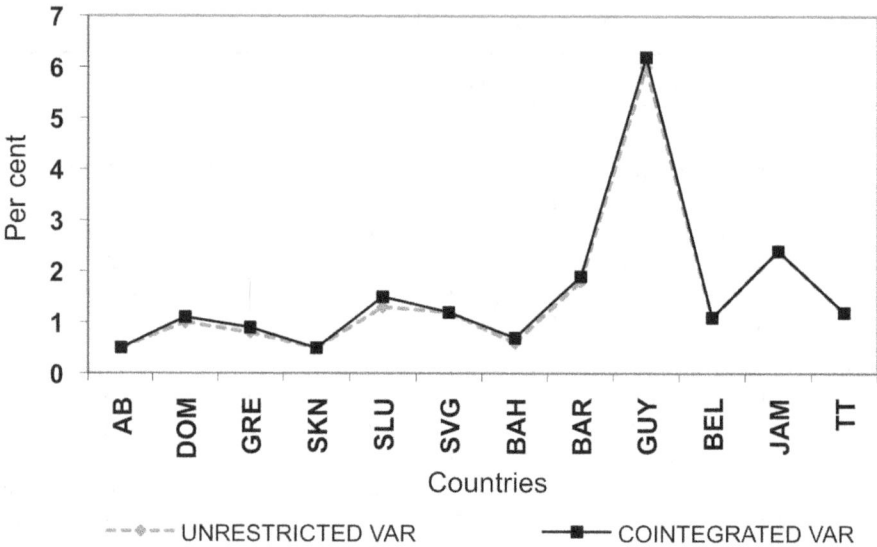

Figure 7.2 Generalized impulse response to one standard error price shock

responses shows that this is not the case. They are broadly similar in each case. The money shocks are generally larger than the price shocks. However, figure 7.1 shows that the money shocks from the orthogonalized system are similar, as are the price shocks from the generalized system shown in figure 7.2.

Table 7.2 shows that a 1 standard error shock in AB raises money by 3.7 per cent. In the fourth quarter, income would be 0.2 per cent higher and prices 0.2 per cent lower (this curious lower price response to a money supply increase is estimated for AB and BAH; all other cases show the a priori expected positive response of prices to a money shock). After 50 quarters income would fall by 0.6 per cent, prices by 1.9 per cent and money by 2.1 per cent. Figure 7.3 shows the impulse response graphs for the orthogonalized and generalized impulse responses for each country. Table 7.2 indicates this in three cases, where the fourth quarter impact on income is negative (SVG, GUY and TT). However, in eight cases, it is positive, by at least 0.2 per cent. SLU income grows by 1.0 per cent.

As we did before, in order to obtain an assessment of the overall effect of each of the money and the price shocks, we calculated the cumulative effect over eight quarters (the medium term) for each of the countries, along with their overall average. These are reported in tables 7.4 and 7.5, respectively.

Table 7.4 shows that an orthogonalized response from 1 standard error money supply increase will increase output on average by 2.8 per cent cumulatively over eight quarters. This average obscures the fact that some negative output growth responses are recorded. As the fourth quarter responses in table 7.2 shows, for example, three negative cases are SVG, GUY and TT. Nine of the twelve cases show an increase in y over the eight quarter. The exceptions are SVG, GUY and TT.

We notice that the output response in the VAR system was similar with a 2.1 per cent increase. Unlike the less than proportional increase estimates in the VAR system, the price response in this VECM system is estimated to be exactly directly proportional.

Table 7.2 Cointegrating VAR: Orthogonalized Impulse Response Functions

	1SE Shock to Money (%)								
	On Impact			After 4 Quarters			After 50 Quarters		
	y	p	m	y	p	m	y	P	m
ECCB									
AB	0.0	0.0	3.7	0.2	−0.2	2.5	−0.6	−1.9	−2.1
DOM	0.0	0.0	4.7	0.4	0.7	3.2	1.1	1.3	2.4
GRE	0.0	0.0	3.5	0.3	0.5	2.7	0.5	1.3	1.8
SKN	0.0	0.0	6.4	0.3	0.1	1.6	0.0	0.2	0.2
SLU	0.0	0.0	2.7	1.0	0.3	3.0	3.3	0.6	3.9
SVG	0.0	0.0	5.9	−0.1	0.6	4.4	0.5	2.1	2.7
Non-ECCB									
BAH	0.0	0.0	3.1	0.7	−0.4	2.6	1.6	−0.5	1.6
BAR	0.0	0.0	3.3	0.6	0.0	3.0	0.6	0.2	1.5
GUY	0.0	0.0	4.9	−0.1	1.4	4.6	−0.9	6.5	5.6
BEL	0.0	0.0	3.2	0.4	0.6	2.7	1.6	1.1	2.8
JAM	0.0	0.0	3.4	0.5	1.1	3.3	0.8	3.1	3.9
TT	0.0	0.0	3.3	−0.1	0.7	4.2	−3.5	7.2	8.1

The average 1 standard error increase in money shock calculated from the fourth column in table 7.2 is 4.0 per cent, which is the same as the estimated increase in prices across the twelve economies shown in table 7.4. From a Quantity of Money Theory perspective ($MV = Py$), this again implies that the income velocity of money is not constant. A direct proportional relationship between M and P with constant velocity would imply no change in y from the

Table 7.3 Cointegrating VAR: Generalized Impulse Response Functions

	1SE Shock to Prices (%)								
	On Impact			After 4 Quarters			After 50 Quarters		
	y	p	m	y	p	m	y	p	m
ECCB									
AB	−0.2	0.5	0.3	−0.2	1.6	0.3	0.5	3.3	3.5
DOM	0.0	1.1	−0.2	0.0	1.0	0.7	−0.1	0.9	0.8
GRE	0.0	0.9	−0.1	−0.5	1.3	0.6	−0.8	1.4	0.6
SKN	0.0	0.5	0.4	−0.5	1.4	1.1	−1.3	1.7	0.4
SLU	−0.3	1.5	0.4	−0.8	1.8	0.5	−1.5	1.7	0.2
SVG	−0.1	1.2	−0.1	−0.4	1.1	0.2	−0.5	0.9	0.4
Non-ECCB									
BAH	−0.3	0.7	−0.3	−2.1	1.9	−0.3	−3.0	2.1	−0.7
BAR	0.0	1.9	0.3	−0.2	3.7	0.6	−0.2	3.4	2.5
GUY	0.2	6.2	0.8	0.9	10.8	3.6	3.2	−1.6	1.4
BEL	0.2	1.1	0.3	−0.1	2.2	0.8	−1.2	2.0	0.8
JAM	0.0	2.4	0.0	−0.4	7.1	3.6	−1.0	6.0	4.9
TT	−0.1	1.2	0.2	0.2	1.9	1.0	1.5	−0.1	0.0

AB
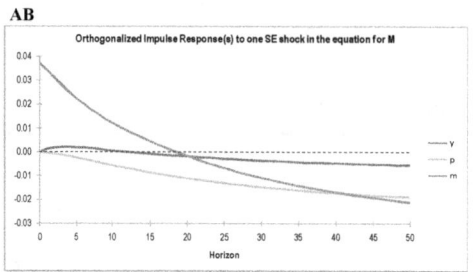

AB
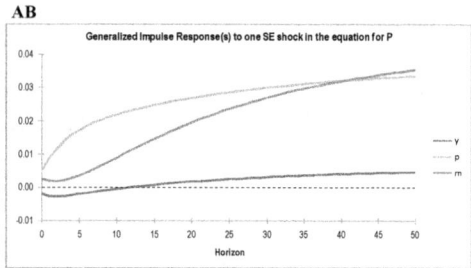

DOM
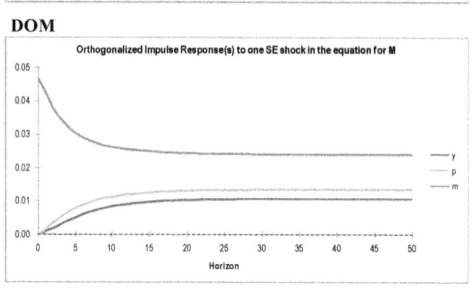

DOM
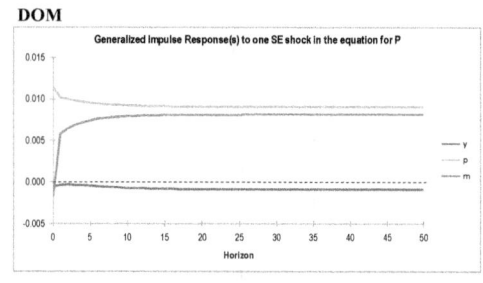

GRE
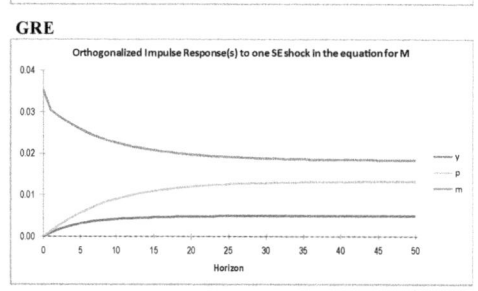

GRE
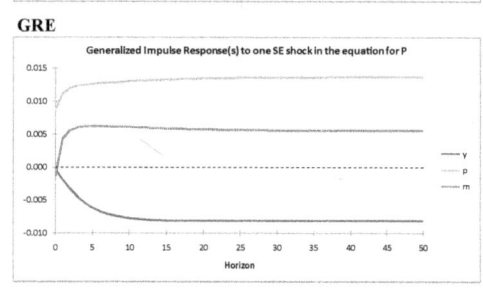

SKN
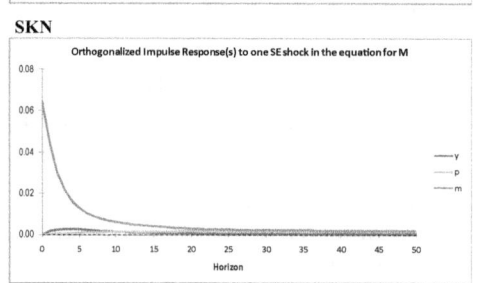

SKN
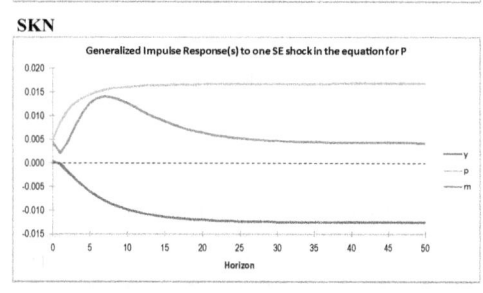

SLU
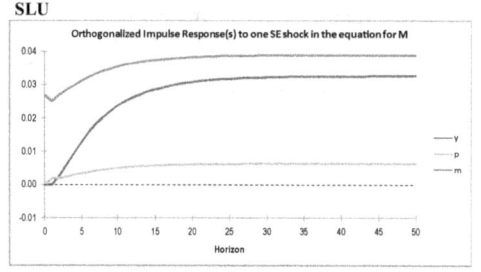

SLU
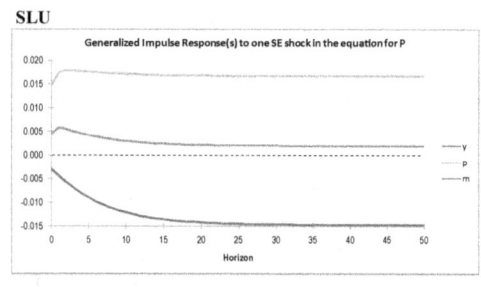

SVG
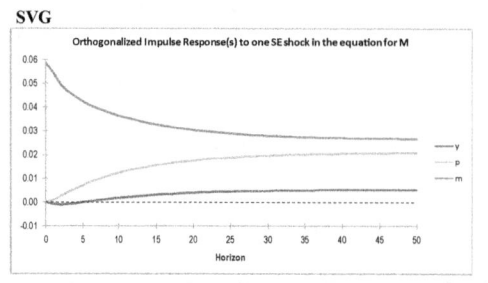

SVG
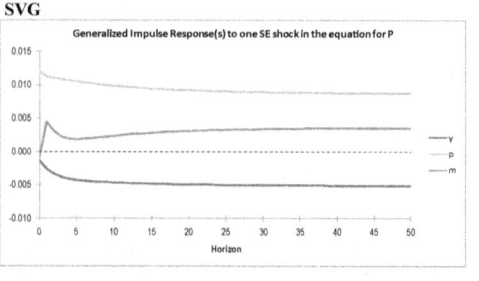

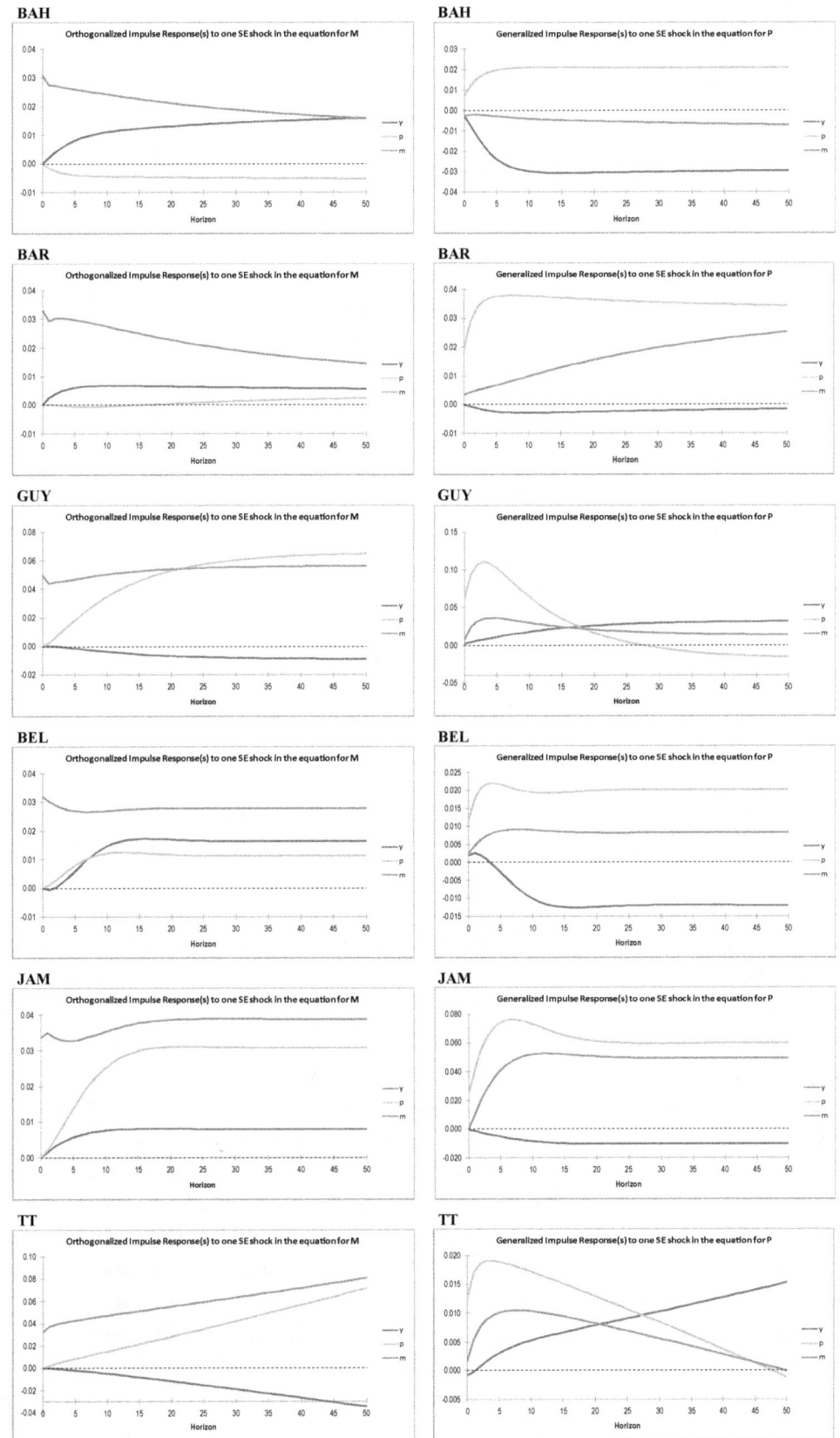

Figure 7.3 Impact effect of a one standard error monetary and price shock: VAR and VECM

Table 7.4 Cointegrating VAR: Cumulative Orthogonalized Impulse Response

	1SE Shock to Money (%)		
	Cumulative Impact After 8 Quarters		
	y	p	m
ECCB	(Impact Quarter Index = 100)		
AB	101.3	98.2	125.5
DOM	103.5	105.5	135.4
GRE	102.2	104.0	127.8
SKN	101.8	100.7	123.8
SLU	108.9	102.5	130.3
SVG	99.9	105.0	150.1
Non-ECCB			
BAH	105.7	97.2	126.8
BAR	104.4	99.7	130.4
GUY	98.9	113.5	151.3
BEL	104.2	105.5	128.4
JAM	104.0	110.1	134.6
TT	98.5	106.2	143.5
Average	102.8	104.0	134.0

Fisher Quantity Theory identity. However, the money shock, in this case, has given rise to an increase in output. We have to be cautious in drawing out implications from this small closed economy modelling. Nevertheless, the results offer some basis for theoretical interpretations.

Table 7.3 shows that a generalized impulse response from a 1 standard error shock to prices in AB increase prices by 0.5 per cent. This is associated on average with a 0.2 per cent reduction in output and a 0.3 per cent increase in money in the same quarter. After four quarters, both income and money still show the same respective 0.2 per cent decline and 0.3 per cent increase. However, the rate or price increase is raised to 1.6 per cent in the fourth quarter. After fifty quarters, as those shocks worked through the system, prices would be 3.3 per cent higher, output 0.5 per cent higher and money supply 3.5 per cent higher. Notice that the sum of effects on y plus p minus m is zero. This is because the cointegrating relationship constrains them.

Table 7.5 reports that on average across all countries, the cumulative impact of a generalized impulse response to a 1 standard error increase in prices (prices increase by 1.6 per cent on average) will decrease output to 97.3 per cent of its former value (a 2.7 per cent fall) over eight quarters. Ten of the twelve estimations show a cumulative decline in output over eight quarters. Table 7.3 reported that after four quarters output responses were negative or zero in all but two of the twelve countries. GUY and TT are the exceptions in this case. An explanation could reside in the distinctive structure of their economies. In the case of TT, the closed economy model showed a decline. However, this closed economy model shows an increase in output, which may

Table 7.5 Cointegrating VAR: Cumulative Generalized Impulse Response

	1SE Shock to Prices (%)		
	Cumulative Impact After 8 Quarters		
	y	p	m
ECCB	(Impact Quarter Index = 100)		
AB	98.2	113.9	103.2
DOM	99.6	109.2	105.7
GRE	95.8	111.3	104.7
SKN	96.1	111.7	108.6
SLU	93.4	116.7	104.1
SVG	96.7	110.1	101.9
Non-ECCB			
BAH	84.5	116.4	97.6
BAR	98.4	135.1	105.8
GUY	108.5	224.4	131.0
BEL	98.6	119.2	106.8
JAM	96.3	171.8	131.5
TT	102.0	117.2	107.7
Average	97.3	129.8	109.1

be due to responsiveness of the oil and gas sectors that drive that economy. In the case of GUY, the history of inflation and economic decline make interpretation more difficult.

On the whole, the results suggest an overall output decline in response to a general price increase, which accords with economic theory.

In the long run, the variables diverge in TT, which is unstable (see figure 7.3). In response to a monetary shock, in SKN, the variables rapidly converge back to their original levels. Elsewhere, the shocks have long-run impacts determined by the long-run money demand function. The short- to medium-term effects of a shock to prices tend to be negative for output (2.7 per cent decline on average across the countries) and positive for a money shock (2.8 per cent increase on average across the countries). From these results, and from the graphs of the response functions in figure 7.3, the long-run effect on output does not support notions of money neutrality (since output showed some increases in the long run to the money shock). However, there is evidence that an inflation shock will, on average, bring about a decline in output.

7.2 Conclusions

At the heart of our restricted VECM is the Fisher equation ($MV = PY$), with the logarithm of velocity ($v_t = y_t + p_t - m_t$) treated as a measure of disequilibrium to which the other variables adjust. This implies the over-identifying restrictions of coefficients of 1, 1, −1 on the right side variables. Although the evidence for the over-identifying restrictions is not strong, it aids economic interpretation. Twenty-nine of the thirty-six adjustment coefficients were correctly signed, and there was evidence of adjustment to this long-run equilibrium in all but TT.

The unrestricted VAR estimates of chapter 6 provided better estimates than those obtained from the VECM estimations in chapter 7, as is indicated by the larger 1 standard error shocks evidenced in figures 7.1 and 7.2. This may be expected since the latter were subject to additional restrictions. The Fisher equation does not impose long-run neutrality of money, just that changes in money are matched by changes in nominal output, where the adjustment can be either by prices or output. In the short run, over eight quarters, in response to a 1 standard error shock, which will be different in different countries, money is estimated to increase by 34.0 per cent (see table 7.4). However, the average increase in prices was only 4.0 per cent, and output rose by 2.8 per cent. Table 7.4 shows that the impacts are not consistent across the countries. Some countries have falling incomes and some rising incomes, and the same is true for prices. However, the rising income and prices impacts are dominant across the countries. Therefore, there is some evidence of sticky prices effects here. Although, again, these effects were not consistent across all countries, and some countries did show some decreases in income. Examination of the impact over fifty quarters (the long run) does not change this general effect (see graphs in figure 7.3).

The generalized impact response results show that the overwhelming effect of a price shock is to cause a decline in output. On average across the twelve countries, over eight quarters, the prices are estimated to increase by 29.8 per cent (see table 7.5). This led to an average fall in income across the countries of 2.7 per cent, with money increasing by 9.1 per cent. Since these economies are small open economies, it could be argued that this may be due to the intolerance of such economies to inflationary shocks, and that they would need to adjust rapidly or pay a high price – a foreign exchange crisis, as indeed JAM and GUY have.

Overall, therefore, estimates of the cointegration VECM provide some evidence that inflation shocks in these Caribbean countries were associated with falling income. This was also supported by unrestricted VAR estimates. The system did not show, however, monetary shocks being strongly linked to price inflation and negatively to output. This does not mean that monetary shock does not have inflationary implications, but rather that these particular estimations did not provide evidence of this. Although, of course, there are strong theoretical reasons to think that such a relationship does exist. These results may be seen as providing some support for the argument that inflation should be the primary macroeconomic target, and money should be given the role of an intermediate target, as discussed in chapter 1(Loayza and Soto 2002; Mishkin 2000).

Chapter 8

Caribbean External Balance Adjustment: The Marshall-Lerner Condition and J-Curve Effects

Introduction

The economies of the Caribbean are small open economies and some of the shocks to them come from the international system. In the previous chapters, we developed closed economy models of their economies to examine the monetary transmission mechanisms, that is, the way in which monetary policy affects their real economy, notably, real output. In this chapter, we develop several ways to estimate two well known open economy relationships to examine the efficacy of these mechanisms in bringing about external balance adjustments in these economies.

In open economies nominal exchange rate devaluations, either within a fixed or flexible exchange regime, are mechanisms through which corrections towards equilibrium may take place. Theoretically, nominal devaluations are mechanisms that should respond to relative price movements in order that a currency may not be overvalued. We examined the issue of overvaluation of a currency in chapter 2. Although the nominal exchange rate is an everyday aspect of international trade, economic theory tells us that the *real* exchange rate is the nominal exchange rate corrected for relative prices, which determines international trade flow. The issue of whether a real devaluation is likely to result in an improvement in the balance of trade is highly relevant to these small economies, notably so in light of the significant negative domestic output effect of inflation identified in the two previous chapters. Moreover, this is especially relevant because devaluation is often a primary focus of IMF policy recommendations, which these countries generally have to consider. We shall consider the balance of payments effects through the analysis of two primary mechanisms: the *Marshall-Lerner condition* (MLC) and the *J-Curve effect*.

The standard international trade theory is that devaluation will improve the balance of trade in the long run, if the Marshall-Lerner condition holds. The condition states that the sum of the export and import price elasticities of demand is greater than one. However, devaluations may worsen the balance of trade in the short run through terms of trade effects. This pattern of short-run deterioration and long-run improvement is known as the J-Curve effect. In this chapter, we will examine evidence of these effects to determine whether the conditions exist among these countries, which would indicate that exchange rate adjustments may lead to balance of payments improvements.

The policy implication of this is important. If the structure of these economies is such that the MLC is not satisfied, then it may be that the cost of adjustment to inflation may be greater than it may first appear, especially in light of the above evidence of the adverse output impact of inflation shocks. Real devaluations may have insignificant trade effects, so that the adjustments have to take place mostly through a reduction in output. That is, an inflationary shock may lead to an output fall on the domestic front, and a fall in trade competitiveness on the international front. If the response to the latter is a nominal exchange rate devaluation to restore international competitiveness in the real exchange rate, this may not be an efficient mechanism to restore that trade balance. The notion is that an asymmetry between inflation and output may exist when inflation rises and when inflation falls. This would imply that measures to increase employment in these countries, which already suffer from high unemployment, are more likely to be unsuccessful.

A priori, this already appears to be the case in some countries with historically high inflation, where adjustment to low inflation appears difficult to attain. If this is the case, the benefits to prudent monetary policy, discussed earlier, becomes even more pertinent. The benefits of prudent monetary policy may be even more important, and the punishment for monetary slackness more severe than may seem. Of course, in the countries with fixed exchange rates (the ECCB countries, the Bahamas, Barbados and Belize), the real exchange rate effects will take place through changes in relative domestic and foreign prices. This, in effect, may well make the process more manageable by focusing attention on the domestic monetary policy–inflation nexus. Only in those countries with floating rates (Guyana, Jamaica, and Trinidad and Tobago) will any effects take place through nominal devaluations of the exchange rates, as well as through relative inflation rates.

8.1 The Model

The data used in this chapter is annual data, which will constrain our methodology due to the paucity of observations. The data used in the previous estimations were quarterly data, which allowed large sample properties to be attained. The trade data for the Caribbean countries are only published on an annual basis, as indeed are the output data. We could interpolate these annual series to obtain quarterly series, but this would lead to severe estimation problems because the variations that we pick up in the estimations would be, in great part, those that we introduced in the interpolation. Hence, we are restricted to using the annual data series.

The balance of trade is usually measured by the difference between exports and imports. Here, it will be convenient to work with the ratio of exports and imports, since in a logarithmic model this gives the MLC exactly, rather than as an approximation a balance of payment equilibrium.

The ratio of nominal exports to nominal imports, B, is given by the ratio of the volume of exports, X, multiplied by domestic prices, P, to the volume of imports, M, multiplied by foreign prices, P^*, and the nominal spot exchange rate S:

$$B_t = (P_t X_t) / (P_t^* S_t M_t) \qquad (8.1)$$

Or, using lower case letters for logarithms, we get:

$$b_t = x_t - m_t - (s_t - p_t + p_t^*) = x_t - m_t - e_t \qquad (8.2)$$

where $e_t = (s_t - p_t + p_t^*)$ is the real exchange rate. Note that this is defined in terms of the real exchange rate using general price indices, rather than the terms of trade. Long-run export and import demand are given by the following:

$$\begin{aligned} x_t &= \alpha_x + \beta^* y_t^* + \eta_x e_t + \gamma_x t \\ m_t &= \alpha_m + \beta y_t + \eta_m e_t + \gamma_m t \end{aligned} \qquad (8.3)$$

The trends capture terms of trade effects (for example, for primary product producers), unmeasured quality improvements or policy measures, such as trend liberalization. We assume supply elasticities are large, so that exports and imports are determined by demand. This is certainly plausible for imports, but may not be true for exports.

The long-run balance of trade can then be written as follows:

$$b_t = x_t - m_t - e_t = (\alpha_x - \alpha_m) + \beta^* y_t^* - \beta y_t + (\eta_x + \eta_m - 1) e_t + (\gamma_x - \gamma_m) t \qquad (8.4)$$

$$b_t = \alpha + \beta^* y_t^* - \beta y_t + \eta e_t + \gamma t + u_t \qquad (8.5)$$

The coefficient on e_t should be positive for a devaluation (an increase in e) to bring about an improvement in the balance of payments from an initial equilibrium. This is the familiar and sometimes contentious (Krugman and Taylor 1978) MLC, which implies that the sum of the export and import price elasticities are greater than one. We can then ask the following questions:

- Is there a long-run balance of payments equation (that is, is equation 8.5 a cointegrating relation)?
- Does the MLC hold is $\eta > 0$?
- Is there a J-Curve, a non-monotonic adjustment to equilibrium?

There are a number of ways that equation 8.5 may cointegrate. To estimate long-run effects we require that the balance of payments cointegrates with domestic and foreign income, and with the real exchange rate. All the variables may be $I(1)$, and there is a single cointegrating vector that constitutes the balance of payments equation. This is the interpretation that we shall use.

Alternatively, there are three other possibilities:

1. The first is that b_t itself may be $I(0)$, reflecting balance of payments sustainability. This implies that the balance of payments will adjust back to equilibrium after it experiences a shock due to the underlying factors at work in the economy.
2. The real exchange rate may be $I(0)$, reflecting purchasing power parity. This means that the real exchange rate is mean reverting to its long-run equilibrium rate in response to any shocks. For example, if the real exchange rate becomes overvalued (that is, uncompetitive) due to an increase in domestic prices, then the nominal exchange rate would, in this case, be devalued, to bring about the long-run equilibrium rate. The overall real exchange rate is, therefore, mean reverting to its long-run equilibrium rate.
3. The output gap $y_t - y_t^*$ may be $I(0)$, reflecting convergence. This implies that the rate of growth of the two countries is the same, hence the output gap remains constant and any shocks to either output last only a short time, as the output revert back to their relative long-run relationship. Therefore, it is important to test for the order of integration of the variables in our series at the start of the investigation.

8.2 Investigating Balance of Trade Effects

Our investigation follows a procedure developed in Boyd, Caporale and Smith (2001), where we examined real exchange effects on the balance of trade of eight industrial countries. This involves the following tests:

1. ADF tests for a unit root in the variables b_t, e_t and y_t
2. Granger block non-causality test on the b_t, e_t and y_t
3. Engle-Granger test for cointegration in long-run balance of payments relationship in equation 8.5
4. Johansen Maximum Likelihood (ML) test for number of cointegrating vectors
5. Johansen ML estimation of cointegrating vector in equation 8.6 and the Marshall-Lerner condition
6. Generalized impulse response functions to seek graphical evidence of J-Curve

8.3 Unrestricted VAR Estimations, Results and Interpretation

8.3.1 ADF Test for a Unit Root

Results from the ADF test for a unit root for the variable are reported in the first three columns of table 8.1. The variables were $I(1)$ in twenty-five of the thirty-six cases. We will treat the variables

Table 8.1 ADF Test for Order of Integration of Variables

Countries	Period	b_t	e_t	y_t
ECCB				
AB	1978–2002	*I(0)*	*I(1)*	*I(1)*
DOM	1978–2003	*I(0)*	*I(0)*	*I(0)*
GRE	1978–2003	*I(1)*	*I(1)*	*I(1)*
SKN	1981–2003	*I(0)*	*I(1)*	*I(1)*
SLU	1980–2003	*I(1)*	*I(0)*	*I(1)*
SVG	1977–2003	*I(1)*	*I(1)*	*I(1)*
Non-ECCB				
BAH	1976–2002	*I(1)*	*I(1)*	*I(0)*
BAR	1981–2003	*I(1)*	*I(1)*	*I(1)*
GUY	1974–2003	*I(0)*	*I(1)*	*I(2)*
BEL	1986–2003	*I(1)*	*I(1)*	*I(2)*
JAM	1976–2004	*I(1)*	*I(0)*	*I(1)*
TT	1980–2004	*I(1)*	*I(1)*	*I(1)*

as $I(1)$ to carry out the procedure, but this assumption is not beyond question. Assuming that the variables are $I(1)$, we can write the long-run relationship for the balance of trade as in equation 8.5:

$$b_t = \alpha + \beta^* y_t^* - \beta y_t + \eta e_t + \gamma t + u_t$$

8.3.2 Granger Block Non-causality Tests

Using the unrestricted VAR, we are able to examine the pattern of causality between the variables with Granger block non-causality tests, testing the significance of each variable in the determination of the other two for b_t, e_t and y_t. The results are reported in table 8.2. These block non-causality tests are derived from the unrestricted VAR estimates of equation 8.5. The probability values, for testing the null hypothesis that the coefficients of the lagged values of b in the block of equations explaining e and y are zero, are reported in the table. For example, in the case of the first reported test with a probability of the null hypothesis being true of 0.239, we would not reject the non-causality null at the 5 per cent level of significance. Hence, there is no significant evidence that b_t determines the other two variables e_t and y_t.

In less than half of the cases (five and three, respectively), b_t, and e_t are Granger causal on the other variables. However, in the majority of cases (nine out of twelve), y_t is Granger casual with respect to the other two variables. This implies that there is little evidence that y_t is endogenous with respect to the other two variables. This may be a signal that y_t may be treated as a long-run forcing variable in latter estimations. Since there is little evidence that y_t is endogenous with respect to the other two variables, we may effectively treat it as weakly exogenous in this system.

8.3.3 Engle-Granger Test for Cointegration

We also used the unrestricted VAR estimations to carry out Engle-Granger tests for cointegration (these are essentially Augmented Dickey-Fuller tests for a unit root on the residuals u_t for each equation in the VAR). The results of these are reported in the final column of table 8.2. Cointegration implies stationarity of the residual so that the unit root null hypothesis has to be rejected. The *unit root null was rejected in only three cases: AB. SLU and GUY.* This suggests that the relationship specified in equation 8.5 does not provide evidence of a cointegrating relationship in b_t in 9 of the 12 cases – at least, as measured by this procedure.

8.4 Cointegrated VAR and VECM Estimations, Results and Interpretation

In this section, we carry out estimations based on the Johansen Maximum Likelihood procedure.
The deviation from long-run equilibrium may be defined as follows:

$$z_t = \alpha + \beta^* y_t^* - \beta y_t + \eta e_t + \gamma t - b_t \tag{8.6}$$

The number of cointegrating vectors among these four variables is an empirical matter, which will be investigated. For the moment, however, we will treat this as the only cointegrating vector. We define $w_t^* = (b_t, e_t, y_t, y_t^*)'$, and we can then model the dynamic adjustment by a pth order vector autoregression, which can be written as a vector error correction model in the cointegrating relationship z_t:

$$\Delta w_t^* = \mu + \alpha z_{t-1} + \sum_{i=1}^{p} \Gamma_i \Delta w_{t-1}^* + u_t \tag{8.7}$$

where μ includes unrestricted deterministic elements, and α is a 4 × 1 vector.[1] This VECM can be regarded as the reduced form for a structural cointegrating vector autoregressive distributed lag (VARDL) model, which includes exogenous variables.

8.4.1 Johansen ML Tests for Number of Cointegrating Vectors

Since we use annual data, and are limited in the degrees of freedom, VARs of order one were used and y_t^* was treated as exogenous. Estimates of the number of cointegrating vectors using Johansen Maximum Likelihood method are reported in table 8.3. In nine of the twelve cases, the trace statistic suggests one cointegrating vector at 10 per cent. In the three remaining cases, no cointegrating vector is identified. To be consistent with our treatment of the sample group, we assumed a single cointegrating vector, although there is weak evidence for this.

---

[1] Sometimes we treat y_t^* as exogenous and sometimes as endogenous. In testing for cointegration we treat it as exogenous so that α is a 3 × 1 vector. In order to generate the impulse responses, however, we excluded this variable. We could have treated it as endogenous, but in view of the relatively small number of observations we chose, we did not choose this option.

Table 8.2 Unrestricted VAR Estimates: Granger Block Non-Causality Tests and Engle-Granger Test for a Unit Root

Country	Block Non-causality Null:			Engle-Granger Test for a Unit Root in Equation 8.5
	$b_t \not\Rightarrow e_t, y_t$	$e_t \not\Rightarrow b_t, y_t$	$y_t \not\Rightarrow b_t, e_t$	
ECCB				
AB	0.239	**0.016**	**0.048**	reject
DOM	**0.005**	**0.000**	0.198	dnr
GRE	0.484	0.685	**0.030**	dnr
SKN	0.077	0.879	**0.009**	dnr
SLU	**0.028**	0.651	0.488	reject
SVG	0.997	0.196	0.840	dnr
Non-ECCB				
BAH	0.165	0.824	**0.004**	dnr
BAR	**0.011**	**0.010**	**0.012**	dnr
GUY	**0.001**	0.398	**0.000**	reject
BEL	**0.044**	0.609	**0.017**	dnr
JAM	0.331	0.629	**0.044**	dnr
TT	0.399	0.101	**0.000**	dnr

8.4.2 Johansen ML Estimates of the Cointegrating Vector and the Marshall-Lerner Condition

As emphasized in Pesaran and Smith (1998), cointegrating VAR analysis involves a large number of choices about specification, including:

- number of endogenous and exogenous variables
- treatment of the deterministic elements
- lag order used
- judgement about the order of integration of the variables
- number of cointegrating vectors chosen
- just-identifying restrictions used to identify them

Estimates and inference are sensitive to the search procedure used and the methods used to make those choices.

Johansen ML estimates of the cointegrating coefficients are reported in table 8.3. Normalized on $b_t = -1$, the expected signs of the coefficients for the variables are $e_t > 0, y_t < 0$ and $y_t^* > 0$, as shown in equation 8.6. These estimates did not provide many instances of significant cointegrating vectors. In only three cases, one for each of the three variables, were coefficients simultaneously significant and had the correct sign: e_t for JAM; y_t for TT; and y_t^* for JAM. Overall, therefore, there was no evidence of a long-run cointegrating relationship.

Table 8.3 Cointegrated VAR (1) Vector Estimates and VECM Error Correction Coefficients Estimates: SE[a] and Probability Values[b]

Country	CV Trace@10% (1)	e_t (2)	y_t (3)	y_t^* (4)	α_b (6)	α_e (7)	α_y (8)
AB	0	−23.1 (60.2)	−19.8 (53.7)	3.2 (11.9)	0.044 [0.312]	0.017 [0.082]	**0.025**[c] **[0.034]**
DOM	1	0.5 (1.8)	**1.6 (0.8)**	−2.2 (1.9)	**0.880 [0.000]**	**0.110 [0.000]**	0.066 [0.322]
GRE	1	−8.7 (5.6)	−3.5 (2.9)	4.7 (3.9)	−0.056 [0.133]	**0.089 [0.000]**	0.006 [0.574]
SKN	1	**−3.8 (1.4)**	−1.2 (0.9)	−0.4 (1.4)	0.310 [0.247]	**0.113 [0.016]**	−0.08 [0.294]
SLU	0	25.4 (25.7)	1.0 (1.2)	0.9 (4.8)	0.106 [0.313]	**−0.027 [0.004]**	−0.034 [0.421]
SVG	0	3.9 (2.8)	1.1 (0.7)	−3.8 (2.6)	**0.352 [0.025]**	−0.036 [0.177]	−0.035 [0.318]
BAH	1	90.5 (468.8)	62.7 (293.9)	−93.8 (488.1)	−0.001 [0.862]	**−0.002 [0.000]**	**−0.004 [0.001]**
BAR	1	**−8.1 (1.8)**	**−8.5 (1.5)**	**7.6 (2.5)**	−0.172 [0.306]	**0.080 [0.000]**	**0.114 [0.003]**
GUY	1	**−1.63 (0.6)**	−1.2 (0.4)	0.9 (1.0)	−0.018 [0.895]	**0.635 [0.000]**	0.007 [0.920]
BEL	1	4.4 (3.2)	−2.1 (1.1)	−2.1 (1.5)	0.084 [0.455]	**−0.078 [0.014]**	**0.092 [0.041]**
JAM	1	**0.16 (0.07)**	1.40 (0.18)	**2.97 (0.57)**	**1.02 [0.000]**	−0.009 [0.977]	**−0.174 [0.019]**
TT	1	−1.35 (0.78)	**−2.84 (0.81)**	0.13 (1.69)	0.208 [0.074]	**0.245 [0.002]**	**−0.126 [0.001]**

[a]Figures within parentheses indicate SE values.
[b]Figures within square brackets indicate probability values.
[c]Figures in **bold** indicate that the coefficient estimate is significant.

In order for the MLC to be satisfied – a devaluation (an increase in e_t) to bring about an improvement in the balance of payments – the coefficient on e_t must be positive, that is, $\eta > 0$. This was statistically significant, with the correct sign only in the single case of JAM. In none of the twelve cases did the estimated parameters all have the correct sign. This particular procedure, therefore, provided poor evidence in support of the MLC for this group of countries.

8.4.3 Generalized Impulse Responses and the J-Curve Effects

To examine the dynamic responses of the VECM in more detail, generalized impulse response (GIR) functions were calculated. Unlike orthogonalized impulse responses, these functions are invariant to the ordering of the variables (Pesaran and Smith 1998). Since the GIR use the information in the historical covariance matrix to calculate them, we dropped foreign output from this specification. We examined the balance of trade, in the form of the export–import trade ratio (b_t) GIR functions, to a 1 standard error depreciation in the real exchange rate (e_t increases by 1 SE). With a competitive real depreciation, an initial worsening in the balance of trade may be expected to be followed by an improvement, as export demand responds to the fall, and the export price and imports also responds to the increase in imports price. This is the expectation of the effect. These effects are based on the expectations that, in the short run, price effects will dominate, whereas in the long run, quantity adjustments will prevail. Unlike the shocks examined in the unrestricted VAR system in the previous chapter, shocks within the cointegrating VAR are, by construction, permanent, so that the 1 SE devaluation represents a permanent devaluation through time. Therefore, assuming the Marshall-Lerner condition holds, a devaluation should at first worsen b_t, then eventually bring about an improvement over the long run.

Figure 8.1 shows the GIR for the twelve countries of our sample. Under the classic circumstances, this should lead to an initial worsening of the trade ratio, b_t, with the curve moving down the y-axis, as b_t moves into a deficit, this would then be followed by a movement up the graph as b_t improves and moves up towards a new long-term balance. We get the shape that corresponds to effect in six cases, but only in three (DOM, SLU and SVG) did the outcome correspond to a positive balance improvement in the long run for the balance of payments. In the other three cases (GRE, SKN and BEL), although the GIR showed the correct shape, the long-run equilibrium had a negative balance of payments. In the other six cases, two countries (AB and TT) had the incorrect shape for the curve, implying a worsening of the balance of payments following the real exchange rate shock. The remaining four (BAH, BAR, GUY and JAM) displayed curves that were essentially flat. BAH was flat with a negative balance; BAR was flat and positive; GUY was flat and positive but very close to zero (0.01); and JAM flat and negative, but very close to zero (0.005).

8.4.4 VECM Feedback Coefficients

If we regard world output as exogenous and define $w_t = (b_t, e_t, y_t)'$, the VARDL of equation 8.7 takes the following form:

$$\Delta w_t = \mu + \alpha z_{t-1} + \sum_{i=1}^{p} \Gamma_i \Delta w_{t-1} + \sum_{i=0}^{p} \delta_i \Delta y^*_{t-1} + u_t \quad (8.8)$$

Writing equation 8.8 out explicitly, ignoring the short-run dynamics and work income, we get the following:

$$\begin{aligned} \Delta b_t &= \alpha_b z_{t-1} + \mu_{10} + u_{1t} \\ \Delta e_t &= \alpha_e z_{t-1} + \mu_{20} + u_{2t} \\ \Delta y_t &= \alpha_y z_{t-1} + \mu_{30} + u_{3t} \end{aligned} \quad (8.9)$$

The adjustment coefficients are reported in columns 6, 7 and 8 in table 8.3. In this analysis, the feedback in the VECM takes place through α_e and α_y significantly, in nine and six of the twelve cases, respectively. In a previous application of this procedure, used to examine eight

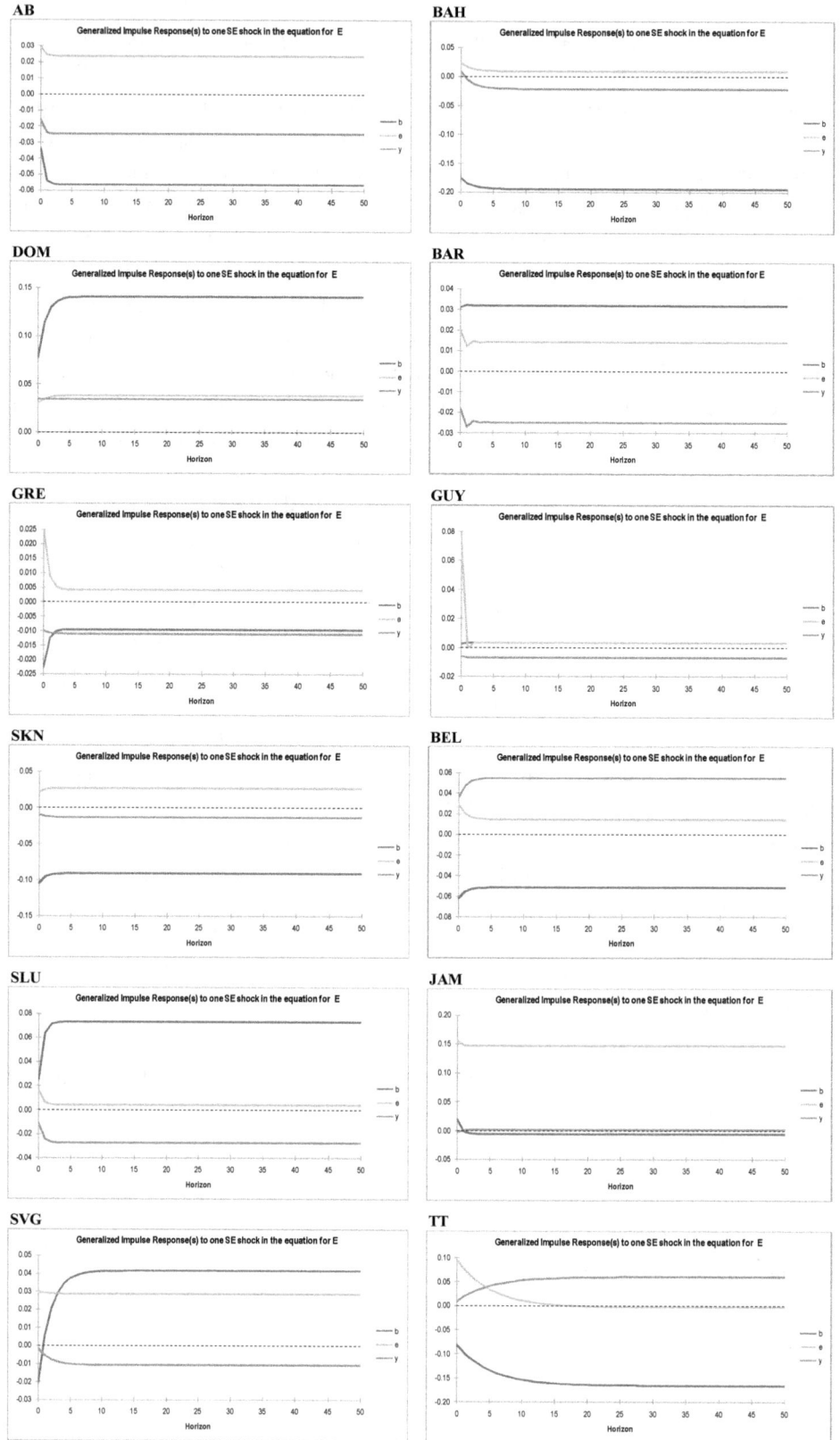

Figure 8.1 Generalized impulse response of balance of payments and income to a real exchange rate shock

industrial countries (Boyd, Caporale and Smith, 2001), a notable feature of those results was that virtually all of the VECM feedback took place through the trade equation. For the G8 industrial countries, $\alpha_e = 0$ and $\alpha_y = 0$. That means we were able to treat e_t and y_t as weakly exogenous, and condition on them to give a single-equation autoregressive distributed lag (ARDL). In the case of this analysis for the Caribbean countries, we are unable to estimate an ARDL, since there are significant feedbacks on more than one variable.

8.5 Conclusions

In this chapter, we sought to do three things:

1. Test for the long-run relationship in b_t
2. Test for the MLC to support the balance of payments improvement over the long run
3. Find evidence of the effects, the short-run movements that gives rise to this overall effect

We used the following four economic models, which differ in the degree to which they condition on exogenous variables, to test for the long-run relationship in b_t:

1. Granger non-causality tests
2. Engle-Granger test for cointegration
3. Cointegrating VAR
4. Cointegrating VECM

Overall, poor evidence of a long-run relationship was found, and support for a long-run relationship in terms of the MLC and J-Curve effect was also poor. This is in marked contrast to the Boyd, Caporale and Smith (2001) study of eight OECD countries, which found that "although there is considerable heterogeneity, overall the results suggest that the MLC holds in the long run with statistically significant results in five out of the eight cases", and that "[O]verall, there was considerable evidence that the real exchange rate does have a significant impact on the trade balance, although, in keeping with the literature, the evidence is mixed".

In respect to the three objectives mentioned above, the overall results of the Boyd, Caporale and Smith (2001) analyses imply the following: Long-run sustainability of b_t implies that b_t should be $I(0)$, implying that b_t is mean reverting. The ADF test reported in table 8.1 showed b_t as $I(0)$ in four of the twelve cases, but it has to be noted that the power of the test, with T = 25, is low. The Engle-Granger results, reported in the last column of table 8.2, also showed little evidence of a cointegrating relationship. Only three of the twelve cases showed evidence of a long-run relationship in b_t. Johansen ML tests for cointegration (column 2 in table 8.3) showed more evidence of cointegration (nine of twelve cases at 10 per cent, with the exceptions of AB, SLU and SVG), but the signs and significance of the parameter estimates are poor. Only BA estimates were all statistically significant, but the b_t variable had the wrong sign. An increase in the real exchange rate, e_t, should lead to an improvement in b_t, but table 8.3 reports it as negative, at –8.1. Statistical evidence for the long sustainability of the balance of payments variable among these countries, therefore, is not strong. However, the power of some of the tests themselves is not strong.

For devaluations to improve the balance of payments in the long run, economic theory suggests that the Marshall-Lerner condition should be satisfied. In order for the MLC to be satisfied – a devaluation (an increase in e_t) should bring about an improvement in the balance of payments – the coefficient on e_t must be positive, that is, $\eta > 0$. This was statistically significant, and with the correct sign only in the single case of JAM. The coefficients had the wrong sign in the three other cases (SKN, BAR and GUY), where the coefficients were statistically significant. This particular procedure, therefore, provided very poor evidence in support of the MLC for this group of countries. This is in marked contrast to the evidence from industrial countries (Boyd et al. 2001). This suggests that these Caribbean economies are unlikely to improve their international competitive position through competitive devaluation. This further may have the implication that devaluation in response to relative price inflation and overvaluation of domestic currencies for these small economies may, in fact, be more costly than we tend to believe. If the disadvantages of high relative inflation cannot be rolled back by changes in relative exchange rates (devaluations), then such countries may have to pay the price of high relative inflation in terms of a decline in real output, or at least a reduction in their rates of growth. If this is the case, the role of monetary policy in guarding against inflation becomes crucial in the process of financial stabilization and economic growth.

Graphical evidence of J-Curve effects was sought using GIR functions from the VECM systems (see figure 8.1). We get the shape that corresponds to a J-Curve effect in six cases, but only in three (DOM, SLU and SVG) did the outcome correspond to a positive balance improvement in the long run for the balance of payments. In the other three cases (GRE, SKN and BEL), although the GIR showed the correct shape, the long-run equilibrium had a negative balance of payments. In the other six cases, two countries (AB and TT) had the incorrect shape for the curve, implying a worsening of the balance of payments following the real exchange rate shock. The remaining four countries (BAH, BAR, GUY and JAM) displayed curves that were essentially flat. This confirms the lack of a positive response in b_t arising from a real exchange rate devaluation, noted for the Marshall-Lerner condition.

Chapter **9**

Conclusions

In the research for this book, we were interested in the features of sound monetary policies that may form the basis for economic growth and sustained economic development. To obtain an insight into these processes, we analysed how monetary policy effects were transmitted to the real economy. We took, as the basis for this study, an examination of twelve Caribbean countries. These countries vary in size and resource endowment. Over the last quarter of the twentieth century, they underwent a varied economic performance experience. A feature of their varied economic performance is the availablity of mineral resources. With the exception of Trinidad and Tobago, the countries with significant mineral resources (Guyana and Jamaica) seem to have fared considerably worse than those without notable mineral resources (such as Barbados and the Eastern Caribbean countries). This led us to think that the economic successes and problems that arose since the 1960s may in part have been due to the monetary policies that have been implemented.

The economics literature has an interest in whether monetary policy is better implemented within a *discretionary* or *rule* regime. Contemporary Caribbean monetary institutions exhibit characteristics of both regimes to differing degrees. At the *discretionary* end of the spectrum are the stand-alone central banks of Barbados, Belize, Guyana, Jamaica, and Trinidad and Tobago. They operate within what is essentially a discretionary framework. Nevertheless, they display a significant degree of variation in their operations. At the other end of the spectrum is the *currency union* of the ECCB, with its rigid *rules*-based *currency board arrangements,* which it administers to the member countries (Anguilla, Antigua and Barbuda, Dominica, Grenada, Montserrat, St Kitts and Nevis, St Lucia, and St Vincent and the Grenadines). An interesting middle ground is covered by the Central Bank of the Bahamas. It incorporates a rules-based currency board element into its otherwise discretionary institutional framework. The currency board element is present in the form of a statutory mandate to ensure that external reserves are maintained at 50 per cent of the value of total notes and coins and demand liabilities of the bank. These countries, with the exception of Anguilla and Montserrat, provided us with the sample of twelve English-speaking Caribbean economies to conduct our analysis.

An important aspect of the analysis was the fact that all the countries in the study have a common colonial background. In chapter 2, we explained that the monetary policy of all the British colonies, including those of the Caribbean, were administered under a currency board regime that constrained the monetary authorities from implementing policies that would result in excessive money supply expansion. Their common colonial economic history and institutional monetary policy framework allowed us to attribute recent economic performance to post-colonial economic policies, allowing for the particular structural characteristics of the economies.

In seeking to explain the impact of monetary policy on these economies, we set out with two objectives: a *substantive* one and a *methodological* one.

9.1 The Substantive Objective

The *substantive objective* was to provide an economic explanation of the fundamental monetary features of these Caribbean economies and to investigate the role of monetary policy in the determination of their relative economic performance. In chapter 2, we began our investigation by paying particular attention to the institutional framework within which the policies were developed. We found that the evolution of institutions provided valuable insights into the contemporary features of Caribbean monetary policy. We were able to analyse the aims and objectives of the monetary institutions and link these to economic theories, policy approaches and policy impact. In this way, we developed a rigorous analysis grounded in the historical characteristic features of the monetary institutions and policies of the twelve countries, and linked these to their inflation and output performances.

The colonial monetary institutions of all the countries were firmly based on currency board arrangements administered under special legislation, related to the colonial territories known as Orders in Council, or other legislative instruments. The entire colonial monetary system was based on colonial monies being fully backed. This, in effect, meant that the money supply of the British colonial territories was fully backed by sterling, which in turn meant that the possession of colonial notes, in essence, meant being in possession of sterling. This was no pernicious colonial peculiarity, but rather a direct result of the British government historical quest that the British money supply should have its value anchored in a real way to silver, in the first place, and then gold. We saw that in 1844, the prime minister of the day, Sir Robert Peel, introduced the Bank Charter Act, so that the pound, as a measure of value, could have an intrinsic value tied to gold of a certain weight and fineness. This legislation installed the framework of what was to follow and, has determined in important ways the operational framework of contemporary monetary institutions, such as the ECCB and the Central Bank of Bahamas. The stated primary motive was to protect the value of the pound, and prevent the various banks licensed to issue notes from excessive printings that would reduce the value of the pound. The danger of excessive increases in the money supply was a lesson not heeded in the post-colonial era by some countries, notably Guyana and Jamaica, in our sample. A heavy price in terms of output loss and financial crises resulted.

The full backing of the pound, in terms of gold (the gold standard), and the convertibility of the pound provided the substantive basis on which monetary arrangement in all the British territories, in the homeland and the possessions, would be carried out. Hence, the currency board arrangements and the convertibility of colonial currencies into pounds can be justly seen as the direct counterpart to this. In this way, the attributes desired by Peel for the pound became the attributes required of the monies of the colonial territories.

The primary motive for all this was to imbue the currency of the entire British Empire with certain intrinsic qualities that would encourage people to have confidence in the currency as both a measure of value and a store of value. Excessive printing of money, as had long been recognized, would quickly lead to people losing confidence in a currency, and its function as a store of value would be eroded as a consequence. This, in effect, is simply saying, in modern parlance, that excessive increases in the quantity of money would lead to inflation.

In the post independence era, among some of the countries that adopted stand-alone central banks and eschewed their historical currency boards frameworks, we saw a rapid movement to what could be rightly termed excessive monetary growth. In the first four years of their operation, the central banks of Guyana, Jamaica, and Trinidad and Tobago were all subject to crises associated with excessive supply of money (Thomas 1972). It is noteworthy that for the independence years 1962–2006, the annual average rates of growth in the money supply for Jamaica were 21.0 per cent and 18.4 per cent for M1[1] and M2, respectively. For the ECCB countries, for the period 1986–2006, the annual average rates of growth of money supply were 9.8 per cent and 9.1 per cent. For Jamaica, for the same period, the comparable annual average growth rates were 24.7 per cent and 19.4 per cent, respectively. On average, the Jamaican money supply growth rates were *annually* more than twice those of the ECCB countries.

We also saw strong statistical evidence of a positive relationship between the rate of growth in the money supply and the rate of inflation among this group of countries. We observed a significant negative relationship between the rate of inflation and the rate of growth of output among our sample countries. The analysis indicated that there was evidence to support the argument that the institutional arrangements of the central bank that served to restrain inflation were associated with relative economic growth in the economies.

We saw that the very small states of the Eastern Caribbean retained a joint monetary arrangement based closely on their historical precedent, and that this has served them well. In spite of the volatility of international trade over the latter part of the twentieth century and into the twenty-first, an important benchmark noted was the EC dollar retaining unchanged its value against its US dollar peg since 1976, when it was first pegged to the US dollar. This peg began with the ECCA, and thus preceded the establishment of the ECCB, which began operations in 1983.

This stability in the nominal exchange rate of the EC dollar is due to the continuance of its historical currency board arrangements and the full foreign exchange backing of the EC dollar. The legal framework allows for only a 60 per cent backing. However, the ECCB consistently

---

[1] M1 is the money supply narrowly defined to include: notes and coins in circulation and demand deposits. M2 is a money supply broadly defined to include: M1 plus quasi-money.

maintained the full backing of the EC dollar and so inspired a degree of confidence in the currency that may have otherwise been lost.

The currency board arrangement is not a panacea. There are important financial tensions in the EC dollar area, especially with regard to fiscal and governance matters on the financial side, and all manner of political economy issues generally. Nevertheless, the support provided by the currency board arrangements within the Eastern Caribbean Currency Union has provided a bulwark of support that many countries in the Latin American and Caribbean region have not possessed. Indeed, the exchange rate performance of the ECCB worldwide has been remarkable, quietly remarkable perhaps, but it has nevertheless attracted some attention in the literature (Rose 2000; Obstfeld and Rogoff 1995).

Throughout the transition from colonial dependencies to independent nation states, the caution evident in the Eastern Caribbean backing of their currency retained in the regulatory monetary arrangements point to a consistently high priority for monetary stability. This served to constrain fiscal deficit expenditure, limit the growth in money supply that served to protect the value of the currency and reduce the risk of inflation. This, in turn, has provided a relatively stable foundation on which to develop their small and fragile economies. Despite their small size, absence of any significant mineral resources and high degree of openness, these ECCB countries have achieved consistent economic growth and an absence of the balance of payments crises experienced by larger more resource rich Caribbean neighbours.

In general, therefore, on this substantive monetary policy analysis aspect, we concluded that the essential difference between the twelve countries is not between the currency-union/currency-board ECCB and non-ECCB countries. It is also not between rules versus discretionary frameworks. The difference is between institutional arrangements and operations that encouraged monetary stability and those that were too accommodating of government deficit expenditures. Therefore, the distinction lay between the nine countries (the six ECCB countries plus Barbados, Belize and the Bahamas) that developed institutional arrangements (rules against accommodating discretionary arrangements) encouraging monetary stability, whether hardwired in the case of currency board arrangements or through consistently prudent policy approaches. The discretionary approach of accommodation of government deficit expenditure of the remaining three countries (Guyana, Jamaica, and Trinidad and Tobago) gave less priority to monetary stability.

9.2 The Methodological Objective

The methodological objective was to see whether we could develop common econometric models that could tell a consistent long-run story about two central theoretical policy processes: the monetary transmission mechanism and the determinants of external balance.

We were interested in an analysis of the *monetary transmission mechanism*: the mechanisms through which monetary policies affect the real economy. In the standard two sector goods and money market IS/LM model to be found in textbooks, the main transmission mechanism is to be found in the investment function; where investment is usually written as a function of the real interest rate. If price is given, this amount to investment is a function of the nominal interest rate that is determined in the money market. It follows that, if price is not given, we must be interested in the rate of inflation as a determinant factor.

Our modelling exercises were designed to estimate various behavioural relationships to see if links arising from monetary policies could be traced through to output or external trade effects. In this way, we estimated various specifications to see if we can find significant statistical evidence of *monetary transmission mechanisms*. We used various time-series modelling techniques and procedures to carry out these estimations.

Economic theory tells us that the dynamics of inflation play a central role in monetary policy. Indeed, we noted above that even in the simple IS/LM analysis, where investment is written as a function of real interest rates, this implies a role for the rate of inflation in the determination of investment.

We therefore began our time-series modelling with an examination of the behavioural characteristics of inflation. The *univariate analysis* carried out showed that all the ECCB countries, along with the Bahamas, Barbados and Belize, showed low mean inflation rates, low variation in rates and low inflation persistence (with the exception of Antigua and Barbuda, which did not show low persistence). In contrast, Guyana and Jamaica show high mean rates, high variations and high persistence in inflation. The standard autoregression specifications used enabled us to discern differences between the countries' inflation performance, which may be attributed to policy responses conditioned by institutional structure. The ECCB countries, the Bahamas, Barbados and Belize showed inflation experiences that contrasted with those of Guyana and Jamaica, with Antigua and Barbuda and Trinidad and Tobago falling somewhere between the low inflation of the former and the high inflation/persistence/variation of the latter.

The *Granger block non-causality* tests on y_t, p_t, m_t sought to test the extent to which each of the variables individually determined the other two. The test showed an almost equal degree of determination between the three variables. That is, in seven of the twelve cases, p_t and m_t, respectively, significantly determined the other two variables. In eight of the twelve cases, y_t was seen to significantly determine p_t and m_t. Therefore, although not conclusive, the evidence does support the notion that money and prices determine the level of income. There is also evidence, however, that income determines prices and money with an almost equal degree of simultaneous determination between these sets of variables. This is supportive of the notion that money and output may be linked in a complex dynamic relationship mediated through price expectations, such as through an Expectation Augmented Phillips Curve hypothesis. This is consistent (or at least, not inconsistent) with the evidence of the previous descriptive statistics and the univariate analyses.

In chapter 6, the impact of money supply and price inflation policy shocks was examined through *orthogonalized and generalized impulse response functions* (tables 6.4 and 6.5, respectively), generated from *unrestricted VAR* estimates.

We estimated an unrestricted VAR in y_t, p_t, m_t in a closed economy specification, using quarterly data, and examined orthogonalized impulse response behaviour of these variables from a money supply shock and the generalized impulse response from a price shock. The orthogonalized impulse response showed that cumulatively, over eight quarters, a 3.8 per cent increase in money supply shock would increase prices by 1.2 per cent and output by 2.1 per cent, on average across the twelve economies. On the basis of these results, there seems to be a less than proportionate sticky prices response, accompanied by some growth in real output. The generalized impulse response of the variables to a 1.5 per cent increase in price shock saw real output fall approximately proportionately 1.6 per cent, on average across the twelve economies. The unrestricted VAR estimates, therefore, showed some real output increase from a positive monetary response, but that output responded negatively to an inflation shock.

In chapter 7, we examine the long-run relationship between y_t, p_t, m_t by using vector error correction models. The impact of a money supply and a price inflation policy shocks was again examined through *orthogonalized and generalized impulse response functions*. We saw that orthogonalized impulse responses from a 4 per cent money supply increase will on average increase output by 2.8 per cent cumulatively over eight quarters. This was largely in line with the money supply shock from the unrestricted VAR estimates in chapter 6. The generalized impulse response of the variables to a 1.6 per cent increase in price shock from cointegration estimates saw real output fall approximately, more than proportionately, by 2.7 per cent, on average across the twelve economies cumulatively over eight quarters. The cointegrating VECM estimates, therefore, also showed a real output fall from an inflation shock.

In general, therefore, both the VAR and VECM showed the money shock to be expansionary and the inflation shock to be contractionary in real output. These results may be seen as providing some support for the argument that inflation should be the primary macroeconomic target, and that money should be given the role of an intermediate target, as was raised in chapter 1 (Loayza and Soto 2002; Mishkin 2000).

To investigate the open economy aspects of the economies, we tested for the Marshall-Lerner condition and J-Curve effects in order to assess the efficacy of these mechanisms in adjusting to external balance in these Caribbean economies. In this respect, we sought to do three things:

1. Test for evidence of long-run stability in the balance of payments relationship
2. Test for evidence of the Marshall-Lerner condition that devaluations may bring about long-run improvements in the balance of payments
3. Find evidence that J-Curve effects may exists – that is, that a devaluation a short-term worsening of the balance of payments will be followed by long-term improvements

To test for the long-run relationship in the balance of payments, we used four economic models that differed in the degree to which they condition on exogenous variables:

1. Granger non-causality tests
2. Engle-Granger test for cointegration
3. Cointegrating VAR
4. Cointegrating VECM

Overall, very poor evidence of a long-run stable relationship was found, and support for a long-run relationship in terms of the MLC and J-Curve effect was also very poor. This is in marked contrast to evidence found for eight OECD countries (Boyd, Caporale and Smith 2001), where "although there is considerable heterogeneity, overall, the results suggest that the MLC holds in the long run with statistically significant results in five out of the eight cases". In this study of twelve developing countries, we were able to obtain only a single instance of a statistically significant parameter with the correct sign that satisfied the MLC – the case of Jamaica. We have to note that degrees of freedom limitations may have a role to play in the estimations. Nevertheless, the lack of evidence in this respect is noteworthy.

The marked contrast between the evidence arising from the industrial countries study (Boyd Caporale and Smith 2001) and this study of small open economies suggests that the latter countries are unlikely to improve their international competitive position through competitive nominal exchange rate devaluations. If the disadvantages of high relative inflation cannot be rolled back by changes in relative exchange rates (devaluations), then such countries may have to pay the price of a decline in real output, in order to correct balance of payments instability. If this is the case, the role of monetary policy in guarding against inflation becomes crucial in the process of financial stabilization and economic growth, and indeed many commentators argue this.

Overall, in this study of the impact of monetary policy on inflation and output in these twelve Caribbean countries, the weight of the evidence suggests that the monetary institutional framework, either hardwired in terms of currency board arrangements or behavioural in terms of consistent prudent monetary policies, can serve to restrain excessive monetary expansion. The evidence also suggests that excessive monetary expansion generally leads to inflation, which may persist for a long time, and such inflation, in turn, retards economic growth, and is likely to generate balance of payments, exchange rate and foreign exchange crises.

9.3 Lessons and Policy Implications

The countries of the Caribbean are a group of nation states that stretches in an arc of over 4,000 kilometres (2,485 miles) from Florida (the Bahamas) in the north to Venezuela (Trinidad and Tobago) in the south. Anglophone Caribbean economies that are the subject of this study are linked not so much by proximity (with 4,000 kilometres of travel), but rather by a common economic and colonial heritage. Indeed, some of these states have common borders with, and are closer neighbours to, some Latin American countries, rather than each other. Jamaica, for example, is much closer to Haiti and Cuba than to its English-speaking Caribbean neighbours. Similarly, Trinidad and Tobago is much closer to Venezuela that to its English-speaking Caribbean neighbours.

The bond between the English-speaking Caribbean countries is their common economic and social history forged in the crucible of their colonial history. Of course, this bond is neither definitive nor exclusive, since there are important links between the various countries of the region. Nevertheless, the anglophone Caribbean countries possess an economic and analytical identity that is both important and undeniable.

Technical economic studies of these small open economies are usually confined to analyses of the major economies of Barbados, Guyana, Jamaica, and Trinidad and Tobago, with peripheral reference, if any, to the other smaller economic nations. This study is unusually comprehensive because the analyses are conducted for twelve economies: the four countries noted above and eight others covering all the English-speaking independent states of the Caribbean. Consequently, comparable data and analyses are conducted for St Lucia as for Jamaica, and all the other countries included in this study.

In this book, we essentially investigate the relationship between monetary policy and economic growth and development. In technical jargon, our central concern is to investigate the monetary transmission mechanism in Caribbean economies, that is, how monetary policy affects output in the economies. The evidence and lessons of the Caribbean experience, we suspected, were not obvious enough to commentators and policymakers, so we sought to examine the issue in both a solid general way, providing a readable analysis, as well as in technical methodological ways that employ modern techniques of statistical analysis.

The World Bank, in its 1978 omnibus study of Caribbean economies, under the supervision of Hollis Chenery, *The Commonwealth Caribbean: the Integration Experience*, denoted Barbados, Guyana, Jamaica, and Trinidad and Tobago as the more developed countries (MDCs) and Antigua, Dominica, Grenada, Montserrat, St Kitts, St Vincent and Belize as the less developed countries (LDCs) of the region, based on early 1970s data. The per-capita GDP of Jamaica and Trinidad and Tobago were multiples of those of the LDCs. In 1974, the average per-capita GDP for the LDCs was US$503.8, which was 45 per cent of that of Jamaica (US$1,131), whereas Dominica, Grenada and St Vincent recorded low values of US$366.00, US$335.00 and US$375.00, respectively (World Bank 1978, table 1.1). The per-capita GDP of Guyana, at US$510.00, was slightly higher than the LDCs average of US$503.8, and was, of course, considerably higher than the three LDCs just mentioned.

By 2004, however, the levels of per-capita GDP were reversed. Table 2.1 shows that the per-capita GDP of Jamaica and Guyana were by far the lowest among the Caribbean economies. The average per-capita GDP for Antigua and Barbuda, Dominica, Grenada, St Kitts and Nevis, St Lucia, and St Vincent and the Grenadines was more than twice that of Jamaica, at 210 per cent of the per-capita value of Jamaica. The average per-capita GDP for this group of six countries in 2004 was US$7,682. For Jamaica, it was US$3,657. Guyana recorded a per-capita value for 2004 of US$3,973. Although the country groupings are not identical across the time periods, the order of magnitude of the changes indicates significant reversals in relative output growth and, in the case of Guyana, output and population growth dynamics.

We began our analysis from the idea that monetary policy is important in establishing the basis for economic growth and development. This is especially so for nations that trade – referred to as open economies. Our analysis indicates that for the earliest days of modern monetary relations, economic theory and policy were cognizant of the dangers of excessive money supply growth and its adverse impact on the currency as a *medium of exchange* and *a store of value,* and subsequent negative impact on the growth of output. In particular, we saw that from the sixteenth to the twentieth century, Britain guarded against the dangers of excessive growth in the domestic currency (the British pound, £) by linking the supply of the currency to silver at first and then to gold, giving rise to what is known as the gold standard. The gold standard provided statutory rights linking paper currency of no intrinsic value to gold, and combined this with convertibility of the currency. This meant, in effect, that holding the intrinsically worthless paper currency amounted to holding gold. This enabled people to have confidence in holding paper currency, and its use as a medium of exchange and a store of value. Throughout wars, financial crises and economic and political evolutions, when specie backing and convertibility were at times suspended, the basic monetary theory linking confidence in a currency to act as a medium of exchange and a store of value and economic growth remained intact.

It was apparent, from at least the Napoleonic war of 1789–1815, and prior to David Ricardo's (1772–1823) influential contributions, that a domestic currency of a trading nation could be operated on the basis of fiduciary issue, that is, without being linked to a silver of gold standard. Britain, however, was unwilling to risk a fiduciary issue, and set it sights in the early nineteenth century to become an industrial trading nation. Experience of convertibility as the basis for monetary confidence was, however, regarded as an important political basis for establishing the conditions for economic growth and trade. In chapter 2, we noted that Prime Minister Peel introduced the benchmark 1844 Bank Charter Act, which set out the principles and objectives that would underpin the operations of British monetary operations for over a hundred years. It was absolutely clear on putting in place institutional arrangements "according to ancient monetary policy of the country", and that this important reform was aimed at inspiring confidence in the currency so that "legislation could ensure the just reward for industry, and the legitimate profit of commercial enterprise conducted with integrity and controlled by provident calculations" (Peel 1844).

The monetary framework under which all British colonies were administered effectively established the monetary regimes of all British colonies on the same principles as those of the British pound. Under the British currency board system, the supply of currency for any colony was based on their ability to hold equivalent sterling deposits in London banks. These sterling deposits effectively made holding a West African shilling or a Caribbean pound the same as holding a British pound, which under the gold standard would have amounted to holding the equivalent value in gold. With the demise of the gold standard and convertibility, the currency board arrangement meant that holding the colony currency was equivalent to holding pounds. This, of course, conferred significant advantages to Britain (Thomas 1972), but in turn provided a basis for confidence in the colonial currency, as long as the pound maintained its properties as a good medium of exchange and store of value.

The movement of British colonies to political independence after World War Two enabled Caribbean nation states to increasingly manage their economic affairs from the 1960s. The central banks established by newly independent Caribbean nations embarked on a variety of ways to manage their individual currencies.

Over the 1960s, Guyana, Jamaica, and Trinidad and Tobago established stand-alone central banks, followed by the Bahamas and Barbados in the 1970s, and Belize in the 1980s. The Caribbean case is particularly interesting because the central banks developed largely individual ways of carrying out their functions as the monetary authority of their nations with varying degrees of success and failure. The mineral resource rich and ambitious Guyana and Jamaica quickly succumbed to the dangers of excessive money growth from the earliest days of their operations, ostensibly, in their quest for economic development. However, they have seen a relative decline in their economic fortunes with respect to their Caribbean neighbours. Trinidad and Tobago, although showing evidence of similar monetary features, have fared considerably better due to their oil and gas resource endowments.

The Bahamas, Barbados and Belize were from the start more cautious in their monetary policy approach. The Bahamas retained a statutory 60 per cent reserve backing currency board component to their currency operations, and consistently paid considerable attention to maintaining the parity value of their Bahamian dollar with that of the US dollar, since the parity peg was established with the Central Bank of the Bahamas in 1974. This is associated with a trend increase in real output over 1980 to 2001 (see figure 2.2) and the highest per-capita income of the Caribbean countries in this study (see table 2.1).

Barbados and Belize have not retained statutory currency board arrangements. However, they have paid considerable attention to keeping inflation low, and so have guarded against the dangers of excessive monetary growth in their conservative monetary approach. This consistent monetary prudency has been accompanied by significant trended growth in output, especially in the case of Belize, which started from a low absolute level (see figure 2.2A), and Barbados, with high per-capita income (see table 2.1).

The tiny island states of Antigua and Barbuda, Dominica, Grenada, St Lucia, St Kitts and Nevis, and St Vincent and the Grenadines, along with Anguilla and Montserrat, have retained the common currency administered under a currency board framework administered by the ECCB. A currency board is an effective way of establishing confidence in a currency. The supply of EC dollar is no longer backed by gold or sterling anymore but by internationally traded currencies that comprise their foreign reserves. This gives the EUS dollar a level of credibility that would be difficult for a currency of a small open economy to otherwise possess. In fact, the EC dollar has not fallen in value against the US dollar in nominal terms since its initial fixed rate peg against the US dollar at US$1.00 = EC$2.70 was established by the ECCA, the predecessor to the ECCB, back in 1976. In this regard, it can be said to have served well as a medium of exchange and a store of value with respect to the US dollar.

The economic theories that underlie the negative impact of inflation on economic growth are a long-standing part of macroeconomics. In open economy macroeconomics, a rise in inflation is likely to reduce net exports due to a loss in price competitiveness in the face of a fixed exchange regime. A reduction in net exports, *ceteris paribus*, is likely to be associated with a decline in output. Net exports are determined by real exchange rates, which are in turn determined by nominal exchange rates, corrected for domestic and foreign price inflation. Adjustment in the nominal value of exchange rates, for example, through a devaluation in nominal exchange rates, is not guaranteed to restore trading balances. Small trading nations with fragile open economies are unlikely to respond well to nominal corrections taken to correct external imbalances. The lesson from the Caribbean is emphatically that inflation is best avoided. This is because the costs of adjustment in financial, economic and social terms are likely to be high, and the benefits from adjustment are not guaranteed.

Monetary stability that minimizes inflation relative to trading partners is increasingly recognized as an important factor in establishing the conditions for economic growth and development, and has given rise to the focus on inflation targeting as the primary objective of macroeconomic policy. The objective of increasing living standards depends crucially on long-term growth in real output. There is a growing consensus in the macroeconomics literature that low long-term inflation, as a result of stable monetary conditions, seems to be a necessary condition to attain this goal. The primary lesson seems to be the one long ago learned by monetary authorities, that the inflation that undermines the value of a currency also undermines the ability of an economy to achieve sustained economic growth and development.

In *The Economic Consequences of the Peace,* Keynes wrote the following:

> Lenin is said to have declared that the best way to destroy the Capitalist System was to debauch the currency . . . As the inflation proceeds and the real value of the currency fluctuates wildly from month to month, all permanent relations between debtors and creditors, which form the ultimate foundation of capitalism, become so utterly disordered as to be almost meaningless; and the process of wealth-getting degenerates into a gamble and a lottery . . . There is no subtler, no surer means of overturning the existing basis of society than to debauch the currency. The process engages all the hidden forces of economic law on the side of destruction, and does it in a manner which not one man in a million is able to diagnose. (Keynes 1919, 220–21)

An interesting feature of our sample countries is that they provide examples of both discretionary-prudent and discretionary-imprudent monetary policy effects, and a textbook case of a currency board administered monetary union for a group of very small trading nations. The institutional framework within which monetary policies are developed is varied and complex. The evidence suggests that the absence of a statutory framework or the political will to maintain a stable currency is likely to lead to economic stagnation and prolonged financial crises, even in the presence of significant mineral resource endowments.

References

Acocella, Nicola. 1998. *The Foundations of Economic Policy: Values and Techniques*. Cambridge: Cambridge University Press. (Orig. pub. in Italian as *Fondamenti di Politica Economica* by La Nuova Italia Scientifica, 1994; trans. Brendan Jones, repr. 2000.)

Agung, Juda. 2000. "Financial Constraint, Firm's Investments and the Channels of Monetary Policy in Indonesia". Applied Economics 32: 1637–46.

Alesina, Alberto, and Lawrence H. Summers. 1993. "Central Bank Independence and Macroeconomic Performance: Some Comparative Evidence". *Journal of Money, Credit, and Banking* 25, no. 2 (May): 151–62.

Arestis, Philip, and Malcolm Sawyer. 2002. "Can Monetary Policy Affect the Real Economy?" The Levy Economics Institute, Economics Working Paper Archive no. 355.

Atkins, Fiona, and Derick Boyd. 1998. "Convergence and the Caribbean". *International Review of Applied Economics* 12, no. 3: 381–36.

Baksh, Sherman, and Roland C. Cragwell. 1997. "The Monetary Transmission Mechanism in Small Open Economies: A Case Study of Barbados". *Savings and Development*, no. 2: 179–92.

Bank of Jamaica. 2007. http://www.boj.org.jm/bank_history.php

Bank of Korea. 1998. "Korea's Experience of the Monetary Transmission Mechanism". In *The Transmission of Monetary Policy in Emerging Market Economies*, ed. Steven Kamin, Philip Turner and Jozef Van't Dack. Policy Papers no. 3. Basle: Bank for International Settlements.

Barro, Robert J., and David B. Gordon. 1983. "A Positive Theory of Monetary Policy in a Natural-Rate Model". NBER Working Paper no. 0807, National Bureau of Economic Research, Cambridge, MA.

Bennett, Karl. 1995. "Economic Decline and the Growth of the Informal Sector: The Guyana and Jamaica Experience". *Journal of International Development* 7, no. 2: 229–42.

Bernanke, Ben S., and Mark Gertler. 1995. "Inside the Black Box: The Credit Channel of Monetary Policy Transmission". *Journal of Economic Perspectives* 9, no. 4: 27–48.

Birchwood, Anthony, and Rudolf Matthias. 2007. "Structural Factors Associated with Primary Fiscal Balances in Developing Countries". *Applied Economics* 39: 1235–43.

Bird, Graham. 2001. "Conducting Macroeconomic Policy in Developing Countries: Piece of Cake or Mission Impossible". *Third World Quarterly* 22: 37–49.

Blackman, Courtney. 1982. *The Practice of Persuasion: Selected Speeches*. Bridgetown: Central Bank of Barbados.

———. 1998. *Central Banking in Theory and Practice: A Small State Perspective*. Caribbean Centre for Monetary Studies Monograph Series no. 26. St Augustine: CCMS, University of West Indies.

———. 2006. *The Practice of Economic Management: A Caribbean Perspective*. Kingston: Ian Randle.

Blinder, Alan S. 1999. *Central Banking in Theory and Practice*. Cambridge, MA: MIT Press.

Bourne, Compton. 1977. *Inflation in the Caribbean*. Kingston: Institute of Social and Economic Research, University of the West Indies.

Boyd, Derick. 1988. *Economic Management, Income Distribution and Poverty in Jamaica*. New York: Praeger.

Boyd, Derick, G.M. Caporale and Ron Smith. 2001. "Real Exchange Rate Effects on the Balance of Trade: Cointegration and the Marshall-Lerner Condition". *International Journal of Finance and Economics* 6, no. 3 (July): 187–200.

Boyd, Derick, and Ron Smith. 2002. "Some Econometric Issues in Measuring the Transmission Mechanism, with an Application to Developing Countries". In *Monetary Transmission in Diverse Economies*, ed. Lavan Mahadeva and Peter Sinclair. Cambridge: Cambridge University Press.

Branson, William H. 1989. *Macroeconomic Theory and Policy*. 3rd ed. New York: Harper and Row.

Carare, Alina, and Mark R. Stone. 2003. "Inflation Targeting Regimes". IMF Working Paper, WP/03/09. Monetary and Exchange Affairs Department. January. http://papers.ssrn.com/sol3/papers.cfm?abstract_id=879084&rec=1&srcabs=882276

Carlin, Wendy, and David Soskice. 2005. "The 3-Equation New Keynesian Model: A Graphical Exposition". University College London Discussion Paper 05–03. http://www.econ.ucl.ac.uk/papers/working_paper_series/0503.pdf.

———. 2006. *Macroeconomics: Imperfections, Institutions and Policies*. Oxford: Oxford University Press.

Carrasquilla, Alberto. 1998. "Monetary Policy Transmission: The Colombian Case". In *The Transmission of Monetary Policy in Emerging Market Economies*, ed. Steven Kamin, Philip Turner and Jozef Van't Dack. Policy Papers no. 3. Basle: Bank for International Settlements.

Clarida, Richard, Jordi Gali and Mark Gertler. 1999. "The Science of Monetary Policy: A New Keynesian Perspective". *Journal of Economic Literature* 37 (December): 1661–707.

Clauson, G.L.M. 1944. "The British Colonial Currency System". *Economic Journal* 54, no. 213 (April): 1–25.

Cornia, G., Richard Jolly and Francis Stewart, eds. 1988. *Adjustment with a Human Face: Ten Country Case Studies*, vol. 2. Oxford: Clarendon Press.

Cottarelli, Carlo, and Angeliki Kourelis. 1994. "Financial Structure, Bank Lending Rates, and the Transmission Mechanism of Monetary Policy". IMF Working Paper no. 39, International Monetary Fund, Washington, DC.

Davies, Glyn. 2002. *A History of Money from Ancient Times to the Present Day*. 3rd ed. Cardiff: University of Wales Press.

de la Rocha, Javier. 1998. "The Transmission Mechanism of Monetary Policy in Peru". In *The Transmission of Monetary Policy in Emerging Market Economies*, ed. Steven Kamin, Philip Turner and Jozef Van't Dack. Policy Papers no. 3. Basle: Bank for International Settlements.

Diaz, Francisco. 1998. "Monetary Policy and Its Transmission Channels in Mexico". In *The Transmission of Monetary Policy in Emerging Market Economies*, ed. Steven Kamin, Philip Turner and Jozef Van't Dack. Policy Papers no. 3. Basle: Bank for International Settlements.

Downes, Andrew. 2003. *Productivity and Competitiveness in the Jamaican Economy*. Cave Hill, Barbados: Sir Arthur Lewis Institute of Social and Economic Studies, University of the West Indies.

———. 2004a. *Economic Growth in a Small Developing Country: The Case of Barbados*. Cave Hill, Barbados: Sir Arthur Lewis Institute of Social and Economic Studies, University of the West Indies.

———. 2004b. *Market Reform and Resilience Building in Small Developing Countries*. Cave Hill, Barbados: Sir Arthur Lewis Institute of Social and Economic Studies, University of the West Indies.

Eastern Caribbean Central Bank (ECCB). 1984. *The Eastern Caribbean Central Bank: Its Responsibilities in the Financial System*. Basseterre, St Kitts: ECCB.

East Caribbean Currency Authority (ECCA). 1982. *East Caribbean Currency Authority: Its Role and Functions in the Financial System*. Basseterre, St Kitts: ECCA.

Edwards, Sebastian. 2002. "The Great Exchange Rate Debate after Argentina". NBER Working Paper no. 925, National Bureau of Economic Research, Cambridge, MA.

Eyzaguirre, Nicolas. 1998. "Monetary Policy Transmission: The Chilean Case". In *The Transmission of Monetary Policy in Emerging Market Economies*, ed. Steven Kamin, Philip Turner and Jozef Van't Dack. Policy Papers no. 3. Basle: Bank for International Settlements.

Farrell, Terence W. 1990. *Central Banking in a Developing Economy: A Study of Trinidad and Tobago*. Kingston: Institute of Social and Economic Research, University of the West Indies.

Fisher, Stanley. 2001. "Exchange Rate Regimes: Is the Bipolar View Correct?" *Journal of Economic Perspectives* 15, no. 2 (Spring): 3–24.

Frenkel, J.A., and H.G. Johnson, eds. 1976. *The Monetary Approach to the Balance of Payments*. London: Allen and Unwin.

Friedman, Irving S. 1981. "The Role of Private Banks in Stabilization Programs". In *Economic Stabilization in Developing Countries*, ed. William R. Cline and Sidney Weintraub. Washington, DC: Brookings Institution.

Friedman, Milton, and Anna Jacobson Schwartz. 1963. *A Monetary History of the United States, 1867–1960*. Princeton: Princeton University Press.

Fry, Maxwell. 1988. *Money, Interest, and Banking in Economic Development*. Baltimore: Johns Hopkins University Press.

Garrat, Anthony, K. Lee, M.H. Pesaran and Y. Shin. 2000. "A Long Run Structural Macroeconometric Model of the UK". In *Econometric Modelling: Techniques and Applications*, ed. Sean Holly and Martin Weale. Cambridge: Cambridge University Press.

Gemech, Firdu, and John Struthers. 2003. "The McKinnon–Shaw Hypothesis Thirty Years On: A Review of Recent Developments in Financial Liberalization Theory". Paper presented at Development Studies Association Annual Conference on Globalization and Development. Glasgow.

Gertler, Mark. 1988. "Financial Structure and Aggregate Economic Activity: An Overview". *Journal of Money, Credit, and Banking* 20, no. 3 (August): 559–88.

Ghosh, Atish R, Anne-Marie Gulde and Holger C. Wolf. 1998. "Currency Boards: The Ultimate Fix?" IMF Working Paper WP/98/8, International Monetary Fund, Washington, DC.

Girvan, Norman. 1980. "Swallowing the IMF Medicine in the 'Seventies". *Development Dialogue* 2: 55–74.

Girvan, Norman, Richard Bernal and Wesley Hughes. 1980. "The IMF and the Third World: The Case of Jamaica, 1974–80". *Development Dialogue* 2: 113–55.

Goldstein, M., and M.S. Khan. 1976. "Large versus Small Price Changes in the Demand for Imports". *IMF Staff Papers*, no. 23: 200–225.

Greenspan, Alan. 1997. "Rules vs. Discretionary Monetary Policy". Paper presented at the fifteenth anniversary Conference of the Center for Economic Policy Research at Stanford University. Stanford, CA. http://www.federalreserve.gov/BoardDocs/Speeches/1997/19970905.htm

Guillaume, D., and David Stasavage. 2000. "Improving Policy Credibility: Is There a Case for African Monetary Unions?" *World Development* 28, no. 8: 1391–407.

Gulde, Anne-Marie. 1999. "The Role of Currency Board in Bulgaria's Stabilization". *Finance and Development* 36, no. 3 (September).

Handa, Sudhanshu, and Damien King. 2003. "Adjustment with a Human Face? Evidence from Jamaica". *World Development* 31, no. 7: 1125–45. http://www.unc.edu/~shanda/research/human_face_wd.pdf

Harris, Wentworth. 1992. "Management of a Multi-national Central Bank: A Case Study of the Eastern Caribbean Central Bank". Paper prepared for the CEMLAC Policy Seminar: Aspects of Central Bank Management, Belize, 2–3 November. Eastern Caribbean Central Bank, St Kitts and Nevis.

Hart, Richard. 1990. "An Historical Approach to Industrialisation in the English-Speaking Caribbean Area (17th Century to 1970)". Typescript in Richard Hart's collection.

———. 1998. "Changing Perspectives on Development in the 1940s and 1950s". Typescript in Richard Hart's collection.

———. 1999. *Towards Decolonisation: Political, Labour and Economic Development in Jamaica, 1938–1945*. Kingston: Canoe Press.

Hollander, Jacob H. 1910. "The Development of the Theory of Money from Adam Smith to David Ricardo". *Quarterly Journal of Economics* 25: 429–70.

Honohan, P., and P.R. Lane. 2000. "Will the Euro Trigger More Monetary Unions in Africa?" Research Paper no. 176, World Institute for Development Economics Research. http://ideas.repec.org/p/wop/wobaie/2393.html

Honohan, Patrick. 1994. "Currency Board or Central Bank? Lessons from the Irish Pound's Link with Sterling, 1928–79". *CEPR Discussion Paper* no. 1040. http://www.cepr.org/pubs/dps/DP1040.asp

Iljas, Achjar. 1998. "The Transmission Mechanism of Monetary Policy in Indonesia". In *The Transmission of Monetary Policy in Emerging Market Economies*, ed. Steven Kamin, Philip Turner and Jozef Van't Dack. Policy Papers no. 3. Basle: Bank for International Settlements.

International Monetary Fund (IMF). 2006, 2007. International Financial Statistics. http://www.esds.ac.uk

Jefferson, Owen. 1972. *The Post-War Economic Development of Jamaica*. Kingston: Institute of Social and Economic Research, University of the West Indies.

Jung, Woo S. 1986. "Financial Development and Economic Growth: International Evidence". *Economic Development and Cultural Change* 34, no. 2 (January): 333–46.

Kakes, Jan. 2000. "Identifying the Mechanism: Is There a Bank Lending Channel of Monetary Transmission in the Netherlands?" *Applied Economics Letters* 7: 63–67.

Kamin, Steven, Philip Turner and Jozef Van't Dack, eds. 1998. *The Transmission of Monetary Policy in Emerging Market Economies*. Policy Papers no. 3. Basle: Bank for International Settlements.

Keynes, J.M. 1913. *The Economic Consequences of the Peace*. London: Macmillan.

———. 1919. *Indian Currency and Finance*. London: Macmillan.

———. 1925. "The Gold Standard Act". *Economic Journal* 35, no. 138: 311–13.

———. 1930. *Treatise on Money*. London: Macmillan.

Khan, Glenn A. 1998. "Monetary Transmission Mechanisms: Their Operation Under Fixed and Floating Rate Regimes". Occasion Paper Series no. 6, Caribbean Centre for Monetary Studies.

King, Damien. 2000. "The Evolution Structurel Adjustment and Stabilisation Policy in Jamaica". Economic Commission for Latin America. http://www.eclac.org/publicaciones/xml/7/4587/lcl1361i.pdf

Krugman, Paul, and Lance Taylor. 1978. "Contractionary Effects of Evaluation". *Journal of International Economics* 8: 445–56.

Lanyi, Anthony, and Rusdu Saracoglu. 1983. "The Importance of Interest Rates in Developing Countries". *Finance and Development* 20, no. 2 (June): 20–23.

Lewis, Gordon K. 1968. *The Growth of the Modern West Indies*. New York: Monthly Review Press.

Loayza, Norman, and Klaus Schmidt-Hebbel. 2002. "Monetary Policy Functions and Transmission Mechanisms: An Overview". In *Monetary Policy: Rules and Transmission Mechanisms*, ed. Norman Loayza and Klaus Schmidt-Hebbel. Santiago: Central Bank of Chile.

Loayza, Norman, and Raimundo Soto. 2002. "Inflation Targeting: An Overview". In *Inflation Targeting: Design, Performance, Challenges*, ed. Norman Loayza and Raimundo Soto. Santiago: Central Bank of Chile.

Lopes, Francisco L. 1998. "The Transmission Mechanism of Monetary Policy in a Stabilising Economy: Notes on the Case of Brazil". In *The Transmission of Monetary Policy in Emerging Market Economies*, ed. Steven Kamin, Philip Turner and Jozef Van't Dack. Policy Papers no. 3. Basle: Bank for International Settlements.

MacKinnon, J.G. 1991. "Critical Values for Cointegration Tests". In *Long-Run Economic Relationships: Readings in Cointegration*, ed. R.F. Engle and C.W.J. Granger. Oxford: Oxord University Press.

Mankiw, N. Gregory. 1994. *Monetary Policy*. National Bureau of Economic Research Studies in Business Cycles, no. 29. Chicago: University of Chicago Press.

Mankiw, N. Gregory, and Mark Taylor. 2003. *Macroeconomics*. 5th ed. New York: Worth.

———. 2008. *Macroeconomics*. European ed. New York: Worth.

Masson, Paul, Miguel A. Savastano and Sunil Sharma. 1998. "Can Inflation Targeting Be a Framework for Monetary Policy in Developing Countries?" *Finance and Development* (March). International Monetary Fund, Washington, DC. http://www.worldbank.org/fandd/english/0398/articles/0100398.htm

Maurin, Alain, Sandra Sookram and Patrick Kent Watson. 2006. "Measuring the Size of Hidden Economy in Trinidad and Tobago, 1973–1999". *International Economic Journal* 20, no. 3 (September): 321–41.

McCullum, Bennett T. 2003. "Inflation Targeting for the United States". Paper for the Shadow Open Market Committee, 19 May. http://wpweb2.tepper.cmu.edu/faculty/mccallum/ITforUS5.pdf

McKinnon, Ronald I. 1973. *Money and Capital in Economic Development*. Washington, DC: Brookings Institution.

Meltzer, Allan H. 1995. "Monetary, Credit and (Other) Transmission Processes: A Monetarist Perspective". *Journal of Economic Perspectives* 9, no. 4: 49–72.

Mendoza, Enrique G., and Fernando Fernandez. 1994. "Monetary Transmission and Financial Indexation: Evidence from the Chilean Economy". IMF Papers on Policy Analysis and Assessments 94/17, International Monetary Fund, Washington, DC.

Mikesell, Raymond F., and James E. Zinser. 1973. "The Nature of the Savings Function in Developing Countries: A Survey of the Theoretical and Empirical Literature". *Journal of Economic Literature* 11, no. 1 (March): 1–26.

Mishkin, Frederic S. 1995. "Symposium on Monetary Transmission Mechanism". *Journal of Economic Perspectives* 9, no. 4: 3–10.

———. 1997. "Inflation Targeting: A New Framework for Monetary Policy?" NBER Working Paper no. 5893, National Bureau of Economic Research, Cambridge, MA.

———. 1999a. "Inflation Targeting". In *Encyclopaedia of Macroeconomics,* ed. Howard Vane and Brian Snowdon. Cheltenham, UK: Edward Elgar.

———. 1999b. "International Experience with Different Monetary Policy Regimes". *Journal of Monetary Economics* 43: 579–605.

———. 2000. "From Monetary Targeting to Inflation Targeting: Lessons from the Industrialized Countries". Paper prepared for the Bank of Mexico Conference on Stabilization and Monetary Policy: The International Experience. November, Mexico City. http://www-1.gsb.columbia.edu/faculty/fmishkin/PDFpapers/00BOMEX.pdf

Mizen, Paul, ed. 2003. *Central Banking, Monetary Theory and Practice: Essays in Honour of Charles Goodhart.* Cheltenham, UK: Edward Elgar.

Montiel, Peter. 1990. "The Transmission Mechanism for Monetary Policy in Developing Countries". IMF Working Paper no. 47. International Monetary Fund, Washington, DC.

Montiel, Peter, and Jonathan D. Ostry. 1991. "Macroeconomic Implications of Real Exchange Rate Targeting in Developing Countries". IMF Working Paper 91/29. International Monetary Fund, Washington, DC.

Morsink, James, and Tamim Bayoumi. 1999. "A Peek Inside the Black Box: The Monetary Transmission Mechanism in Japan". IMF Working Paper no. 137. International Monetary Fund, Washington, DC.

New School. 2006. "The Bullionist Controversy". http://cepa.newschool.edu/het/schools/bullion.htm

Newlyn, W.T., and D.C. Rowan. 1954. *Money and Banking in British Colonial Africa.* Oxford: Clarendon Press.

Obstfeld, Maurice, and Kenneth Rogoff. 1995. "The Mirage of Fixed Exchange Rates". *Journal of Economic Perspectives* 9, no. 4 (Fall): 73–96.

Palley, Thomas I. 1997. "Optimal Monetary Policy in the Presence of a Monetarist Transmission Mechanism". *Economics Letters* 55:109–14.

Peel, Robert. 1844. Introduction of the Bank Charter Act 1844 to the House of Commons. *Hansard* 74, 3rd ser.: 720–54. http://www.historyhome.co.uk/polspeech/bank.htm

Pesaran, M.H., and Yongcheol Shin. 1999. "An Autoregressive Distributed Lag Modelling Approach to Cointegration Analysis". In *Econometrics and Economic Theory in the 20th Century: The Ragnar Frisch Centennial Symposium,* ed. S. Strom. Cambridge: Cambridge University Press.

Pesaran, M.H., and R.P. Smith. 1998. "Structural Analysis of Cointegrating VARs". *Journal of Economic Surveys* 12: 471–506.

Polak, J.J. 1957. "Monetary Analysis of Income Formation and Payment Problems". *IMF Staff Papers* 6, no. 1: 1–50.

Poole, W. 1970. "Optimal Choice of Monetary Policy Instruments in a Simple Stochastic Macro Model". *Quarterly Journal of Economics* 84: 197–216.

Ramlogan, Carlyn 2004. "The Transmission Mechanism of Monetary Policy". *Journal of Economic Studies* 31, no. 5: 435–47.

Rogoff, Kenneth. 1985. "The Optimal Degree of Commitment to an Intermediate Monetary Target". *Quarterly Journal of Economics* 100 (November): 1169–89.

Rose, Andrew K. 2000. "One Money, One Market: The Effect of Common Currencies on Trade". *Economic Policy* 15, no. 30: 9–45.

Schuler, Kurt. 1992. "Currency Boards". PhD diss., George Mason University, Fairfax, VA.

Seerattan, Dave. 2006. "The Effectiveness of Central Bank Intervention in the Foreign Exchange Markets in Selected Flexible Exchange Rate Countries". *Journal of Business, Finance and Economics in Emerging*

Economies 1, no. 1. [Monograph, Caribbean Centre for Money and Finance, University of the West Indies, St Augustine, Trinidad and Tobago.]

Shabbir, Ahmad. 2008. "Monetary Transmission Mechanism in Fiji and PNG". *International Research Journal of Finance and Economics*, no. 5. http://www.eurojournals.com/finance.htm

Sharpley, J. 1984. "Jamaica 1972–80". In *The IMF and Stabilisation: Developing Country Experience*, ed. T. Killick. London: Heinemann.

Shaw, Edward S. 1973. *Financial Deepening in Economic Development*. New York: Oxford University Press.

Sirivedhin, Tanya. 1998. "Financial Reform and the Monetary Transmission Mechanism: The Case of Thailand". In *The Transmission of Monetary Policy in Emerging Market Economies*, ed. Steven Kamin, Philip Turner and Jozef Van't Dack. Policy Papers no. 3. Basle: Bank for International Settlements.

Svensson, Lars E.O. 2003. "The Inflation Forecast and the Loss Function". In *Central Banking, Monetary Theory and Practice: Essays in Honour of Charles Goodhart*, ed. Paul Mizen. Cheltenham, UK: Edward Elgar.

Tarp, Finn. 1993. *Stabilization and Structural Adjustment: Macroeconomic Framework for Analysing the Crisis in Sub-Saharan Africa*. London: Routledge.

Taylor, John. 1993. "Discretion versus Policy Rules in Practice". *Carnegie-Rochester Conference Series on Public Policy* 39: 195–214.

———. 1995. "The Monetary Transmission Mechanism: An Empirical Framework". *Journal of Economic Perspectives* 9, no. 4 (Fall): 11–26.

Taylor, Lance. 1981. "IS/LM in the Tropics: Diagrammatics of the New Structuralist Macro Critique". In *Economic Stabilization in Developing Countries*, ed. William R. Cline and Sidney Weintruab. Washington, DC: Brookings Institution.

———. 1983. *Structuralist Macroeconomics: Applicable Models for the Third World*. New York: Basic Books.

Theil, H. 1956. "On the Theory of Economic Policy". *American Economic Review* 46: 60–66.

———. 1964. *Optimal Decision Rules for Government and Industry*. Amsterdam: North Holland.

Tinbergen, J. 1952. *On the Theory of Economic Policy*. Amsterdam: North Holland.

———. 1964. *Economic Policies, Principles and Design*. Amsterdam: North Holland.

Thomas, C.Y. 1972. *The Structure, Performance and Prospects of Central Banking in the Caribbean*. Kingston: Institute of Social and Economic Research, University of the West Indies.

Tobin, James. 1969. "A General Equilibrium Approach to Monetary Theory". *Journal of Money, Credit and Banking* 1 (February): 15–29.

Trev, R.H. 2006. "British Banknotes". http://homepage.ntlworld.com/trev.rh/Notes/notes.htm

United Nations Development Programme (UNDP). 2000. *Human Development Report 2000*. http://hdr.undp.org/reports/global/2000/en/

Van Wijnbergen, Sweder. 1982. "Stagflationary Effects of Monetary Stabilization Policies: A Quantitative Analysis of South Korea". *Journal of Development Economics* 10, no. 2 (April): 133–69.

———. 1983. "Interest Rate Management in LDCs". *Journal of Monetary Economics* 12, no. 3 (September): 433–52.

Vinals, J., and J. Valles. 1999. "On the Real Effect of Monetary Policy: A Central Banker's View". *CEPR Discussion Paper* no. 2241 (September).

Walsh, Carl E. 2002. "Teaching Inflation Targeting: An Analysis for Intermediate Macro". *Journal of Economic Education* 33, no. 4: 333–47.

———. 2003. *Monetary Theory and Policy*. Cambridge, MA: MIT Press.

Watson, P.K. 2003. "Evaluating Monetary Policy Measures in a Small Primary-Exporting Country: The Case of Trinidad and Tobago". *Social and Economic Studies* 52, no. 3: 143–66.

Weliwita, Ananda, and E.M. Ekanayake. 1998. "Demand for Money in Sri Lanka during the Post-1977 Period: A Cointegration and Error Correction Analysis". *Applied Economics* 30: 1219–29.

Williams, Oral, Tracy Polius and Selvon Hazel. 2005. "Reserve Pooling in the Eastern Caribbean Currency Union and the CFA France Zone: A Comparative Analysis". *Savings and Development* 24, no. 1: 39–59.

Williamson, John. 1995. *What Role for Currency Boards?* Policy Analyses in International Economics no. 40. Washington, DC: Institute for International Economics.

Woodford, Michael. 1999. "Optimal Monetary Policy Inertia". Institute for International Economic Studies, Stockholm University. Seminar Paper no. 666.

World Bank. 1978. *The Commonwealth Caribbean*. Baltimore: Johns Hopkins University Press.

———. 2000. *World Development Indicators (WDI)*. CD-ROM. Washington, DC: World Bank.

———. 2006, 2007. *World Development Indicators (WDI)*. http://www.esds.ac.uk

Worrell, Delisle, and Compton Bourne. 1989. *Economic Adjustment Policies for Small Nations: Theory and Experience in the English-Speaking Caribbean*. New York: Praeger.

Worrell, Delisle, Desiree Cherebin and Tracy Polius-Mounsey. 2001. "Financial System Soundness in the Caribbean: An Initial Assessment". IMF Working Paper, WP/01/123, International Monetary Fund, Washington, DC.

Index

adjustment coefficients, 75, 97, 98, 106, 115
Akaike Information Criterion (AIC), 69
Anguilla, 11, 22, 119, 128
Antigua and Barbuda (AB), 9, 11, 12, 22, 33, 35, 60, 61, 65, 81, 82, 86–89, 92, 93, 98–101, 104, 105, 111–19, 123, 126–28
appreciation in the domestic currency, 51
Asset backing and convertibility, 39
augmented Dickey-Fuller (ADF) equation, 68, 78–82, 94, 110, 111, 117
Australia, 43
autoregression, 6, 7, 67, 68, 78, 80, 84, 94, 112, 123
autoregressive distributed lag (ARDL), 112, 117

backing of a currency, 4
Bahamas, the (BAH), 3, 4, 9–13, 22, 29–37, 40, 56–61, 65, 66, 81–84, 87, 89, 92, 98–101, 104, 105, 108, 111–28
Bahamas Monetary Authority (BMA), 29
balance of payment, 4, 18, 47, 108
balance sheet mechanism, 52
Bank Charter Act 1844, 5, 13–16, 120, 127, 143
Bank of England, 2, 3, 11, 13, 15–17, 20, 23, 27–31
Bank of Jamaica, 22, 23, 25, 30, 137
Bank of Korea, 53
banknotes, 13, 15, 16, 38, 39
Barbados (BAR), 3, 4, 9–13, 19, 22, 23, 26–29, 32–40, 62, 65, 66, 80–89, 92, 93, 98–101, 104, 105, 108, 111–23, 126–28, 137–39

Basle Facility, 1968, 25
bauxite/alumina, 30, 41
Belize (BEL), 3, 4, 9–12, 31–37, 40, 56, 62, 65, 81–89, 92–94, 99, 101, 104, 105, 108, 111–15, 118, 119, 122, 123, 126–28, 140
Belize Board of Commissioners of Currency, 32
Belize, Monetary Authority of, 32
bills of exchange and promissory notes, 14
black market, 51
Board of Commissioners of Currency, 21
Brazil, 3, 43, 47, 49, 53, 55, 56, 58, 141
Bretton Woods, 45
British Caribbean Currency Board (BCCB), 11, 22, 26, 27, 30
British colonial empire, 10, 14, 24
British colonies, 2, 11, 22, 32, 39, 120, 127
British Commonwealth countries, 24
British Currency School, 13
British Government Securities and Treasury Bills, 22
British pound (£), 14, 21, 127
BWI$, the, 22

Canadian banks, 22
Cement Marketing Company, 10
central bank independence, 46
Central Bank of Belize, 32
Central Bank of the Bahamas, 29
Central Bank of Trinidad and Tobago, 26, 30
Central Banks, 2, 6, 8
CFA Zone, 56

Chile, 3, 43, 47, 49, 53–55, 141
Coinage Act 1816, 15, 17
Cointegrating
   vector autoregression (VAR), 101, 104, 105, 117, 124
   vector error correction model (VECM), 67, 117, 124
   vectors, 68, 69, 75, 76, 97, 98, 110, 112, 113
cointegration, 75, 76, 78, 96, 98, 106, 112, 117, 124, 145
Colonial Currency Authorities, 20
colonial monetary institutions, 120
Colonial Office, 10
conservative monetary policies, 32, 78
Consumer Price Index, 60, 61
convertibility, 2, 8, 13, 15, 16, 21, 23, 39, 121, 127
Cowles Commission, 72
credibility, 2, 3, 16, 28, 29, 45, 128
credibility of the central bank, 29
credible monetary policy, 56
Credit Channel, 52, 137
Crown Agents for the Colonies, 21
Cuba, 10, 125
currency board, 3–5, 14, 16, 27, 29, 32, 39, 40, 84, 119, 120, 122, 127, 128
Currency Board of Commissioners, 22, 23
currency boards, 19, 21, 24, 140, 143
Currency Board's Agents in London, 22
currency officers, 20, 21
currency overvaluation, 17
currency union, 4–6, 11, 27, 84

demand for money function, 97
developing countries, 2, 3, 6, 25, 43, 46–58, 125
developing economies, 40, 42, 43, 49, 54, 57
discretionary policy, 3, 4, 9, 84
dollarization, 55
Domestic Asset Price Channel, 51
domestic currency, 56, 126, 127
domestic investments required the permission of the Colonial Office, 24
Dominica (DOM), 65, 81, 82, 86–89, 92, 99, 101, 104, 105, 111–15, 118, 128
dynamic structural economic model, 67

East African Currency Board, 21, 56
East Caribbean Currency Authority (ECCA), 26– 29, 121, 139

Eastern Caribbean
   Central Bank (ECCB), 5, 9, 11–14, 22, 26–40, 81, 82, 84, 87, 89, 92, 99, 101, 104, 105, 108, 111, 113, 119–23, 128, 139, 140
   countries, 11, 29, 32–35, 37, 40, 82, 84, 108, 121–23
   Currency Union, 122, 145
   dollar, 14, 26
economic
   development, 1, 8, 10, 14, 24, 25, 37, 39, 57, 58, 119, 128, 140
   growth and development, 1–4, 10, 14, 25, 46, 58, 126, 129
   performance, 1, 2, 6, 9, 31, 39, 47, 58, 119, 120
emerging market economies, 4, 43, 50
endogenous variables, 67, 85, 87
Engle-Granger, 69, 110, 112, 113, 117, 124
   test for cointegration, 110, 117, 124
European Union, 42
exchange rate
   channel, 50, 51, 54–56, 58
   devaluations, 107, 125
   regime, 2, 51, 79
      fixed, 40, 41, 51
      floating, 51
exogenous variables, 67, 85, 112, 113, 117, 124
Expectation Augmented Phillips Curve Analysis, 94

Falkland Islands, 21
Federation of the West Indies 1958–1962, 22
feedback coefficients, 97–99
fiduciary issue, 16, 127
financial
   intermediation, 48
   repression, 48
   stability, 1, 2, 4, 5, 32, 34, 46
   stabilization, 4, 6, 47, 55, 118, 125
Fisher equation, 105, 106
Fisher Quantity Theory, 104
foreign exchange crises, 4, 6, 35, 46, 125
Friedman Rule, 2

General Theory, The, 39, 50
generalized impulse response functions (GIRF), 73, 88, 114
gold, 2, 4, 8, 13–20, 38, 39, 120, 121, 127, 128

gold standard, 5, 13, 15–21, 38, 39, 121, 127
Gore, James, 10
government deficit, 2, 6, 26, 28, 30, 31, 84, 122
grains of gold, 17
Granger block non-causality, 94, 110, 111, 123
   causal, 86, 87, 111
   causality tests, 49
   non-causality, 78, 86, 117, 124
Grenada (GRE), 9–12, 22, 33, 35, 61, 65, 80–82, 87, 89, 92, 94, 99, 101, 104, 105, 111–15, 118, 119, 126, 128
Guyana (GUY), 3, 4, 9–13, 22, 23, 26–41, 56, 57, 60, 62, 65, 81, 82, 84, 87, 89, 92–95, 98–101, 104–6, 108, 111–15, 118–23, 126–28, 137

Haiti, 125
History of Colonial Currency, The (Chalmers), 19

identification problem, 70, 71, 75, 86, 97
identifying restrictions, 70, 75, 87, 96–98, 105, 106, 113
impulse response function, 7, 53–57, 67, 71, 73, 74, 77, 78, 85, 86, 88, 110, 123, 124
Indian Currency and Finance (Keynes), 20, 141
Indonesia, Bank of, 55
industrial economies, 3, 43, 46, 49, 57
inflation
   persistence, 79, 84, 123
   shock, 93, 105, 124
   targeting, 2, 3, 39, 43, 46, 50, 54, 129
instruments, 2, 43, 45–50, 54–56, 58, 120
interest rate, 2, 3, 34, 42–60, 65–67, 71, 85, 123
International Financial Statistics, 31, 33, 60, 61, 65, 81, 141
International Monetary Fund (IMF), 31, 34, 47
International tourism, 12
interpolated, 59, 60–63, 65, 86, 108
investment function, 42, 43, 50, 122
IS/LM
   in the Tropics, 48, 144
   model, 42, 122
Israel, 43

Jamaica (JAM), 3, 4, 9–13, 21–41, 56, 57, 60–66, 81, 82, 86–89, 92–95, 98–101, 104–6, 111–15, 118–28, 137–41, 144
   population, 12

J-Curve effect, 107, 108, 118, 124
Johansen
   Maximum Likelihood, 69, 110, 112
   ML estimates of the cointegrating coefficients, 113
   ML tests, 117
   trace 10 per cent test, 98
joint-stock bank with limited liability, 15

Keynesian, 2, 24, 25, 39, 138
Korea, 43, 53, 54, 137, 144
KPSS test, 68

Lenin, 129
Lewis, Sir W. Arthur, 23, 24n6
Loanable Funds Theory of Savings and Investment, 50
long-run
   equilibrium, 112
   impact of a price shock, 94
loss function, 44

Marshall-Lerner Condition, 7, 107–10, 113–14, 118, 124, 125, 138
McKinnon–Shaw model, 48
medium of exchange, 15–17, 24, 126–28
Mexico, 4, 55, 139, 142
Modigliani MIT–Penn–SSRC (MPS) model, 52
monetary authority, 3, 11, 22, 28, 29, 127
   instruments, 49
   policy rule, 2, 14, 39
   policy shocks, 7, 50, 56
   stability, 4, 8, 9, 19, 21, 23–30, 39, 40, 122
Monetary Policy Committee, 3
monetary transmission mechanism, 1, 6, 17, 42–59, 77, 94, 122, 126, 139, 141, 143, 144
Money and Banking in British Colonial Africa, 19
money demand, 45, 48, 55, 85, 96–98, 105
money demand function, 55, 98, 105
money shock, 78, 88, 94, 95, 104, 105, 124
money supply multipliers, 42
Montserrat, 11, 22, 119, 126, 128

Napoleonic war of 1789–1815, 127
neo-structuralist approach, 48, 49
New Keynesian, 43, 44

New School, 14, 39
nominal exchange rate, 51, 55, 60, 61, 65, 107, 108, 110, 121, 125
non-standard distributions, 98
non-stationary, 79
null hypothesis, 68, 75, 86, 87, 94, 111, 112

oil/gas based economy, 12
one-size-fits-all monetary policy approach, 48
Orders in Council, 120
Organisation of Eastern Caribbean States (OECS), 14, 22
orthogonalized, 73, 88, 93, 94, 99, 100, 114, 123, 124
    impulse response functions (IRF), 73, 74
    impulse responses, 88, 94, 114, 124,
output gap, 43, 44, 71, 110
output shock, 93
over-expansionary monetary policy, 46, 58

Palestine Currency Board, 21
parallel market, 51
per-capita GDP, 13, 126
persistence of inflation, 78–80, 85
Phillips Curve, 44, 71, 94, 123
policy instruments, 43, 47, 49, 143
policy rules, 2
primary commodity-producing outposts, 10
principal–agent relations, 52
prudent
    monetary policies, 4, 41, 125
    policy, 40, 122

Quantity of Money Theory, 93, 101

Rand Monetary Area, 56
random walk with drift, 78
real exchange rate, 46, 67, 107–10, 115, 117, 118
real money demand, 45
repo rate, 3
reserve backing, 40, 128
Reserve Bank of New Zealand, 3
reserve currency, 2
resource rich economies, 36
Resumption of Cash Payments 1819, 15
Robert Peel, Sir, 15, 16, 123
rupee group, 18
Russia, 4

Schwartz Bayesian Criterion (SBC), 69
secretary of state for the colonies, 20
seignorage, 45
silver standard, 14
South Africa, 43, 56
St Kitts and Nevis (SKN), 65, 81, 87, 89, 92–94, 99, 101, 104, 105, 111–15, 118, 128
St Lucia (SLU), 9, 11, 12, 22, 24, 33, 35, 37, 59, 61, 65, 66, 81, 82, 87–89, 92–94, 98–101, 104, 105, 111–19, 126, 128
St Vincent and the Grenadines (SVG), 65, 81, 82, 86–89, 92, 94, 98–100, 101, 104, 105, 111, 113–18, 128
stabilization policies, 49
standard error shock, 73, 74, 88, 93, 100, 104, 106
stationary, 68, 75, 78–80, 82, 94
sterilized, 51
sterling
    area, 4, 19, 24, 25, 32
    area agreement, 4, 32
    group, 18, 19, 20, 21
    standard, 21, 24
sticky prices, 50, 88, 93, 94, 106, 124
stochastic trend, 68
stock markets, 51
store of value, 17, 24, 121, 126–28
structural shocks, 72, 73
structural vector autoregression (VAR), 71
structuralist
    approach, 48
    models, 43
Suspension of Cash Payments by the Bank of England Act 1797, 15
Sweden, 43
Switzerland, 43, 137–139, 141, 144

Taylor Rule, 2, 44, 71
Thailand, 43, 56, 144
Tobin's q theory, 51
Treasury Bill rate, 57, 61
trend stationary, 68
Trinidad and Tobago (TT), 4, 9–13, 22, 23, 26–41, 53, 56, 58, 62, 65, 80–84, 87, 89, 92, 93, 98–101, 104–8, 111–15, 118–28, 138, 139, 142
    oil/gas based economy, 12
    windfall associated with having an oil and gas, 35

unit root, 68, 69, 75, 78–80, 82, 110, 112
United Kingdom, 10–13, 16, 18, 19, 21, 22, 42, 43, 61
United States, 11, 12, 13, 16, 18, 19, 39, 42, 43, 139, 142
univariate, 7, 77, 78, 84, 93, 94, 123
univariate analysis, 93
University of Guyana, 23
University of the West Indies (UWI), 23, 138–141, 144
unrestricted reduced form, 72
    vector autoregression (VAR), 88, 96, 99, 111
urban–rural distribution of the populations, 12

variance decomposition, 57
vector autoregressions (VAR), 7, 54, 56, 67, 69, 70, 74–77, 84–89, 94–100, 106, 110–15, 123, 124

vector error correction model (VECM), 7, 69, 74–77, 96–100, 105, 106, 112, 114–18, 124
velocity of circulation of money, 95
Venezuela, 10, 125

West African
    Currency Board, 19, 21
    Dependencies, 19
    pound, 20
white noise, 68, 78, 79
World Bank, 12, 34, 35, 38, 59, 60, 62, 65, 81, 126, 145
World Development Indicators (WDI), 34, 60, 65, 81, 145
World War Two, 10

www.ingramcontent.com/pod-product-compliance
Lightning Source LLC
Chambersburg PA
CBHW080739300426
44114CB00019B/2637